BET ✓

W9-AOE-688

Culture
and
Practical
Reason

Culture and Practical Reason

Marshall Sahlins

The
University
of Chicago
Press

Chicago
and London

Wingate College Library

MARSHALL SAHLINS is professor of
anthropology at the University of Chicago. He
is the author of *Social Stratification in
Polynesia, Moala: Culture and Nature on a
Fijian Island, Tribesmen,* and *Stone Age
Economics.*

The University of Chicago Press,Chicago
60637
The University of Chicago Press, Ltd.,
London

©1976 by The University of Chicago
All rights reserved. Published 1976
Printed in the United States of America
80 79 78 77 76   987654321

Library of Congress Cataloging in Publication Data

Sahlins, Marshall David, 1930–
   Culture and practical reason.

   Bibliography: p.
   Includes index.
   1. Ethnology. 2. Dialectical materialism.
3. Structural anthropology. I. Title.
GN345.S24   301.2   75-27899
ISBN 0-226-73359-9   7- 25- 77

Contents

v

071255

Tout ce qui est, est d'une manière déter-
minée, a des propriétés caractérisées.

Emile Durkheim
"Représentations individuelles et
représentations collectives," 1898

Preface

This book amounts to an anthropological critique of
the idea that human cultures are formulated out of
practical activity and, behind that, utilitarian interest. The idea at issue I generally call "praxis
theory" when attention is centered on forms of
economic activity or "utility theory" when it
concerns the logic of material advantage supposed
to govern production. "Praxis" I should like to
confine mainly to the sense of productive action, its
principal sense in Marxist writing, including, as in
that literature, both the objective and subjective
aspects of the process: on one hand, the historically given means and relations of production; on
the other, the experience men have of themselves
and the objects of their existence in the course of
productively transforming the world through a
given instrumental mode. "Utility" likewise may be
thought of in subjective and objective dimensions,
although many theories rather underspecify which
practical logic they take as the basis of cultural
order. For some, however, it is clear that culture is
precipitated from the rational activity of individuals
pursuing their own best interests. This is "utilitarianism" proper; its logic is the maximization of
means-ends relations. The objective utility theories
are naturalistic or ecological; for them, the determinant material wisdom substantialized in cultural
form is the survival of the human population or the
given social order. The precise logic is adaptive
advantage, or maintenance of the system within

natural limits of viability. As opposed to all these genera and species of practical reason, this book poses a reason of another kind, the symbolic or meaningful. It takes as the distinctive quality of man not that he must live in a material world, circumstance he shares with all organisms, but that he does so according to a meaningful scheme of his own devising, in which capacity mankind is unique. It therefore takes as the decisive quality of culture—as giving each mode of life the properties that characterize it—not that this culture must conform to material constraints but that it does so according to a definite symbolic scheme which is never the only one possible. Hence it is culture which constitutes utility.

The argument of the book, as this brief synopsis must imply, involves a complex dialogue of theories, at once among themselves and in relation to the kinds of cultural systems they seek to explain. The scene is set in chapter 1 by a description of certain difficulties encountered by historical materialism in the analysis of so-called primitive societies. From this discussion it seems reasonable to conclude, at least provisionally, that Marxism and the received anthropological structuralisms are only relative theoretical accounts, respectively appropriate to specific cultural universes or historical epochs. Yet in the second chapter it is suggested that the issues that divide Marxism from cultural theory have profound analogues in the history of anthropological thought on "primitive" society. This elucidation of the controversy betweeen practical and cultural reason within anthropology then makes it possible to criticize historical materialism in chapter 3 and to draw bourgeois society into the kingdom of symbolic order in chapter 4. This last engages the title of the work, *Culture and Practical Reason,* in a double entendre characteristic of the book's constant movement between the opposition of theory and theory and the confrontation of theory and object; for the intention of chapter 4 is to suggest the symbolic structure in material utility.

The final chapter offers first conclusions from the entire exercise: on utility versus meaning at the level of cultural theory, and Western versus "primitive" at the level of fact.

The book thus argues a position—for the meaningful—in a dispute with practical thought that is classic not only in anthropology but in all of social science (not to mention philosophy). It is a debate, moreover, to which knowledge of any society or any history is pertinent. Clearly, I could not hope (or want) to escape being taxed on the documentation I offer on the controversy; nor, regrettably, could I expect that the resolution offered will escape being categorized within the procrustean opposition of "idealism" and "materialism" by which the discussion customarily proceeds. As for documentation, I would only defend the choice of anthropological theories and findings as a privileged site for such debate. This because the anthropological concept of culture poses the challenge to practical reason in its most powerful form—and also because, as I shall argue in a moment, this same concept leaves behind just such antique dualisms as mind and matter, idealism and materialism. Within anthropology itself, I have chosen certain authors and certain societies to situate and exemplify the main arguments. Naturally the selection was guided by what seemed to best serve these purposes; but here surely the limitations and idiosyncrasies of an individual experience must have their effect. For that reason, one cannot but welcome commentary based on other sources and other disciplines. It could well confirm the essential point: that the contest between the practical and the meaningful is the fateful issue of modern social thought.

As for the charge of "idealism" that an insistence on the meaningful appears to invite, this, it seems to me, must take its ground in precisely the kind of preanthropological, presymbolic epistemology of subject/object relations whose transcendence was the historical condition of a concept of culture. To return to this language now would be to rob the concept of its determinate properties. It would reduce the problem of culture to the terms of the endemic Western antinomy of a worldless subject confronting a thoughtless object: ineradicable opposition of mind and matter, between the poles of which 2,500 years of philosophy has succeeded in plausibly drawing the line of reality at every conceivable position, from the idealism of Bishop Berkeley to the materialism of Vladimir Ilych. To engage culture in the same problematic is merely to ask whether it represents the subject's "real" experience or his ideal conceptions; whereas, in truth, it is the social condition of the possibility of either and both. Boas, we shall see, was to formulate the modern notion of culture out of discontent with exactly this unmediated subject/ object frame. Passing successively from physics to psychophysics, then to geography, linguistics, and ethnology, he would discover at each stage the same sort of discontinuity between the subjective and the objective, and at each stage too a more general, collective (less Kantian, more cultural) reason for the discontinuity. Ultimately, on the ethnological plane the interposed term became the collective tradition, informing subjective perception by an historic conception. Here was the specifically anthropological contribution to the established dualism: a tertium quid, culture, not merely mediating the human relation to the world by a social logic of significance, but constituting by that scheme the relevant subjective and objective terms of the relationship.

In this book, I take the position that meaning is the specific property of the anthropological object. Cultures are meaningful orders of persons and things. Since these orders are systematic, they cannot be free invention of the mind. But anthropology must consist in the discovery of the system; for as I hope to show, it can no longer be content with the idea that custom is merely fetishized utility.

Acknowledgments

I must especially thank those who suffered through part or all of one or another manuscript version of this book and offered their criticism with their encouragement: Firthjof Bergmann, James Boon, Vern Carroll, Remo Guidieri, Paul Kay, Raymond Kelly, Julius Kirshner, Barbara Sahlins, David Schneider, Bob Scholte, Judith Shapiro, Michael Silverstein, George Stocking, Jr., Stanley Tambiah, Michael Taussig, and Terence Turner.

A generous invitation on the part of the Department of Anthropology, Lehman College of the City University of New York, permitted me to give these ideas public expression in a series of lectures in April 1973. I am grateful to Professor Lucy Saunders for both the welcome opportunity and the kind hospitality.

1 Marxism and Two Structuralisms

The question that first inspired this book was whether the materialist conception of history and culture, as Marx formulated it theoretically, could be transferred without friction to the comprehension of tribal societies. Since it appeared to me that it could not, the question became, What is the real nature of the difficulty?

I hasten to add that the reference is to the materialist system as it is stated methodologically in passages of the *Economic and Philosophic Manuscripts of 1844, The German Ideology,* the "Theses on Feuerbach," *A Contribution to the Critique of Political Economy,* the *Grundrisse, Capital,* and other works of Marx which will be cited hereafter. The general social theory set forth in these studies is commonly referred to as "historical materialism." It is well known that Marx never used the term "historical materialism" (or "dialectical materialism") to describe his philosophy. The need for such labels arose later—and this may be symptomatic of the problem that will concern us. Serious students of Marx have claimed that he failed to systematize adequately the practices he actually used in the more concrete analyses of history and of capitalist society. Accordingly, the present work might be thought of as a response on two levels to the disparity, since it takes an epistemological gap between practice and concept as an occasion to reflect on the adequacy of material praxis to account for the cultural order.

Such reflection necessarily develops into an internal critique of anthropological theory as well. Still, I believe that the encounter with tribal and peasant societies has generated something novel and authentic in anthropology, especially in its concept of culture, and I am moved to defend it. It would be a dismal—although conceivable—comment on our supposed "science" if the materialist interpretation as Marx developed it in

1

the mid-nineteenth century could be applied without problem to the tribal world. A hundred years of thought and fieldwork, all that mental and physical discomfort, would have been largely for nothing—an immense detour into the uncharted hinterlands of mankind that merely brought us back to the starting point. Nothing we learned about human culture in the villages of the Indians, the Africans, or the Polynesians would have contained any real surprises. On the contrary, anthropology, handmaiden to imperialism, beyond its contributions to the spread of Western ideology and polity, would reveal itself as a grand intellectual distraction, bourgeois society scratching its head.

That could be. On the other hand, the received materialism has had its difficulties with anthropological knowledge. To determine the source of the problem would be of the highest service to anthropological and Marxist theory alike. For by the very fact that anthropology is the creature of a bourgeois society whose supposed superior virtues it does not credit, its greatest aim must be the same as that of a critical materialism: "to help men out of their self-made prison of uncomprehended economic determinism" (Schmidt 1971, p. 41). That is the spirit of this book.

The resistance of tribal society to materialist theory has had many expressions. There were clear anticipations of the problem in the works of Marx and Engels: caution about the pertinence of the material dialectic where the means of production do not confront the producers as reified and alienated forces; circumspection about the formative powers of the economic base relative to "natural" bonds of "blood"; observation of the immutability of archaic village communities (see especially Marx 1964; 1967 [1867], 1:358; Engels 1972 [1891]; Marx and Engels 1936, pp. 405–6). So that now for every claim of the universality of the materialist interpretation there is a counterclaim of its relativity. For every assertion of its applicability to all of history (Althusser and Balibar 1970; Terray 1972) there is a reservation of its specificity to the growth and decline of capitalism (Petrovic 1967; Schmidt 1971). The disagreement is over the theoretical status of historical materialism as *the* science of history or—the owl of Minerva taking wing at dusk—the critical self-awareness of late capitalist society.

Meanwhile, within the anthropological academy proper, historical materialism has not been an unqualified success. Of course, there are ideological resistances, but there are also serious criticisms. This chapter takes up some main issues in certain recent debates between Marxism and the two anthropological structuralisms, British and French. But first, a few ground rules for such discussion.

It would be sheer "terrorism" on the Marxist side to dismiss these anthropological arguments as bourgeois idealism (cf. Sartre 1963). But it would be just as uninformative for anthropology to adopt the same terrorism in reverse, writing off the Marxist challenge as a "vulgar economic determinism," a naive "reflectionist" understanding of the relations between economic base and political-ideological superstructures. There are enough concrete examples in Marx, not to mention the well-known explications in Engels's correspondence, to justify leaving such criticisms aside. The issue joined in the debate with British structuralism is a real one: the relevance of the Marxist analytic frame to a society that does not know an organizational distinction between base and superstructure; that is, where the two are formally the same structure. In turn, this morphological or institutionalist problem is only an aspect of the deeper issue in the controversy between Marxism and French structuralism.

"Controversy" may not be the correct word. In some instances there is an uneasy accommodation. The love-hate affair raging between structuralists and Marxists testifies to the accuracy of Luc de Heusch's ethnographic report from the Latin Quarter to the effect that the French intelligentsia is the most nervous in Europe. Still, the usual modes by which the two are opposed, the synchrony of structuralism to the diachrony of Marxism, the idealism of the former to the materialism of the latter, make it difficult to understand why they should even contemplate a synthesis. True that some militants reject structuralism out of hand for its apparent quietism. But Lévi-Strauss says he is a Marxist, in some sense (1965, p. 61; 1966, p. 130), even as Godelier finds Marx was a structuralist (1972). Moreover, this attraction of opposites has an analogue in anthropology proper, in the fascination Lévi-Strauss holds for Anglo-Saxon ethnologists, despite their habitual hard-headed empiricism. What structuralism seems to offer, even beyond a conception of the continuity in history that Marx recognized for certain precapitalist societies, is an explicit statement of the culture in the praxis, the symbolic order in the material activity.

This too Marx was among the first to recognize. But to adopt a distinction of Althusser's, to recognize an important fact, to *see* it, is not the same as developing the *concept* of it. Marx's general formulations of cultural theory would subordinate the societal logic of production to the instrumental logic of work, and withal transpose the symbolic *coordinates* of social being into the *consequence* of that being. The relation between productive action in the world and the symbolic organization of experience—this is the issue between Marxism and French structuralism; as it is also the issue in the provincial debates of anthropology over practical and cultural reason. The disagreement is over the adequacy of praxis to constitute the human order.

The following discussion seeks to establish the framework of this disagreement, and of all its corollaries, equally fundamental, concerning the relations between structure and event, culture and nature, ideology and economy. Perhaps the importance of the question, as well as the difficulties Marxism and structuralism discover in escaping from each other, is summed up by the observation that the Marxist vision of a socialist future, the mastery by society of society's mastery over nature, is very similar to the idea that Lévi-Strauss and Boas before him have entertained of the primitive past. What is more, is this not the essential anthropological understanding of culture itself?

Marxism and British Structuralism:
The Worsley-Fortes Controversy

When Peter Worsley (1956) subjected Meyer Fortes's studies of the Tallensi (especially 1945, 1949) to a Marxist critique, he adopted a strategy that seemed more analytic than dialectic. "It is necessary," he wrote, "to break a kinship system, which is a unitary system of relations between persons, into its *component purposive systems* of different kind (economic, procreative, ritual, etc.) and to examine the relations between these systems" (1956, p. 64; emphasis mine). Yet here there is an even more striking departure from the received materialism. The analytic dissection Worsley performs on the Tallensi lineage system is rather the opposite of the procedure Marx used to demystify Western capitalism. Worsley is obliged to dismember an apparent unity in order to posit hidden relationships among its parts; for Marx, the problem was to discover the unity among parts—the economy, law, the state—which presented themselves as distinct and autonomous.

This difference in method is, I suggest, the theoretical counterpart of a difference in the cultural object. The materialist synthesis achieved by Marx was a triumph over the peculiar and deceiving appearance of bourgeois society. Lukács explains: "Economics, law and the state appear here as *closed* systems which control the whole of society by virtue of the perfection of their own power and by their own built-in laws." Historical materialism, Lukács concludes, "was an epoch-making achievement precisely because it was able to see that these apparently quite independent, hermetic and autonomous systems were really aspects of a comprehensive whole and that their apparent independence could be transcended'' (Lukács 1971, p. 230). But the Tallensi, as Worsley describes them, present this problem in reverse:

> We have seen that those persons to whom one stands, for example, in a particular *political* relationship are also the same persons to whom one stands in other relationships—moral, religious, educational etc. The ties linking individuals in Tale society are not ties of unitary interest alone; there is a complex network of interlocking ties which bind people together. This multiplicity of ties is mainly expressed in the idiom of kinship. Political relations between groups are similarly expressed in kinship terms, although the content of such relations is obviously of a different nature from the content of the relations between actual kin. Thus kinship is the framework of the whole social system: the many ties that link people together coincide with those of direct kinship, and this shapes the structure of the whole society. [1956, p. 63]

Worsley is thus compelled to find a diversity in the institutional unity— on the model of a method for discovering the unity in an institutional diversity. To get a clearer picture of this theoretical inversion, allow me to reproduce Marx's most famous statement of materialist principle:

> The general conclusion at which I arrived and which, once reached, continued to serve as the leading thread in my studies may be briefly summed up as follows: In the social production which men carry on, they enter into definite relations that are indispensable and independent of their will; these relations of production correspond to a definite stage of development of their material powers of production. The sum total of these relations of production constitutes the economic structure of society—the real foundation, on which rise legal and political superstructures and to which correspond definite forms of social consciousness. The mode of production in material life determines the general character of the social, political, and spiritual processes of life. It is not the consciousness of men that determines their existence, but, on the contrary, their social existence determines their consciousness. [Marx 1904 (1859), pp. 11–12]

Marx of course goes on to outline the dialectics of change: conflict between the developing material forces and the established relations of production, leading to social revolution, transformation of the economic base and, consequently, more or less rapid transformation of the ''entire immense superstructure.'' Both dynamic and determination in the theory, diachronic movement and synchronic relationship, presuppose a differentiated cultural order. The society envisioned in materialist theory is divided into "component purposive systems"—economy, polity, ideology—each organized by specialized institutions (market, state, church, etc.). Marx's own formulation of historical materialism contains a definite structural a priori—but of a kind that anthropology has recognized as particular and historical.

For the absence of just that differentiation between base and superstructure presumed by the materialist conception is the hallmark of the "primitive" in the array of human cultures. The term has had no sensible use in anthropology except to designate a *generalized* structure. In the tribal cultures, economy, polity, ritual, and ideology do not appear as distinct "systems," nor can relationships be easily assigned to one or another of these functions. To put it positively, society is ordered by a single consistent system of relationships, having the properties we recognize as "kinship," which is deployed or mapped onto various planes of social action. Tribal groups and relations are "polyvalent" or "multifunctional": they order all the activities which in Western civilization are the subject of special institutional developments. Kinship, which in the West is one of these specializaitons, confined to the domestic corner of social life, is *the* design of a society such as that of the Tallensi. Yet kinship is "superstructure" from the perspective of classic materialism, even as it is base in the structure of tribal society. For the Tallensi, kinship relations between father and son, husband and wife, brother and brother, are the main relations of production. They are also jural-political and ritual relations. Religion is the ancestor cult, as polity is the lineage and production is the patriarchal compound.[1]

1. "In fact the ideology of kinship is so dominant in Tale society, and the web of genealogical connexions so extensive, that no social relationships or events fall completely outside the orbit of kinship. In this respect the Tallensi resemble very many other primitive societies among whom, as Firth puts it, kinship is the articulating principle of social organization. Just because kinship acts as a major determinant of social behaviour in every aspect and department of social life, it is the basis of the machinery of social integration in societies of this type, as many studies on Africa, Oceania, and America have shown. . . .
   "Among the Tallensi kinship relations are a major determinant of the pattern of organization of all activities through which the ruling interests of the people are satisfied. This holds for all departments of Tale social life—for the activities concerned with the production and consumption of food and all material goods, for those involved in the reproduction and rearing of offspring, for those concerned with maintaining the rights and duties of individuals and corporate units toward one another, and for religious and ceremonial activities" (Fortes 1949, pp. 338–40).

Hence the necessity sensed by Worsley to fragment kinship into its "component systems." Thus assimilating the totality of one society to the divisions of another, Worsley undoes the work of history by a work of the mind. But the "material analytic" must then discount the kinship properties of economic relations and so reduce the famous "determination by the economic base" to an ecology of practical interest and a psychology of economic motive. For the anthropology of tribal societies, the important lesson must be that this argument from material necessity is not intellectually accidental. In part, the character of Worsley's critique was imposed by the theory prevailing in British anthropology. The species of materialism which understands kinship as the "idiom" of practicalities is, on the one hand, an adaptation to existing theoretical conditions within the discipline. Worsley's is the antithesis to the structuralist thesis developed by Radcliffe-Brown and forwarded by Fortes, and as pure negation it shares the premises of its theoretical opposite. Especially it retains that conception of social form as the "expression" of an underlying "principle" which was central to Radcliffe-Brown's work. It is content to substitute the principle of economic interest for that social solidarity, seeing the first as the "objective basis" of the second, but thus making of materialism another kind of sentimentality. This theoretical influence on Worsley's materialism I reserve for later discussion. The more important implication of the controversy with Fortes is an ontological one: what it says about the nature of the object in dispute, Tallensi society. If Worsley's materialism was in part constrained by the theoretical climate, it was on the other hand imposed by the Tallensi themselves. This same resolution of kinship to practical reason represents a logical transformation of historical materialism in the face of a generalized cultural order that it did not originally envision.

The concrete form of Tallensi society is a silent third part to the controversy but is the dominant force of its logic. The stages in Worsley's permutation of historical materialism are connected by the way the Tallensi system is constituted. At an initial moment of analysis, Worsley is compelled to exchange the real content of Tallensi relations of production for their abstract forms (e.g., cooperation), with the intention of understanding the former as an "idiom" of the latter. The relations of production adduced by Worsley are formal-technical facts: the collaboration and authority required in agricultural production; the demographic limits on compound size and density; the implications for fusion and fission of the differential distribution of agricultural resources; the necessary social scale of food sharing and thus of social solidarity; the relations of cooperation and

competition that ensue between people by virtue of their common dependence on uniquely valuable resources (permanent fields); and the like. From
such technical conditions. Worsley would derive the *content* of the relationships entailed—or sometimes, more modestly, the "objective significance"
(p. 42) of this content. By the age of nine or ten, for example, Tale children
begin to participate in the domestic economy under their father's authority;
it is "during this period," Worsley writes, "that the identification of father
and son which gives *shape* and strength to the lineage system, begins to
develop" (p. 42; emphasis mine).[2] Likewise, it is in the facts of sharing
food and working together that brothers develop that "solidarity of siblings" which is the bond of lineage (p. 42). The "practical basis" of filial
submission and attachment is the economic value of land, as it is likewise a
basis for disengagement when land is scarce (pp. 42 ff.). In this way, from
a number of similar observations, Worsley concludes: "The kinship system is the unifying system in Tale life. But it is itself the form *of expression*
of economic activities. . . . I contend that the significant determining system is the economic system, including production, distribution, and consumption" (p. 64; emphasis mine). Thus, at the first stage of Worsley's
analysis, the kinship system ordering production is dissolved into its real
"purposive systems"—whose reality at the economic level is an abstract
technical dimension—only to reappear later as the "expression" of
economic relations of which it is the content.[3]

In the final analysis, then, the materialism becomes a variety of
"economism." The dynamics of Tallensi lineage structure are laid to
gainful motives, conceived as following obviously from the objective conditions of production. Sons remain under their father's authority after

2. This may be something like the common reproach leveled by psychoanalysts at Marxists,
that the latter speak as if a man has no psyche until he gets his first paycheck.
3. The reduction of concrete, historical relations of production to an abstract shadow structure of productive requirements seems to be a necessary condition for applying the classic
historical materialism to primitive societies—as, for example, the "production units"
corresponding to forms of cooperation, which are in turn "realized" as lineage or village
relations, in Terray's analysis of Guro (1972; see also below, p. 17n); or the basic
organizational "constraints" in Godelier's study of Mbuti Pygmies (1973). Such imposition of the infrastructure-superstructure model is sometimes justified as a "scientific"
passage from the apparent to the hidden realities, but it is more accurately a simultaneous
analytic exchange of the actual for the formal and the historical for the eternal. The
concrete relations of production are taken merely as an appearance of formal-technical
necessities, and the latter abstraction is then reified as the true infrastructure. Hence the
actual historical mode of production is "explained" by impoverishment to dismal
positivist rules of material efficacy. For an analogous procedure in current ecological
reasoning, see below, pp. 85–89.

maturity (patrilocal residence) in order to retain access to the extended family farm; or else shortage of land, a desire to take control of their own labor, or concern for their growing families leads them to break from the parental homestead (pp. 48, 54 ff.). The structural solidarities and cleavages of which Fortes makes so much are more basically a matter of economic sentiment. The logic of lineage form is economic interest.

Between the first and final stages of this theoretical development, Worsley interprets the other "purposive systems" within the kinship system, such as the ancestor cult, by the economic structure that he had similarly analyzed out. One functional moment of a polyvalent kinship relation is thus understood as the effect of another, when each in fact is simultaneously present in the other. Worsley contends, for example, that the jural or ritual relationship between Tale father and son depends on their relationship in production (pp. 41–49, 62). Yet it is evident that their relationship in production also depends on the authority of the father in a patrilineal structure and the ritual piety of the son (Fortes 1949, p. 204). But the basic dilemma in this, as throughout the analysis, is that one cannot determine the kinship properties of the relation by the economic coordinates of the interaction. Nothing in the material conditions or the economic interests specifies the quality of kinship as such. Tallensi farmers are not related as father and son by the way they enter into production; they enter thus into production because they are related as father and son. This is what renders Fortes's reply unassailable (1969, pp. 220 ff.).

Fortes's reply is simply that the structural form of the Tallensi lineage system is not given by the objective properties of production. One might add that kinship is a symbolic attribution—a "primary category of Tale thought" (1949, p. 339)—by definition not a relation of objective nature. The lineage is sui generis, in the sense that its own terms as culture are in no way immanent in the material conditions, and at the same time it is dominant over these conditions in that it orders them in its own terms. Fortes is quite prepared to concede that it may be in the nature of agricultural production that father and son *cooperate,* but it is not in the nature of agricultural production that *father* and *son* cooperate—as opposed to mother and daughter, mother's brother and sister's son, or Don Quixote and Sancho Panza. Fortes had acknowledged in the original ethnography that material necessity is an irreducible matter of fact, but as opposed to such *fact,* he rightly insists that the *logic* in the situation is the set of kinship relations analytically dissipated by Worsley. Hence the effect of the material necessity is determined by the kinship property of the relations—even as the definition of a human existence in lineage terms specifies the economic necessities in the first place.[4]

But if this is the strength of Fortes's position, its vulnerability was the way he phrased it. The weakness in it was that distinction between social form and underlying principle endemic in British structuralism. Worsley's opening was generously provided by a characteristic passage from the last chapter of Fortes's *Web of Kinship*. The essence of Tale kinship, Fortes here suggested, lies "in its function as the primary mechanism through which the basic moral axioms of a society of the type represented by the Tallensi are translated into the concrete give and take of social life" (1949, p. 346)—a proposition cited by Worsley at the very beginning of his critique (1956, p. 38). It was then altogether too easy for Worsley to demonstrate from Fortes's reports that the "concrete give and take of social life" was economically inspired, that both morals and kinship are subject to inflection by economic motives and ecological conditions. Where Fortes had seen the tendency of patrilocal residence, or else the inclination of sons to return to their father's homestead after his death, as an indication of the solidarity of the patrilineage, Worsley could convincingly counter that such behavior is understandable from the uniquely fertile manured farms built up in established compounds. It is the lineage that "translates" the give and take of economic life; manure is thicker than blood. And if it is economically desirable, neither the solidarity nor the cult of the lineage is proof against the inclination of sons to remain apart from fathers, or brothers from brothers.

The difference in the handling of compound fission is particularly instructive. Two ships pass in the night. Fortes had set out the progressive stages of the Tale domestic cycle in a series of diagrams (1949, p. 76; the initial phases of segmentation are reproduced here in simplified form as fig. 1). For Worsley, however, the diagrams were prima facie evidence of "the incorrectness of [Fortes's] analysis of fission in the lineage in terms of conflict between the 'principles' of matricentrality and patricentrality" (1956, p. 57). The objection was to Fortes's claim that "the concept of paternal origin is counterpoised by the concept of maternal origin in every

---

4. "This mode of production must not be considered simply as being the reproduction of the physical existence of the individuals. Rather it is a definite form of activity of these individuals, a definite form of expressing their life, a definite *mode of life* on their part" (Marx and Engels 1965, p. 32).

   The implications of this passage from *The German Ideology* are discussed at length in chapters 3 and 4 below.

Figure 1

Schema of Tallensi compound fission (abridged from Fortes 1949, p.76).

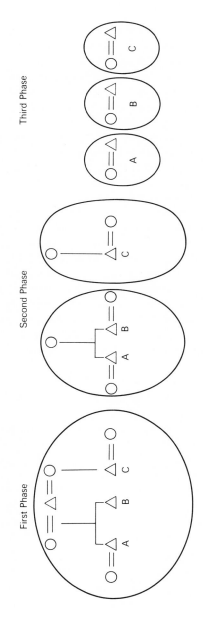

aspect of family life''—that these two concepts of descent ''operate as polar principles in the structure of this field.''[5] But by Worsley's reading, the true ''source'' of compound fission cannot be a conflict of social principles; it is rather an economic differentiation of households. The secession of sons represents a clash of property interests, motivated by the growth of their individual families, their desire for independence, and a shortage of land, either natural or imposed by a system of inheritance which denies them immediate control. Economic differentiation is thus ''the *force* which acts upon other distinctions such as age, sex, and cleavages in the lineage structure'' (Worsley 1956, p. 60; emphasis mine).

But, of course, as Fortes sees it such arguments do not touch his own. Fortes does not deny the ecological constraint or the economic interests; he points them out. But he does insist that *the social effects of practical interest—not to mention the nature of that interest—depend on the structure in place.* Again, the economic logic is socially constituted. As for the fact of manured permanent fields, this may account for people's desire to gain access to them, but it does not account for why sons stay with fathers, or why land is patrilineally inherited. As for family fission, Fortes had himself stressed the economic factor (1949, p. 262 and passim; noted by Worsley 1956, pp. 46–49). His point is that ''economic pressures . . . would not work out in just the way they do were it not for the inherent dichotomy in the structure of the family and the lineage.'' All the

5. For Fortes, this contrast of organizing principle pervades Tale society at every level, and supplies a dialectic of its movement in time and space:

"The structure of this field [of kinship] is determined by the interaction of two categories of social ties, those of parentage and those of marriage. Their interaction gives rise to two concepts of descent that operate as polar principles in the structure of this field. The concept of paternal origin is counterposed by the concept of maternal origin in every aspect of family life. The structural equilibrium of the domestic organization depends on their complementary functions. At the level of corporate social relations we find a similar structural equilibrium in the lineage system and also in the politico-ritual system. . . .

"The polarity of patrilateral and matrilateral kinship regulates the development of kinship relations in time, as well as their configuration at a given time. . . . The patrilineal principle is the primary factor of stability and continuity in the organization of the family and hence of the entire social structure. Conversely, the recognition of kinship ties through the mother is the primary factor of dispersion and segmentation in the family and the social structure. The values symbolized in the concept of patrilineal descent [note that the concept of descent is again a translation of other values] constitute the chief centripetal force, those summed up in the concept of matrilateral kinship the chief centrifugal force in the structure both of the family and of the society at large" (Fortes 1949, pp. 341–42).

economic pressures put together would never account for the sequence of segmentation as such.

Let us reduce the problem to its most elementary form, supposing with Worsley that the division of the joint family from phase 1 to phase 2 were due to demographic economic forces. Yet in material terms the only significance of such "pressure" would have been that (roughly) two-thirds of the original family could continue to live in the same location at the initial economic level. Whether the response should be intensification, privation, or segmentation, and, if the last, which third of the people should go, is not specified by the indeterminant economic "pressure." Different societies may be expected to react differently. As for the Tallensi, the social logic of fission was just what Fortes had discussed in the analysis of their patrilineal order. Sons are differentiated first by their father's marriages, second by their own. It is a phenomenon known generally to the anthropology of partilineal systems: the lineage is internally divided by external alliances and obligations, such that wives and mothers, indispensable to the continuity of the group, become at the same time the genealogical focuses of its segmentation. Such a logic, however, is structural and cultural, in its own properties no sequitur to the character of the economic "pressure."

On the contrary, it would be easy to show by reason and example that the nature of the material pressure is a function of Tallensi social logic (e.g., Fortes 1949, pp. 182–83). The demographic imbalances experienced by the Tallensi are not a direct and intrinsic expression of the productive forces but are an expression of the way these are culturally organized: particularly of the *mode of access to resources,* here governed by such rules as patrilocality, the incorporation of landholding at low levels of lineage segmentation, and the incapacity of sons (even though middle-aged and fathers themselves) to own property in their own right during their fathers' lifetimes. Under these conditions differential growth and mortality among families will prove a continuous source of microecological pressure—of a kind and intensity that simply would not exist if, for example, land were held by higher-level lineage or territorial units with freedom of access enjoyed by all constituent households.[6] From all this, one might conclude in Fortes's favor that economic force *as such* has no social significance or effect. There can be no predicative relation between the

6. For an excellent example of the structural determination of material pressure, both of its intensity and its effects, see Raymond Kelly's article "Demographic Pressure and Descent Group Structure in the New Guinea Highlands" (1969). Note particularly the demonstration of the variation in pressure according to the segmentary level of landholding.

Wingate College Library

indifference of the material function to the form of its realization and the specific properties of a patrilineal order. On the other hand, inasmuch as the material forces are socially constituted, their specific effects are culturally determined. The decisive issue between Worsley and Fortes is not which of these—material circumstance or structure—is a social force, but rather which is a social logic.

Yet if Fortes seems to win the debate, it may not be so much on the merits of his theoretical case. Structural-functional theory, as we have seen, lent credibility to Worsley's critique—so long as he stayed within the analytic of form and "principle" which Fortes himself used. It may be worthwhile to digress for a moment on the nature of that theory.

The vulnerability in Fortes's perspective was an original condition of British social anthropology. Radcliffe-Brown thought he could found a theoretical and comparative "natural science of society" by discovering the general principles manifest in specific social practices (see, for example, Radcliffe-Brown 1950, 1952, 1957). The social world marched on two levels: concrete groups and relationships were the "expression" of more abstract sentiments; the phenomenal form was a circumstantial representation of the underlying principle. The "principles" Radcliffe-Brown adduced, however, were typically abstract reformulations of the customs he was seeking to explain. The equation between father and father's brother in kinship terminology, for example, was understood by the "principle of equivalence of siblings." The interpretation is of course a tautology and as such defeats the original purpose: collapsed into the custom to which it referred, the explanation lacks the depth Radcliffe-Brown would have given it. One might say that Worsley's materialist revaluation of the Tallensi filled an intellectual vacuum within the British school.

But the theoretical stiuation was really worse than that, and Worsley's critique responded in detail to a more serious difficulty. The deficiency in Radcliffe-Brown's procedure became fully apparent only when it was extended comparatively. If in a single instance "principle" is the abstract version of form, the generalization of principle to accommodate a number of distinct forms becomes an exercise in classification. Thus for Radcliffe-Brown the kinship equivalence of a man and his brother, the levirate and sororate, adelphic polyandry and sororal polygyny, as well as the avunculate in patrilineal systems, are so many instances of the principle of "identity of siblings." Mired in such confusion of generalization with classification, Radcliffe-Brown's project was threatened with absurdity. Using the model of the natural sciences, he had intended to explain the particular by the general, to see the concrete form as a specific case of a broader rule. He understood himself to be discovering natural laws of social life, defining natural law "as a statement of the characteristics of a certain class of natural systems" (1957, p. 63). But where the law is thus a taxonomic class, the wider it is, the fewer and more general must be the criteria for inclusion within it. Therefore, the greater the "generalization" or "law," the less it says about anything in particular. In the course of grouping more and more diverse forms under wider and wider principles, Radcliffe-Brown explained less and less about any one of them. The "principles" cannot hope to account for particularity, because they destroy it.[7]

One main response of the British school to the vacuity of taxonomic generalization was to invert the procedure—to make the classes smaller rather than larger. A satisfactory contact with empirical reality could be restored by subdividing the social types and principles into finer and finer varieties of the same, as expressed in particular societies. This "butterfly hunting"—as it was so aptly characterized and criticized by Leach (1966)—can be understood as a retracing of the steps of Radcliffe-Brownian generalization, exchanging the emptiness of the general principle for its variance in a specific case without questioning the formal notions built into the project. With regard to the idea of "principle," however, one aspect of these notions tended to be emphasized, also as if in awareness of the "scientific" stalemate. The social principles were increasingly determined as underlying values and moral sentiments. This too had been in the original conception. Its roots go back at least to the Enlightenment, whence it was transmitted through Saint-Simon and Durkheim, among others, to Radcliffe-Brown (Evans-Pritchard 1954, pp. 21 ff.). "Principle" in this

7. On the other hand, when confronted in comparative studies with an irreducible diversity, Radcliffe-Brown tended to employ another tactic: the idea of the several principles as a universal pool of structural constituents, endemic in the elementary conditions of family and marriage, but variously taken up by different societies (1950; 1952; cf. Fortes 1969). Any particular institution could then be explained ad hoc, as a selective appropriation or a specific combination of the universal principles. In a way, this is the worst sort of historicism, a violation of Lyell's rule of uniformitarianism, inasmuch as it alleges for an unknown past the existence of processes not observable in the phenomenon as we know it; but for Radcliffe-Brown it was a particularly felicitous, no-fail method, since the principles he adduced were often contradictory themselves. So if "the unity of the lineage" accounts for the overriding of generations in certain categories of Omaha kinship, nevertheless the "merging of alternate generations" and the separation of those adjacent would explain the contrasting practices of the Yaralde—despite the presence and unity of Yaralde lineages (e.g., 1952, pp. 48–49).

problematic was the active force behind the form, the "human passions which set it in motion." The phrase is from a key passage of *The Spirit of the Laws* (bk. 3, chap. 1):

> There is this difference between the nature and the principle of government, that the former is that by which it is constituted, the latter that by which it is made to act. One is its particular structure, and the other the human passions which set it in motion. [Montesquieu 1966 (1748), p. 19; Montesquieu footnotes: "This is a very important distinction, whence I shall draw many consequences; for it is the key of an infinite number of laws."][8]

Principle is the necessary human condition for the existence of social form, that which gives a form its distinctive reason. A social structure is thus a kind of crystallization in objective relations of some subjective value—just as, for Montesquieu, each type of government had its proper principle: republican government, virtue; monarchy, honor; and despotism, fear. Here, then, is the source of Fortes's concept of kinship as a "translation" of the basic moral axioms of Tale society into the give and take of social life.[9] And so for Worsley, too, kinship was a "form of expression"—but in this case an expression of basic economic activities. The theoretical conjuncture in British anthropology, which held that kinship was the translation of some deeper reality, was made to order for a materialist critique of the same import. Much of the mutual incomprehension in their debate came about because Worsley was attacking the idea that kinship expresses the social values, whereas Fortes was making the observation that kinship organizes the economic activities.

This being the observed fact of Tallensi society, what do we conclude about the appropriateness of historical materialism? It may be that the argument over the facts was so motivated as to preclude any decision on the validity of the theory. Worsley's own version of materialist theory was

8. On the formulation of the analytic-synthetic method in the natural sciences and its analogic extension to the social sciences, see Cassirer's *Philosophy of the Enlightenment* (1951 [1932]; cf. also Althusser [1969]; and Peters [1946] on the original adoption by Hobbes of Galileo's "resoluto-compositive" method).

9. This conception poses an additional difficulty in the relation between form and principle; for as Lévi-Strauss remarks in a parallel case, the structure is precise but the moral value unspecific—the former logical and the latter merely sentimental—such that the derivation of structure from sentiment is something out of nothing. If Fortes had seriously attempted to reduce Tallensi kinship to such basic values as "reciprocity" (cf. 1949, pp. 204ff.), he would have on one hand come closer to Worsley's economism, and on the other fallen into the same kind of indeterminism (see Hart, in press).

subject to a double determination: by the nature of the structuralist theory it opposed as well as by the structure of the society it explained. It could be that its economism was due to the first, in which case its failure proves nothing about the second, at least not that the type of society is inherently resistant to an authentic Marxism. I have argued, on the other side, that the metamorphosis of Marxism into an economistic or technological determinism was an inevitable outcome of its confrontation with a generalized system such as Tallensi.[10] But it may be enough for the moment to make that suggestion, and too much to think it has be substantiated. In the same way, I would discuss its corollary: merely suggesting the plausibility of the position of Lukács and a number of other Marxists, to the effect that the truth of historical materialism is itself historical.

It was no error, Lukács wrote, to apply historical materialism "vigorously and unconditionally to the history of the nineteenth century." For,

> in that century all the forces which impinged upon society functioned in fact purely as the forms of the "objective spirit" become manifest. In precapitalist societies this was not really the situation. In such societies economic life did not yet possess that independence, that cohesion and immanence, nor did it have the sense of setting its own goals and being its own master that we associate with capitalist society. [1971, p. 238]

But by the same token, namely, that the theory is "the self-knowledge of capitalist society," it has a specific historical status. It is a brilliant *prise de*

---

10. As noted, Terray's (1972) formal application of the Althusser-Balibar explication of materialist method to the Guro is another case in point. This analysis surely merits a detailed consideration in its own right. Of particular interest here are the analogies to Worsley's argument which suggest a regularity to the tribal declension of historical materialism that transcends the theoretical starting-point. Even beyond the parallel deconstitution of the relations of production to technical requirements (in this instance, forms of cooperation abstractly defined), there is striking resemblance to Worsley in Terray's notion that economic relations are then represented or "realized" as kinship. Terray is more consistent than Worsley in recognizing that the kinship "element" is not reducible to the formal requirements of economic cooperation. His concept of "realization" (the term is almost always in quotation marks in Terray) here supposes that kinship is something of the order of biological-genealogical fact, whose (fictive) representation in classificatory terms, for example, prepares the way for an inflection of kinship by economic requirements. (Compare Worsley's "actual kin," above.) This particular parallel is of interest not only in itself, as an indication of the theoretical necessity imposed on materialism by tribal structure, but for its suggestion of a common, and more basic, theoretical tendency: a refusal of the symbolic constitution of social reality; or else of the "reality" of that constitution. Exactly what is entailed in this theoretical choice will become clearer as the present work proceeds.

conscience of a particular type of system, one in which the relations between man and man, like those between man and nature, are reified as economic relations. In the upshot, Lukács goes on to say, historical materialism does make an anthropology possible. Not by a mechanical transfer to precapitalist societies, but precisely by the possibility of avoiding a naive identification of the past with the structure of the present. If, however, historical materialism is transferred without change to earlier society, it encounters a "very essential and weighty difficulty . . . one which did not appear in the critique of capitalism." This difficulty, often noted by Marx and Engels, "lies in the *structural* difference between the age of civilization and the epochs that preceded it" (1971, p. 232; Lukács's emphasis).

Following Lukács, one is tempted to conclude that historical materialism and British structuralism, good or bad, are both special theories, appropriate to different cultural universes. The same conclusion, we shall see, develops from the debate between Marxism and French structuralism. Yet that debate also goes beyond the institutional differences of societies—and beyond all "revisionist" contingencies in the form and application of Marx's materialism. It presents the more fundamental problem of the relation between praxis and the symbolic order. And once that issue is raised, it is no longer a question whether tribal culture is not also materialistically determined, but whether bourgeois society is not also a culture.

Marxism and French Structuralism

The institutional structure of tribal cultures is only one of the anthropological problems historical materialism must face. Another is the seeming resistance of such systems to experience in the world, a certain immunity of the existing order to historical contingency. This resistance in turn goes to a more fundamental property of the tribal social-economic formations: a domination of practical action by cultural conception rather than conception by action.

Since these are essential contentions of French structuralism, it is clear why that structuralism, for all its interest to Marxists, is the most subject to revolutionary criticism. Indeed, it seemed in Paris during the heady days of May 1968 that the obituary to this current philosophical rage of the Latin Quarter had been fittingly composed by practice. As the saying went, "Structuralism has gone down into the streets" (cf. Epistemon 1968; Turkle 1975). Such was the common word on the intellectual barricades.

And if it were remarked that the barricades themselves seemed more nostalgic for 1789 than effective for 1968, the response was, *"Mais enfin,* the enemy hasn't changed." Structuralism had indeed gone down into the streets.

Allow me another anecdote that raises the same paradox. Shortly before the events of May 1968, I had the opportunity to witness an informal debate between an American member of the Russell Tribunal—passing through Paris from Copenhagen, where he had learned of the structuralist vogue from French colleagues—and a Parisian anthropologist. After a long period of question and discussion, the American summed up his views in this way: "I have a friend," he said, "who is doing a sociological study of the equestrian statues in Central Park. It's a kind of structuralism. He finds a direct relation between the cultural status of the rider and the number of legs the horse has off the ground. One leg poised has a different historical and political connotation from a horse rearing on hind legs or another cast in flying gallop. Of course the size of the statue also makes a difference. The trouble is," he concluded, "people don't ride horses anymore. The things in a society that are obsolete, out of contention, those you can structure. But the real economic and political issues are undecided, and the decision will depend on real forces and resources."[11]

The Parisian anthropologist thought about that a moment. "It is true," he finally said, "that people don't ride horses anymore. But they still build statues."

Something more was implied than that the past was not dead—because, as has been said of the American South, it is not even past. It was also intended that economics and politics have modalities other than the "real" competition for power. Just as Durkheim argued against Spencer on the converse issue that the contract cannot be said to form society, since society is already presupposed in the unstipulated rules by which the agreement proceeds, so social competition must be grounded in shared conceptions of resources, finalities, and means—values that are never the only ones possible. The competition does not evolve absolutely, on an eternal and formal rationality of maximization; it develops according to a system of cultural relationships, including complex notions of authority and sub-

11. Compare Ricoeur (1967, p. 801) on the conditions for the triumph of the type of intelligibility called structuralism, namely, "travailler sur un corpus déjà constitué, arrêté, clos et, en ce sens, mort." See Furet (1967) on structuralism and the French political context.

mission, hierarchy and legitimation. And among other means, it is by a literal concretization of this code in statues that history is made to act within the present, at once directly and through its dialectical reappropriation and revaluation.[12]

Indeed the whole reply was a concrete modality of the argument of Lucien Sebag, who wrote in *Marxisme et Structuralisme:*

> C'est qu'il est vain de chercher une réalité qui soit à la fois de l'ordre de la culture et qui ne puisse être traduite en termes d'activité intellectuelle; car les individus, ou les groupes sociaux luttant les uns contre les autres, transformant la nature, organisant leur propre vie en commun mettent en jeu un système de concepts qui n'est jamais le seul possible et qui définit le forme même de leur action. A ce niveau la distinction entre infrastructure et superstructure s'efface car les rapports économiques, sociaux, politiques comme les théories qui en rendent compte au sein d'une société déterminée sont tout autant produits de l'esprit. [Sebag 1964, p. 193]

> [It is vain to seek a reality that is at once of cultural order and cannot be translated in terms of intellectual activity. For individuals and social groups, in struggling against one another, transforming nature, or organizing their life in common, bring into play a system of concepts which is never the only possible one and which defines the very form of their action. At this level the distinction between infrastructure and superstructure disappears, for economic, social, and political relations, like the theories that account for them in a given society, are just as much products of the mind.]

12. "The statues in the square [the Piazza della Signoria in Florence] were admonitory lessons or 'examples' in civics, and the durability of the material, marble or bronze, implied the conviction or the hope that the lesson would be permanent. The indestructibility of marble, stone, and bronze associates the arts of sculpture with governments, whose ideal is always stability and permanence. The statue, in Greek religion, is thought to have been originally a simple column, in which the trunk of a man or, rather, a god was eventually descried. Florentine sculpture, whether secular or religious, retained this classic and elemental notion of a pillar or support of the social edifice. Other Italians of the Renaissance, particularly the Lombards, were sometimes gifted in sculpture, but the Florentines were almost always called upon by other cities when it was a question of public, that is, of a civic, work. The great equestrian statue of the *condottiere* Gattamelate that stands in the square at Padua was commissioned from Donatello; when the Venetians wanted to put up a statue along the same lines (the Colleone monument), they sent for Verrocchio. The state sculptor of the Venetian Republic was a Florentine, Sansovino"—Mary McCarthy, *The Stones of Florence.* (Note, "statue" and "statute" have the same root.)

I defer discussion of the apparent "idealism" in such a position to concentrate on the seeming "conservatism," which has in any case the same principle—the privilege accorded the symbolic construction of practice.

The wave of disillusionment with structuralism for its celebration of the status quo has its origin in the conviction that revolution would be a good thing. But too much is lost in this political simplification. The bare oppositions of synchrony/diachrony, of stasis/change, do not adequately describe the current differences between French structuralism and the going Marxism. Even the simple anecdotes of their confrontation I have offered suggest a curious paradox of historical consciousness. Privileging the determinations of the preexisting state, rather than the modifications ensuing from practice, structuralism invokes the action of the past where Marxism demands only the presence of the action. In appearance an elaborate sequel to *plus ça change, plus c'est la même chose,* structuralism must then accord a unique respect to history. Synchronic in principle, it offers the highest rationale for the study of diachrony. But in truth structuralism is not so much a theory of simple reproduction as it has been a theory of structures that so reproduce.

The issue of *principle* for structuralism is that circumstance itself does not engender form except as it is given significance and effect by the system in place. It is unwarranted to suppose that no theoretical space remains for human action or contingent event. Only that such action—like the spoken word uttered in a novel situation—takes its meaning as a projection of the cultural scheme which forms its specific context, and its effect by a relation of significance between this contingent reference and the existing order. An event becomes a symbolic relation. The process is best known and followed in the linguistic appropriation of experience. As Sapir described it,

New cultural experiences frequently make it necessary to enlarge the resources of a language, but such an enlargement is never an arbitrary addition to the materials and forms already present; it is merely a further application of principles already in use and in many cases little more than a metamorphical extension of old terms and meanings. It is highly important to realize that once the form of a language is established it can discover meanings for its speakers which are not simply traceable to the given quality of experience itself but must be explained to a larger extent as the projection of potential meanings into the raw material of experience. If a man who has never seen more than a single elephant in the course of his life, nevertheless speaks without the slightest hesitation of tens of elephants or a million elephants or a herd of elephants walking two by two or three by three or of generations of elephants, it is obvious that language has the power to analyze experience into theoretically dissociable elements and to create that model of the potential intergrading with the actual which enables human beings to transcend the immediately given in their individual experiences and to join in a larger common understanding. This common understanding constitutes culture. [Sapir 1933, pp. 156–57][13]

For structuralism, meaning is the essential property of the cultural object, as symboling is the specific faculty of man. Meaning of course does not create the real and material forces, but so far as these are engaged by men meaning encompasses them and governs their specific, cultural influence. Nor is it, then, that the forces are without real effect; only that they have no particular effect, as no effective cultural existence, apart from their integration in a given historical and symbolic scheme. Change begins with culture, not culture with change. For praxis theory, by contrast, the decisive and self-sufficient moment is the act. Itself constrained by instrumental necessity, the act necessarily generates cultural form and significance on the basis of given qualities of the real as worked upon—the famous process of human self-creation through labor. The "common understanding" of which Sapir spoke is here not the author of significance but its prior condition or its subsequent representation. The specific construction of culture is the product of a concrete activity which transcends the system to appropriate the novelty and actuality of the material world.[14]

---

13. Thus one can agree with Ricoeur (1967) that the spoken word (*parole,* the act) returning from the event to the system (*langue,* structure), brings with it the evidences of "the real" in a new aspect of polysemy, without however supposing that this represents an opening toward history that structuralism is incapable of conceiving. For Ricoeur's critique not only fails to elucidate the systematic character both of the projection to and the return from the "real," but even more important, does not explain that the "real" involved is never the given quality of the word but is that quality as value and meaning. Hence *parole* throughout represents action *in a system* and a *system in action.* By Ricoeur's own best understanding this "real" is something more than an instrumental and objective fact (see his remarkable essay "Work and Word," 1970; and also Silverstein 1975). Also, for a contrary textual reading on the purported closure of the structuralist concept of system, the idea that *tout se tien,* on which Ricoeur rests his critique, see Gaboriau's "Structural Anthropology and History" (1970).

14. "Le problème n'est pas de nier l'importance capitale du moment de la structure, du moment du concept, mais de ne pas les traiter d'une façon abstraite, de savoir en chaque moment remonter, comme Marx nous l'a enseigné, de la structure à l'activité

At this creative instant of the act, the existing order of culture loses its historical (i.e., constituting) function. The dead hand of the past, it now plays the theoretical role of an impediment to the structures built up from the productive logic; or else it is "soft" and submits to its own desuetude like the good "dependent variable" of an empiricist anthropology. Hence the paradox of historical consciousness: The role assigned to history by materialist explanation risks an impoverishment on one side to residue, on the other side to origins. "History" enters into theory as a survival, the name of a short-run exception to the constituting power of practice. Or else, taken merely as such constituting power of the productive forces, the actual historical content is abstracted, so that the analysis may proceed as a kind of initial situation—as if one had the opportunity, with Malinowski, of being present at the creation (see below, pp. 80–81). Symbol and act, word and world—the two perspectives differ in their epistemological starting points. And the apparent conservatism of structuralism is the *concept* of what everyone will recognize as the fact: that history begins with a culture already there.[15]

What then to make of the opinion of the French Marxist, Charles Parain, who can only conclude from prolonged reflection on the works of Lévi-Strauss that what is to be found there, *"c'est l'embarras du structuralisme face à l'histoire"*? If so, *c'est un embarras de richesse*. Structuralism developed in the first place out of the encounter with a type of society, the so-called primitive, distinguished by a special capacity to absorb perturbations introduced by the event with a minimum of systematic deformation. By its comprehension of that capacity, structuralism takes on the explication of the work of history in its most powerful form, the persistence of structure by means of event. And after all—one can just picture Jean Pouillon's Gallic shrug of the shoulders as he reminds us—"It is not the structuralists who put the structures in history" (1966, p. 785).

What is this "special capacity" of tribal society to reproduce more or

---

humaine qui l'engendre, tenir les deux bouts de la chaîne, le moment de la structure et le moment de la liberté, le moment de la necessité et le moment de l'*activité créatrice* de l'homme" (Garaudy 1965, p. 119).

15. "Ce que nous mettons en cause c'est le possibilité d'isoler des réseaux ou des événements pleinement significatifs par eux-mêmes dans le déroulement de la trame historique; une invention technologique boulverse tout l'édifice des relations sociales; certes, mais elle est elle-même pénétrée de 'spiritualité'; elle est produit d'un certain travail de l'intellect qui n'est pas pensable en termes économiques; il n'y a donc pas 'd'origine' " (Sebag 1964, p. 141; cf. Lévi-Strauss 1971).

less stereotypically in the face of historical vicissitudes? What special light does a structuralist analysis throw upon it? Without claiming any real structuralist competence, I would hazard an answer by rethinking along those lines an ethnographic experience I have previously described in other terms (Sahlins 1962).[16] The example concerns the moiety system and its resistance to demographic variation in the Moalan and Lau Islands of eastern Fiji. It thereby addressed a problem also known to Marx: the so-called stationariness of archaic communities (cf. B. Turner 1974). Besides, it has another value relevant to the debate between Marxism and structuralism—attention to which will perhaps excuse the length of the ethnographic digression. Inevitably it must consider the symbolic organization of economic practice, hence the famous ''idealism'' of structuralism. I hasten to add that the description of Moala and Lau will be so simplified, so abusive of the real complexities, that it would not merit any attention were it not so good an illustration of these points.

''Everything goes in twos,'' A. M. Hocart was told by a Lauan friend, ''or the sharks will bite.'' Similarly for the Moalans, their island and each of its villages are essentially made up of two ''kinds'' of people: the Land People (*kai vanua*) and the Chiefs (*turaga*). The Land People are also known as the ''owners'' (*taukei*) an expression synonymous with first occupants or original settlers. The Chiefs came later, by sea, to assume the rule over a numerous host that had filled the inland regions—so the Land People are also the ''Thousands'' (*Udolu*) or ''Animal People'' (*Yavusa Manumanu*). Having submitted to the Chiefs, the Land People served them in ritual capacities, notably as masters of ceremony and food distribution (*matanivanua*). One can already sense the symbolic productivity of the dualism. A difference of social groups corresponds to the distinction of land and sea on the geographic plane, itself an instance of a general spatial differentiation of interior and peripheral, correlated with oppositions of indigenous and foreign, earlier and later, even animal and cultural; the same groups again are inferior and superior politically, ritual and secular functionally. As it were, the myth of origin is a temporal rendition of these basic distinctions, the setting of a binary logic to time, to reproduce it as narrative (cf. Thompson 1940). But it would be inadequate to consider the contrasts merely as a series of congruent oppositions. Local legends of the

16. I take this opportunity to acknowledge the percipiency of Murray Groves, who in a review article (1963) pointed out the significance of the ''two-section'' system in Moala, an analysis I had failed to make.

coming of the Chiefs as well as many customary practices reveal a definite structure of reciprocities. In its most general terms the reciprocal logic is that each "kind" mediates the nature of the other, is necessary for the realization and regulation of the other, so that each group necessarily contains the other. The ensuing configuration is not so much a simple opposition as a four-part system operated by the replication of a master dichotomy, as in Hocart's representation of the "tribe" in Moala and neighboring islands (fig. 2). This scheme, we shall see, does indeed serve

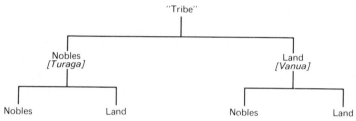

Figure 2   General model of the "tribe" in Moalan group (after Hocart 1929, p. 233).

well as a description of the Moalan polity, taken either as a system of descent groups or as a territorial framework. Yet the same four-class code can be discovered in the relations of kinship and marriage, in ritual and production, in the values of goods and the concepts of space.[17] By following out the meaningful connections between customs at these different levels, we may in a way reproduce the process by which one cultural domain is mapped upon another to create a global order at once of form, content—and action.

Throughout Lau, the claim of Land People to be the true "owners" and men of the soil is acknowledged as genuine; but their cultivations would not prosper without the agency of the Chiefs. The right of the ruling chief to products of the land, especially the first fruits (*sevu*), has thus always been accorded by the "owners" as a guarantee of fertility, without

17. Bourdieu (1971) analyzes a Kabyle structure of this type under the general diagrammatic formula $a:b::b_1:b_2$. He notes of its generative capacity: "doubtless one of the simplest and most powerful [structures] that may be employed by a mythico-ritual system since it cannot oppose without simultaneously uniting (and inversely), while all the time being capable of integrating in a unique order an infinite number of data, by the simple application of the same principle of division indefinitely repeated" (1971, p. 749).

supposing a chiefly proprietary claim in the Western sense. It would be more to the point to understand the chief's intervention as a modality of the paternal right. The specific quality of Fijian chiefly power (*kaukawa* or *mana*) is masculine potency, a virility that has more than one representation in common custom. It appears directly, for example, in the paramount's privileged access to nubile women of his domain; symbolically, in the correspondence between the rites of chiefly investiture and the initiation of young men to sexual and warrior status by circumcision. Yet both these ceremonies are marked by the assumption of the bark cloth (*masi*), the most valuable of "woman's goods" (*yaya vakayalewa*). Hence the passage to higher male status is mediated by a female element—in logical converse of the chief's bestowal of fertility upon the land.[18]

To show the generality of this system, it is only necessary to make the connection between women and the land side of things. Moalan traditions again supply a paradigmatic statement—prepared, moreover, by the idea of the fecundity of the original inland people, the "Thousands." Arriving at the several local settlements, men of chiefly stock secured the rule when they were given firstborn daughters to wife by leaders of the Land. The political effect attributed to this gift can only be appreciated in light of the important kinship practices for which it serves in turn as legendary charter: (1) The superiority of the "side of the man" or wife-takers, the "strong side," to the wife-givers or "weak side"; (2) the superiority of the firstborn and his or her descendents to the line of the cadet; (3) the famous ritual and economic privileges of the *vasu* or sister's son over his mother's brother—such that in the traditional tales the authority of chiefs is reiterated as *vasu* to commoners.[19]

Now by another change of cultural register, this time to rules governing

18. The same rite of investment in bark cloth, here administered by the senior chief, attends the celebration of a warrior's first killing. In these ceremonies also the warrior is given a new name; as the local imagery has it, "the old name is to be cast away like a foreskin" (Tippett 1968, p. 61). The entire rite in its traditional form seems to have been quite similar to the circumcision ceremony (Williams and Calvert 1859, pp. 42–43). Likewise, the celebrations for a successful war party were characterized by a "vulgarity" that shocked the early missionaries. "The songs suggested that the hero in war was to be a hero in sex, and the most successful heroes were addressed in terms of their sex organs, and the sex organs of the living captives were abused by the dancing women" (Tippett 1968, p. 65). To adopt Hocart's type of symbolic shorthand, *Chief = virility = growth of crops = prowess in war.*

19. See Hocart 1929 on the political significance of the *vasu i taukei*, the chiefly *vasu* to the Land; and also Hocart 1915, p. 19.

familial sharing of food and personal possessions, one may develop further details of the relations between Chiefs and Land, men and women, paternal kinsmen and maternal kinsmen. The rules prescribe, first, certain priorities among these categories. The men of the family eat before and apart from the women, who serve the food, while fathers should precede sons, and older brothers eat before younger. Second, there are striking interdictions on the use by a man's descendents of his food leftovers, or of possessions such as clothes that have been closely associated with his person. The junior kinsman would be afflicted by an excess of potency, causing a swelling of the part of the body in contact with the prohibited item. Eating the elder's food, for instance, will produce abnormal enlargement of the throat or stomach. In Moala this effect goes by the Tongan word *fula;* but the older Fijian usage is precisely *bukete vatu,* to be made "pregnant with stone" (Deane 1921, p. 94)[20]

Appropriately then, the one member of the Moalan household exempt from the tabu and its effects is the patriarch's senior wife. A similar immunity is enjoyed by female cross-cousins, who are preferred sexual and marital partners—and opposed in all such dimensions of consummation to a man's sister. Finally, for ruling chiefs, the privilege goes also to the master of ceremony (*matanivanua,* "face of the land"), the same who in the traditions represents the Land People, wife-givers to the Chiefs. The right that is symbolized here, however, is something more than the access of these "talking chiefs" to the goods of the chief, even more than the corollary claims of the wife-givers or maternal kin against the line of the men—reciprocal of the *vasu* claim. By his immunity from the dangers of chiefly virility, the talking chief (like the chiefly wife) becomes the indispensable intermediary of all reciprocal relations between senior and junior kin of the same descent, lest the latter be stricken by the potency of the former. Without this freedom from tabu on the woman's side—which may now be more generally understood as a negation of chieftainship, corollary

20. The link is not only made here with the virility of the Fijian chief. Polynesian ethnologists will be reminded of the celebrated *hau,* the fertile stone-embodied (and stone-shattering) power of the gift in the Maori text analyzed by Marcel Mauss (cf. Sahlins 1972). This logical association is only strengthened by transformations of the term in related languages, such as Tongan *hau,* "a conquerer, a reigning prince," of which the Fijian chiefly title *sau* is also cognate (Tregear 1891, pp. 52–53). It does not seem too wild to consider the phallic-stone images of Polynesian gods as still another representation, e.g., the Hawaiian familial altar or "stone of Kane" (note, *kane* is Haw., "man," and Kane the principal god).

to the concept of a true people of the land, "real owners" (*taukei dina*)—
hierarchy would dissolve into discontinuity. But as it is, every feast given
by a chief is ceremoniously received by a talking chief, with his hand upon
it.

   Similarly in the Tokelau Islands, the "descendants of the man" provide,
but the "descendants of the woman" divide (Huntsman 1971). The Fijian
scheme is cognate with structures well known in western Polynesia, which
may be generally described on the surface level by the rule reserving main
economic and political control to the paternal line, while the "descendants
of the woman," although excluded from succession, retain a ritual authority at once indispensable and inimical to those who would rule.[21] The
system is constructed on a double axis. On the one hand: the patrilateral
relation of authority, represented notably as the distinction between older
and younger brother. This is the armature for the formation of social
groups; it is typically figured as a reciprocal relation in which the junior
serves the senior, who in return takes care of his cadet. On the other hand,
there is an axis of complementarity, coded as the brother-sister tie; this
enters particularity into the alliance between groups—that is, as the mediating bond between the woman's kin by birth and her relatives by marriage.
The Fijian system of Lau is a variant of the same dualism, but permuted
into more complex triadic and four-part representations.[22]

   In Lau, everything really goes by fours. Four is the Lauan numerical
concept of a totality. It takes four groups to make an island, four days of
exchange (of four kinds of goods) to complete a marriage, four nights of
treatment to effect a cure. Traditionally, Moala was organized just the way
Hocart described the "tribe": divided into Great Moala and Little Moala,
each half led by a group of Chiefs ruling over their own Land People.[23]

---

21. Actually we seem to be in the presence of a very widespread and profound Polynesian
    or Malayo-Polynesian pattern. The Fijian talking chief is counterpart to the Maori
    chiefly woman who mediates between tabu and nontabu periods of the economic
    cycle—or, for that matter, of those aristocratic Hawaiian women who played a decisive
    role in the abolition of the tabu by "free eating" (*ai noa*) in the famous "cultural
    revolution" of 1819.
22. For other transformations—in Tonga, Samoa, Futuna—see Panoff (1970); Kaeppler
    (1971); Gifford (1929); Mead (1930); and Gilson (1963); as well as Huntsman (1971)
    on the Tokelaus. See also Mabuchi (1960, 1964) for suggestions on the generality of the
    system in Oceania.
23. The island of Lakeba, in Lau, is composed of the territorial moieties of "The Town"
    (*Na Koro*) and the "Back of Lau" (*Doku ni Lau*). Each moiety again is divisible into
    two sets of villages. "The Town," which is dominant, is headed by the ruling commun-
    ity of Tubou, in relation to which its satellite settlements are "land." Conversely, the

Immediately the mention of such four-part systems will put the anthropologist in mind of a classic type of marriage system, and he would be right in suspecting its existence in Moala.

Moalans prescribe marriages between cross-cousins (i.e., offspring of siblings of the opposite sex). The practice would establish a duality such as we have seen in other relations—a basic combination of opposites, differentially valued—here dividing one's kin into an in-group (parallel relatives) and a set of in-laws ("cross" kin). But there is a further marital stipulation, yielding the complete set of four categories: first cross-cousins are prohibited from marrying; the nearest potential spouse becomes a second cross-cousin (e.g., MoMoBrDaDa, FaMoBrSoDa—these are classed with first cross-cousins in kinship terminology). Technically, the ensuing system is "Aranda" in respect to its four intermarrying segments, although it lacks the terminological elaboration into an eight-section system. Robin Fox's excellent diagram (fig. 3) and discussion of the Aranda system (1967, pp. 195–99) will thus help develop the structural implications. The logical model of second cross-cousin marriage is one of four descent lines—each represented for a specific ego by one of his four grandparents—arranged in certain relations of alliance. The lines are grouped two by two in exogamous moieties, each line united in any given generation with one of the two in the other moiety, and in the succeeding generation with the other of the two opposed lines. Relations among kinsmen are this way analogous in form to the global structure of the "tribe" (fig. 2); as conversely, the representation of tribal categories such as Chiefs and Land in the terms of marriage renders these different levels homologous in content.

It is important to remark, however, that the social formation is at once ternary as well as dual and quaternary. These modes of social order are only different perspectives on the same structure. They are so many elevations of the one social architecture—each a suitable model for independent realization in custom. Taken as a whole, the domain of kinship is composed of two "kinds" of people, own relatives and affinal. By the rule of marriage, this dualistic kin universe is internally differentiated into four lines. The marriage rules, however, preclude the duplication of alliances

---

"Back of Lau" has a ruling village whose chief is descendant from the dominant line of "The Town." The community of Tubou has the same scheme for its several descent groups (cf. Hocart 1929, pp. 10–22). Exactly the same organization appears in Thompson's (1940) description of Kabara Island, Lau.

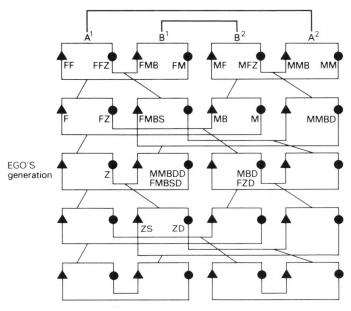

Figure 3   Kinship relations in second cross-cousin marriage (after
                      Fox 1967, p. 196; note that Moalans do not practice
                      actual sister-exchange, but the structural implications
                      are essentially as diagramed here).

between two paternal lines within successive generations, so that over the
short term each family is engaged with two contrasting sets of in-laws,
standing as wife-giver to some, wife-taker in relation to others. This is the
triadic element. From a certain vantage point within the system, the four-
part structure of complementary pairs is most saliently a set of three,
consisting of one's immediate paternal kin, the group of mother's brothers
with regard to whom one is *vasu* or ''sacred blood'' (*dra tabu*), and the
group of the sister's son, subject of a corresponding respect (fig. 4). This
particular image is in a way difficult to focus. It shifts between a triangular
order centered in one's own line and the ranked series of sister's son or
vasu relations which place wife-receivers in the supreme position. The
difficulty is only part of a constituted instability of the system *à trois*.

By comparison, the four-part structure is durable and dominant. For one
thing, it is a necessary condition of the triadic structure. But more, in

continually being canceled as well as reproduced by the quaternary code, the ternary system takes on a fugitive existence within an endemic contradiction between hierarchy and reciprocity. Nothing in the bilateral rule of (second) cross-cousin marriage would prohibit a reversal of the rank order between lines by changing the direction of wife-taking in the third generation—for example, by the marriage of a FFZSD (as of b^1 to C in fig. 4). Meanwhile, the economic relations between wife-takers and wife-givers have been working over time toward the same egalitarian effect. For taken in the larger context of exchange obligations between intermarrying groups, and over the longer term of two generations, the claims of the *vasu* or sister's son amount to the balancing of accounts that had first favored the mother's brother. At the marriage of the woman, sister of the latter, the husband's side would have given somewhat more in feasts and goods than they received, and especially at the birth of the sister's son, his paternal relations must secure his *vasu* rights by a very generous gift to the mother's

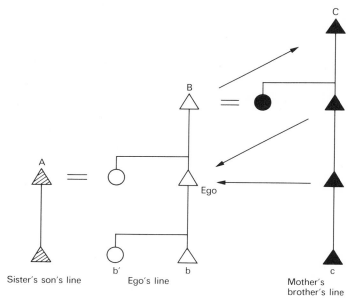

Figure 4   Salient triadic relation in the Moalan kinship order (→, direction of main economic obligations; A>B>C, ritual rank, based on "sacred blood").

kin (*vakalutulutu*). After the exercise of the *vasu*'s claims, then, the economic relations between intermarrying lines have been squared; and accordingly, cross-cousins—a man and his mother's brother's sons—have strong but *mutual* obligations of material aid (fig. 4). Now the children of these men are again preferred marriage partners. Yet since the relation between the cross-cousins has been rendered equal and reciprocal, there is no necessary disposition to repeat in the third generation the direction of wife-giving established in the first. Hence the triadic code is an image constantly produced by the quadratic and almost as often effaced. And with this resolution of hierarchy into the familiar outlines of reciprocity go many other Fijian visions of political centralization.[24]

Let us allow the preceding sketch, incomplete and fragmentary as it is, to stand for the general scheme of eastern Fijian culture. The problem remains of extending such an account of structure to the realm of action, specifically to the practical and historical action claimed by a certain Marxism as its exclusive analytic preserve. A good way to begin is with the construction of the Moalan house and the observation that this construction is in material form and division of labor a tangible representation of the same structure that has already been described—complete with binary, ternary, and quaternary elevations. A man's house is his castle; or as Moalans say, "Every man is a chief in his own house." If so, the society's house is its culture.[25]

Elliptic in outline, the Moalan dwelling house is divided down the long axis into a "chiefly side," traditionally set parallel to the sea, and a "common side" toward the inland. For each side there is an associated end segment: the rear arc of the house (between the main corner posts) is the "upper" end and "goes with" the chiefly side; the opposed front entrance

24. The political implications are discussed below, pp. 43–46. One sees in the economic claims retained in the first instance by wife-givers the corollary to the ritual powers of the wife and the talking chief over the paternal ("strong") side. Hence the Moalan variant of the western Polynesian dualism—since here ritual authority over the paternal line is divided between the kin of the wife and the "descendants of the woman" (sister's son). But then at a deeper level these two are not substantially distinguished by Fijians, since the sister's son, whatever his patrifiliation, specifically shares the "blood" and soul of his mother and her brothers: see Jarré (1946) on birth customs designed to prevent loss of maternal soul with the cutting of the umbilical cord. For an interesting West African analogue of the two-generation balancing of affinal accounts, see Marie (1972).

25. The following account of Fijian "domestic proxemics" is confined to the most general dimensions; for an appreciation of the full possibilities of such structural analyses of domestic space see, among other excellent studies, Bourdieu (1971); Cunningham (1973); Tambiah (1969); and Wagner (1972).

is "lower," traditionally oriented leeward, and "goes with" the common side. These associations (in a standard Lauan four-class system) are practical as well as symbolic, inasmuch as the superstructure of the village community is traditionally the infrastructure of domestic construction. The exterior plan of the house—symbolic exoskeleton of family life which is at the same time a miniature of the political community—mediates the relations between household and village and constitutes the relations of village production. The house is built collectively. But the form of cooperation does not simply follow from the technical dimensions of the task. By custom it was an active, synthetic instance of the meaningful correspondence between polity and domesticity, segments of the community being responsible for segments of the house according to the correlation of structures. And as implied in the following description of traditional house-building, this set of agreements extends outward to the cultural structures of nature:

> The side of the house towards the sea was called the noble side (*yasa turaga*) and with it went the east end, or, if the house were perpendicular to the sea shore, the east side was the noble one, and with it went the sea end. If Tumbou village alone were building, Katumbalevu [chiefly segment of the chiefly moiety] would work on the noble side, and Valelailai [land segment of the chiefly moiety] on the end that goes with it; in housebuilding Valelailai goes with Katumbalevu, that is why they are joined together as Tai [chiefly moiety]; Tumbou quarter [land moiety of Tumbou village] would divide the other side and end.
>
> If the whole of Lakemba were building, The Town [Na Koro, the ranking territorial moiety] took the noble side; Wathiwathi and Waitambu would take the east end on account of Wathiwathi [ranking village of the land division of The Town, with Waitabu "land" relative to it]; Natokolau [or *Daku ni Lau*, the second territorial moiety of the island] took the other side and end . . . [etc.]. [Hocart 1929, p. 126; for a transformation of the structure in women's collective fishing, see pp. 113–14.][26]

26. The orientation of the house with its long axis parallel to the sea is still common in Fiji but is not universal (see Hocart 1929, p. 11; Sahlins 1962, p. 99; Tippett 1968, pp. 163–63). The environing space of the house, however, is coded by the intersection of two systems of orientation, which accounts for the interchange between sea and east in Hocart's discussion. Alongside the morphological code—that is, by geographical features such as land/sea—there is a system of wind directions, again a four-class set of the familiar type. The principal axis is windward/leeward, or *tokalau/ceva,* the former generally easterly and conceived as "above" to the leeward's "below." The windward has

The exterior of the house is partitioned according to the four-class system of the society onto which it gives. A projection of the same lines of distinction through the interior would essentially yield a tripartite space, integrating family life literally within the categories of the larger society (fig. 5).[27] The "upper" and "lower" ends of this three-section space, *loqi*

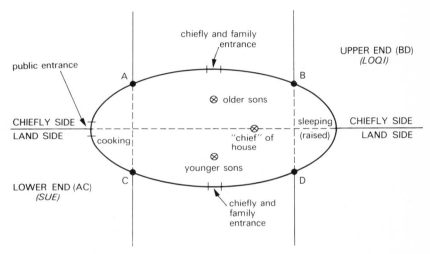

Figure 5   Schematic representation of traditional social spaces of Moalan house.

and *sue* respectively, are as opposed in types of sociability as they are different in rank value. Separated from the rest of the house by a curtain of bark cloth, the upper end shelters the raised sleeping platform of the family

---

a subordinate quarter, *tokalau lutu* or "fallen windward" (generally NNE); and the leeward correspondingly has a "lower leeward," *ceva i ra* (SSW). Elsewhere Hocart (1929, p. 9) notes the common placement of the front or lower door of the house westward; hence, in the preceding description either the chiefly side or the chiefly end will be east, that is, "above" by the compass.

27. There is a striking similarity between this diagram and the total six-part structure developed by Milner (1952) from textual material, especially his representation of "the social unit" according to the remarkable document composed by the *turaga* of Cuva village on the main island of Fiji. Space does not permit a detailed comparison, but there are numerous analogies in the relationships between categories, suggesting a similarity of deeper structure—of which the six-part model would be still another objectification.

elder and his store of valuables, weapons, and agricultural tools. Its use is generally restricted to family members (who also may keep possessions there), but principally to the *turaga* and *marama* of the house (the "chief" and "chiefess"). The relative value of the upper end is distinguishable not only by height, but also by the fine mats placed there, by comparison with the coarse mats of the front entryway and the better but still everyday mats covering the middle section. The lower end of the dwelling is public rather than private and is customarily associated with woman's hearth, culinary utensils, and cooked food rather than with sleeping (sex) and the male sacra.[28] The set of oppositions thus engaged is even broader than these household extremes and brings into play the interesting complexities of the sexual division of labor. The women's hearth indoors stands in manifold contrast to the underground ovens in which men cook, situated by tradition at the outskirts of the village. Thus we have the diagrammatic relation, women:men::inside:outside, we have seen before, in the mythical contrasts of Land (= side of the woman) and Chiefs (= side of the man). It is likewise consistent that the underground ovens are generally reserved for special occasions—for example, nowadays for Sunday—and the woman's hearth for everyday meals. But the logical inversions must also be stressed: the men's cooking is dry, underground, and in the "lower" medium of land; women's cooking is boiling in pots—above, and in the medium of salt water or coconut cream (both "male"). I will return to this complex exchange in a moment, when I discuss production relations.

But first let us complete the tripartite sociology of the house. With the exception of ranking chiefs, who like members of the family are permitted the side doors, all visitors must enter the inferior end and remain respectfully seated or squatting unless invited into the central section. The latter is the common ground of public and domestic, as it is, analogously, of men, women, and children of the house. It is framed, however, by longitudinal and lateral coordinates of rank, set out by the value oppositions of sides and ends of the dwelling (fig. 5), so that in any ritualized activity such as kava drinking or commensality people are distributed spatially according to

---

28. Hearths within the dwelling house have been legally prohibited in Moala. All cooking is done in a separate cookhouse, although the food is still served by women from the lower end of the eating house. Thompson (1940, p. 169) reports for Southern Lau that hearths were traditionally situated in the *sue* to the left of the entryway, but she does not specify the observer vantage (from the door or from inside the house). I have no further information on this point.

their community or familial status. The isomorphism between architectural and general cultural categories is, then, something more than picturesque analogy. Insofar as the house is so divided symbolically, it becomes the construction of a comparable differentiation of behavior. A "model of" society and a "model for"—to adopt Geertz's terms (1973, p. 93)—the house functions as the medium by which a system of culture is realized as an order of action. What is in analysis a set of parallel classifications, or a single structure operating on different planes, is in experience an undivided totality. The four-class code is practice as well as form. Unfolding in a habitation so structured, the relationships between persons are themselves inhabited by the same structure.

These relationships necessarily extend to the objects of family life. Cultural categories and economic goods are here defined in terms of one another: the quality of the mat signifies the virtue of the cultural space; conversely, the collection of different objects in the one space represents a commonality of cultural virtue. ("Intimately associated with the head, which is the center of *mana,* the headrest is tabu private property. It may not be touched by persons of lower rank than the owner. Headrests are kept in the upper [rear] part of the house" [Thompson 1940, p. 171].) It is a process of mutual valuation. What it implies is that economic value is Saussurean, it is the differential standing of a given object in a system of meaningful relationships. (This would only be fair, since Saussure understood linguistic value by the economic.) The effect of the process is to establish structures of differentiation between goods which are isomorphic with, as they substantialize, the categorical distinctions among men.

The commutability of certain goods then appears as a shared social substance, a symbolic attribute by which they are also incommensurable and untransactable with goods of other value. All the main contrasts of Lauan culture are reproduced as classes of material goods and as possibilities of their substitution or exchange. To describe this system of objects would be to rehearse the entire ethnography, for goods too are sea or land, male or female, chiefly or common, ritual or free. As everything goes by twos, every group a complementary combination of superior and inferior, so every meal must contain a marked element of meat, fish, or greens (*i coi*), and an ordinary starchy staple ("true food," *kakana dina*). Whale's teeth are "the head of all things." Their only social measure is a human being: they give a claim on the services, in war or in work, of those who accept them as an offering; they secure the wife to the husband, compensate the warrior for his tribute of a cannibal victim, the father-in-law for the death of the wife, the mother's kin for the birth of her child. Whale's teeth today are sometimes displayed on the upper posts of the house, but customarily they are concealed in the rear section, cohabiting with other objects of potency (*mana*) the sleeping place of senior man. Valuable as they are, whale's teeth cannot be exchanged for any ordinary useful thing or food—anymore, one might say, and for similar reasons, than a younger brother could eat the food of the firstborn. Only two things move regularly against whale's teeth—turtle and pig—the "head" of all sea foods and the "head" of all land foods. But then, a pig may be substituted for a man in sacrifice; and turtle is the "fish that lives" (*ika bula*) or the "man-fish" (*ika tamata*), for whom, should the chief's fisherman fail in the hunt, he shall be obliged to substitute himself. There is a transitive equivalence among whale's teeth, pig, and turtle, based on their common interchangeability with men.[29] Now anthropologists often discover in the tribal economies "spheres of exchange"—the allocation of goods between inconvertible classes, each a separate circuit of transactable items insulated from the others by discrepancies of social value (Firth 1965; Steiner 1954; Bohannan 1955; Salisbury 1962). But the famous spheres of exchange, what are they but the functional moment of a system of objects? And the system of objects? The transposition on another plane of the scheme of society.

An "economic basis" is a symbolic scheme of practical activity—not just the practical scheme in symbolic activity. It is the realization of a given meaningful order in the relations and finalities of production, in valuations of goods and determinations of resources. Consider the Moalan opposition "land/sea." More than a discourse of the interaction between social groups or between men and women, it signifies the cultural organization of a natural distinction. Actual relations of production on sea and land are constituted in agreement with the structures of reciprocity among the categories so designated, and through this sea and land as natural elements are given cultural order. For Moala the relevant reciprocity structures are of two kinds. First, the simple exchange corresponding to the essential complementary dualism of Moalan society: Land and Sea people— including in the latter category the Chiefs as well as master-fisher groups (*kai wai dina*) attached to their service—supply products to each other

---

29. Note also in light of the relation previously discussed between virility and the supreme female good, bark cloth, that the last is specifically coupled with whale's teeth in marital presentations between the kin of bride and groom (cf. Lester 1939–40, p. 281).

from the elements with which they have a natural affinity. Land People, as it is said, are ''not so happy on the water.'' Indeed, villages dominated by Land do very little deep-sea fishing to this day, whatever the feasibility of access to fishing grounds. Their role is to cultivate, especially taro, and to supply taro-coconut puddings and pigs to the feast. Nor should they eat this pig in the presence of the Sea, as the latter must not eat fish before Land—for fish and turtle are what the Sea People provide the Land.[30] The second form of reciprocity is a more complex interchange, corresponding rather to the system of four classes, and dividing land and sea accordingly. Here each side, as it were, provides the substance or nourishment which constitutes the other, and so must produce in the element of the other. This is the essential model of the domestic division of labor, rehearsed all over Fiji at an appropriate moment of the marriage exchanges when the man's side, despite its superior and sea status, supplies a pig feast to the wife's kin in return for a feast with fish.[31] Likewise for ordinary labor, if (some) Moalan men do deep-sea fishing on occasion, it is the women's daily netting and collecting in the lagoon areas that yield the main supply of seafood. Besides that, women weave mats and make bark cloth in the village, whereas all cultivation of food crops in the interior ''bush'' is man's work. Placing this division of labor on the landscape, one recognizes a familiar configuration: women's activities are ''inside,'' in the village and adjoining sea, flanked on either geographical extreme by the men's domains of deep sea and high forest. The tripartite distinction then permutes the land-sea opposition into a typical structure of four (fig. 6).

30. ''We are the Sea People (*kai wai*); our obligation (*tavi*) is to fish. We do not know farming. Our elders [ancestors] did not know it. They were expert sailors. We were Sea Pople in Tailevu, in Gau and in Moala. Our elders did not plant. The chiefs gave us wet-taro patches at [the old village of] Navucinimasi, a place called Vunisinitoba. We did not plant it. Those people over there planted our food. We only fished. They brought our food every day; every day, we brought their food. Nowadays we do not feel like fishing. . . . Our elders knew the yam, but it was the work of the chiefs of the Land to plant taro'' (Sirelli, elder of Nuku Village, 1955).
    Thompson reports that in southern Lau, the Chiefs are poor gardeners by comparison with the Land, but superior fishers (1940, pp. 32–33, 119–20). As implied by Sirelli, only the last remains true in Moala. However, in intervillage and island feasts, as well as tribute feasts to the ruling chief, Land and Sea groups are expected to contribute their respective special foods.
31. This particular symbolism occurs at different moments of marriage and birth feasts in different areas of Fiji (cf. Williams 1859, p. 134; Jarré 1946; Sahlins 1962). In the Nakoroka, Vanua Levu, there are separate women's and men's ovens prepared for certain feasts, the former consisting of fish and yams, the latter pigs, yam, and taro (Quain 1948, p. 73).

For the land is socially bisected into village (*koro*) and bush (*veikau*), while the sea is likewise differentiated into the *wai tui* or "chiefly sea" of the men, beyond the reef, in contrast to the lagoon or inland side of the sea, place of women's activities, called by the same term (*dranu*) as inland fresh waters.[32] In Marx's phrase, the nature known to man is a "humanized nature."

On the other hand, one begins to see the issue in current Marxist critiques of structuralism as an immobile logic of equivalent structures, innocent of any sense of dominance or determination between the levels of cultural order—and therefore of any knowledge of change or event (Terray 1972, pp. 39–41). It is a kind of Kuhnian "paradigm gap," since for structuralism the classic distinction between infrastructure and superstructure no longer makes clear sense. Nor is it easy to understand the "preponderance of the economic factor" by a structuralist understanding of the economic factor. The so-called infrastructure appears as the manifestation of a total system of meanings in action upon the world, a process that predicates also the meaning of practical experience as a relationship in that system. The infrastructure embodies a superstructure: a conceptual logic neither of the world itself—in the sense of an inherent mechanical effectiveness—nor expressing its material properties except as a culturally specific valuation. Any cultural ordering produced by the material forces presupposes a cultural ordering of these forces.

Let me open a brief parenthesis on the institutional conditions of Fijian conceptual categories. Aside from the patent oversimplification, perhaps the main fault of this kind of explication of the cultural text is that it proceeds, in a way, to invent anthropology, without benefit of ethnological understandings already achieved. But at this juncture, with the examples of British and French structuralism simultaneously before us, it seems clear that the strength of each is the complement of the other. I would not claim to make the synthesis, only to observe that the transposition of a given symbolic scheme on different planes is a counterpart to the received understanding of tribal society as a generalized institutional order. On this condi-

32. Correspondingly, salt water as opposed to fresh water is specifically efficacious in purification. Furthermore, the ambiguity involved in the women's exploitation of the higher and male geographic element, the sea, meets with ritual restrictions that would not be out of line with semiological theories of Douglas (1966) or Leach (1964), just as the particular sexual symbolism is also consistent with Fijian concepts of male and female potency; pregnant women are inimical to fishing, as are menstruating women; whereas the purification and termination of these conditions, called "bathing in the sea," is normally the occasion for resumption of fishing.

Figure 6   Division of labor and division of nature.

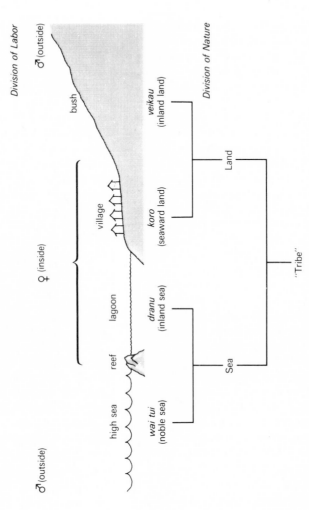

Division of Labor

♂ (outside)

♀ (inside)

♂ (outside)

bush

village

lagoon

reef

high sea

veikau
(inland land)

koro
(seaward land)

dranu
(inland sea)

wai tui
(noble sea)

Land

Sea

"Tribe"

Division of Nature

tion, namely, a consistent set of relationships (primarily kinship) deployed to various functions, the generalization of symbolic relations likewise becomes authentic. It follows too that the isomorphism between diverse codes—social, geographical, mythical, and economic—is neither fantastic nor the product of a pure speculative interest; it is a real condition of social life. If distinctions in environment are metaphorically connected with differences in political status, it is because the same relationships that order production also order polity. To the extent that the institutional relationships remain consistent, the symbolic agreements are never arbitrary. Mediated by the social order, they are always motivated by the cultural experience of the thinking subject. And their determination by the ethnologist is no more an idealism than is their practice by the people. If in the narrow sense of practical activity ''praxis'' is a conceptual scheme, still in the broadest sense the conceptual scheme is a cultural praxis.

There will be much more to say about all this. For the moment I close the parenthesis in favor of the implications of our ethnographic example for structure and event, culture and history.

The key text for Moala is provided by a Mexican poet commenting on the works of the French master. In a long essay on Lévi-Strauss, Octavio Paz perceptively draws out the implication that ''in classification systems, in myths and rituals, history enters into the cycle of recurrent phenomena and thus loses its virulence'' (1970, p. 88). Just so, because the symbolic coordinates of Moalan culture are translated in different modes, the system seems to develop an immunity to changing circumstance. The village of Nuku, for example, has the usual dual organization of land and sea sections, although strictly speaking there has never been a single Land group in the community. Nuku was founded in the latter part of the nineteenth century exclusively by master fishers attached to the chiefs, Sea People par excellence who had migrated from the capital village of Navucinimasi and ulteriorly from the islands of Gau and Bau. Yet by the local conception, certain Nuku groups were Land People. If one suggests to Nuku villagers—as I often did—that all the local groups are Sea People, this is readily admitted. But it will also be explained that one body of the people was first to come to Nuku from the chiefs' village, that they *receive* the fish from the sea and are warriors (*bati*) for the later groups; that is, they are ''Land'' in relation to the true Sea People who arrived afterward. This is an apposite example of ''stereotypic reproduction,'' in Godelier's (1972 [1966]) phrase.

The example is especially capital for its disclosure of the mechanism of cultural reproduction in the face of a historical disconformity. Multilated by history, the moiety system is recreated by the transposition of symbolic correspondences from related domains to the population remaining. A dual division of groups into "Land" and "Sea" is restored by a congruent contrast between original and immigrant peoples. On the conceptual level, this particular procedure is especially facile, insofar as the temporal distinction remains unaffected—if needs be, the myth of settlement can be revised to conform to it—while the social distinction can always be thought one way or another. Yet such is merely the mechanics of the process. More fundamental is the fact that the moiety opposition is always present in village life, even in the absence of its historical existence, because the distinction between Land People and Sea People is continually *practiced* in a thousand details of rite and myth, domestic and public life. That the village has these components is restated in every marriage ceremony, in every exchange of complementary foods, in the way men and women fish and the places they do so, in the construction of the dwelling and the everyday family life that goes on there. Land and sea compose a necessary axis of virtually every group and activity. The social duality is not only conceived; it is lived.

Still, the reconstruction of structure at the expense of event is not achieved without residue (cf. Lévi-Strauss 1966; Sebag 1964, p. 184). If the symbolic scheme seems manipulable without error or failure, history subsists in a certain opacity of the real: there is no escaping the contradiction of a village at once composed of Land People and Sea People, and yet of Sea People alone. The point is of potential significance to a dynamic theory of structure. Hocart observed that dualism has become cheap in Fiji, and that its excessive use must in the end weaken and obscure it (1952, pp. 57–58). So in the Nuku case, the opposition of structure and event is overcome, but at the cost of a social complication which denies the structure even as it is confirmed. One dualism negates the other, is placed across the other, and it seems reasonable to suppose that any system will discover limits to its ability to thus accumulate historical contradictions, or at least that it will become vulnerable to some transformation. From a naturalistic perspective these would appear to be the "adaptive" moments. But in fact structure remains the beginning of historical wisdom. History is not simply an opening into something new—let alone something more practical. As Greimas suggests, the change may also be a closure: a definitive selection of only one of the permutations latent in any given structure (1966, p. 823).

In this respect Fijian society is not static; it contains the embryo of another cultural order. That the established dualism survives a variety of historical attacks only means that it has not yet met the decisive one—the one that overdetermines its own contradictions to release the future already prefigured. "For even in such an apparently symmetrical type of social structure as dual organization, the relationship between moieties is never as static, or as fully reciprocal, as one might tend to imagine" (Lévi-Strauss 1963b, p. 135). Complementary yet unequal, symmetrical but asymmetrical, Fijian dualism contains an endemic contradiction: a conflict, as we have seen, of reciprocity and hierarchy. This is the centralized triad in the balanced two- and four-class systems. In its sharpest form, it is the incompatibility of bilateral cross-cousin marriage and the superiority of wife-takers to wife-givers; for if the second signifies a difference in status by the transfer of woman, the first implies that all such advantage is perfectly reversible. Reciprocity dominates, but in the background of its structural forms moves another, asymmetrical order: a classic system of "generalized exchange" or mother's brother's daughter marriage, which represents the vision of a society which has known how to abandon the pretext of equality for the undisguised development of chieftainship and hierarchy (cf. Lévi-Strauss 1969; Leach 1951).

By the principle of "generalized exchange," a given group consistently receives women from one line and gives its daughters to another; hence, it requires a minimum of three to make the system. And a consistent hierarchy can be maintained among them provided that women of the highest are not passed directly to the lowest. For Fiji this future may have already been accomplished, as it exists among lineages of the neighboring Tongan archipelago, considered by many prehistorians to have been settled from Fiji perhaps two thousand years ago. The Tongans, moreover, have resolved the problem of the paramount chiefs' daughters by maintaining immigrant lines as "foreigners"—including a "House of Fiji" (Fale Fisi)—to whom the highest-ranking women are disposed, even as women of native junior lines move upward toward the ruling chief. If the second device allows the paramount to multiply his supremacy as genealogical senior by his status as sister's son (*fahu*), of the cadet line, the first also removes those who receive the chief's daughter from political contention, since as foreigners they are outside the system. Traditionally these outsiders serve the chiefs as ritual attendants (*matapule*)—a permutation of the correlations wife-givers/wife-takers, native/foreign, herald/chief we saw at work in Lau. This transformation is accompanied by a series of others, whose necessity may be judged by comparison with the logic of the cognate Fijian categories.

In Tonga, the geographic axis of the chief/commoner distinction is rotated from the horizontal to the vertical. Rather than coming by sea—here the source of the chief's foreigners—the founder of the Tongan ruling line, son of the god Tangaloa, descends from the sky to mate with a woman of the earlier, indigenous population (themselves, by one version, offspring of the worm). Hence, sky encompassing sea and land: apposite cosmographic representation of the triadic polity. But that polity also develops an image of dualism, if in a status of background and subordination to the tripartite scheme that reverses their relationship in eastern Fiji. The Tongan dualism, moreover, is transferred from the opposition between "the side of the man" and "the side of the woman" to the distinction between senior and cadet lines, a transfer essentially accomplished by the merging of the two contrasts within a system of generalized exchange. Seen another way, the coding of the relation between senior and cadet as wife-taker to wife-giver harnesses the brother-sister tie to the ranking of older brother–younger brother. One effect is to mark the ritual superiority of women over men, since politically this also amounts to the superiority of the older brother (wife-taking) line. At another level we discover the development of the sacrosanct paramount chief, the Tui Tonga, the chief who remains immobile and inside, toward whom all women flow, who combines overriding maternal power with supreme paternal mana. Tongan dualism is represented, then, by a classic dual chieftainship, sacred and secular, the latter title formally allocated to a junior branch of the ruling line acting in an executive function. This segmentation is indeed the frame of a moiety division that ideally extends to all Tonga, the two sides respectively headed by the senior-sacred and junior-secular chiefs. Yet since the former is to the latter as "side of the woman" to "side of the man," and as the woman is "inside" to the man's "outside," there is in the moiety division a final reversal of Fijian spatial concepts, with the superior now the interior: "The names of the two divisions refer to their geographical placement. The Kauhala'uta [moiety of the Tui Tonga] lived on the inland ('uta) side of the road, while the Kauhalalalo [moiety of the secular chief] lived on the lower or ocean side of the road, in order to protect the Tui Tonga and his people" (Kaeppler 1971, p. 192; see also Gifford, 1924, 1929; Bott 1972; Leach 1972; Biersack 1974).

All the elements of this development also exist in eastern Fiji, but without synthesis or dominance. This includes the anomalous "foreign" groups attached to the chiefly lines, whose external origin remains a fundamental quality of their local identity despite all acculturation. In Moala these are the chief's carpenters—"Samoans" they are reckoned—and the fisher groups from Bau and Gau. One is thus Land and the other Sea, but together they are "different people" or outsiders by comparison with the indigenous Land People, and experts in technical rather than ceremonial functions (both types of activity, however, coming under the notion "work" [*cakacaka*]). While the Land People were by tradition wife-givers to the Chiefs, these foreign experts validate their attachment to the chiefly line by the marriage of their immigrant ancestors to the Moalan paramount's daughters. The system concealed within Moalan dualism is generalized exchange.

In the same way the villages harbor a concentric dualism within the symmetric, a triadic arrangement of the dyad. Traditionally divided by a stream or path into complementary halves, one the site of the chiefly moiety, the community is at the same time centered in a public square where stand the house of the ruling chief and the village temple. But this distinction between center and periphery, sacred and secular, also implies a tertium quid, still another degree beyond, constituted by the external residence of the chief's foreigners. In history, as has been seen, the peripheral location may be translated into a centrifugal movement; for example, the migration of the master fishers of Nuku from their precincts outside the chiefly village of Navucinimasi to their present site in western Moala. And the effect may be, as in the Moalan case, the recreation of the ambiguity between dual and triadic modes within the territorial system of the island as a whole. In western Moala the fisher groups of Nuku joined the neighboring village of "Samoan" carpenters to form a geographic-political division called the "Side Below" (Yasana i ra), in logical discontinuity with the main divisions of "Great Moala" (Moala Levu) and "Little Moala" (Moala Lailai), permuting the ancient territorial moieties into a dissonant structure à trois.[33]

The general point is that when there is such structural contradiction there is also historical direction. Fijian dualism may be proof against many kinds of contingent circumstance. But on the one hand success can weaken that dualism through the accumulation of historical inconsistencies. On the

33. See Sahlins (1962) for ethnographic details. On village form, see Hocart (1970) and Tippett (1968). In Tippett's general plan of Fijian villages (p. 163) can easily be read a four-part structure, the opposition of church to chief's house along the other axis (cf. Quain 1948, p. 83). On the spatial and social relations between the chiefly village and the precincts of the foreign attendants, see Hocart's remarks on Tubou and the Levuka settlement in Lakeba, Lau (1929, passim).

other hand, the internal contradiction: if events are continuously reinter-
preted by a privileged structure, the structure maintains by the same process a privileged eventuality—which is only apparently discontinuous with
itself. The Fijian system is inclined, or at least vulnerable, to a certain
differentiation and centralization of power. It has already, in advance as it
were, a code for representing certain differences in force as relations of
rank as well as rules of marriage. All of Polynesia, which developed out of
the Fijian hearth and everywhere retains the traces, is testimony to this
potential. The most acute observers have been able to see the alternate
structure of the future in the Fijian present:

> No single formula ever does sum up a society; for before a new one
> has finished ousting the older ones, another new one is arising to
> supplant it. . . .
> We can see something of the kind happening in Fiji. We cannot say
> what main interest engrossed the Fijian mind before the passion for
> opposing teams captured it, for this captured it so effectively that it is
> difficult to discern older structures under the dichotomy. In 1912 it
> was still so far from being spent that it could still provide the mould
> for new situations. The Lau School inevitably formed itself into two
> houses, North and South. Once I sent them as an unorganized crowd
> to dive for coral. A master reported that they were merely playing.
> "Divide them into teams," he advised. They were divided into North
> and South. At once began an intense competition . . . until the
> exhausted teams asked for the order to stop.
> Such an incident is also prophetic of decay, for dichotomy was
> becoming so common as to be cheap. It was being extended to all
> occasions. . . .
> Not only does too much use make stale, but the multiplying of sub-
> divisions was bound, as I have pointed out, to obscure the whole
> dualism.
> A new and more solemn interest seems already to have encroached
> upon the old dualism weakened by excess. That newer enthusiasm was
> the service of the chief. He and his family were exalted so far above
> the rest as to upset the old balance of paired groups, a process which
> can be traced to some extent in the narrative traditions of Lakemba.
> The two sides that used to face each other, equal except in precedence,
> have begun to break up into units which all face the chief, like planets
> round the sun. [Hocart 1952, pp. 57–58][34]

34. My suggestions on the relationship between reciprocal and hierarchial structures in Fiji
of course were inspired by Lévi-Strauss's article, "Do Dual Organizations Exist?"

I have tried to suggest certain ways structuralism may be brought into the world, so to speak, in rapprochement with history and with other anthropologies. There is no denying that this has been a particular "reading" of the structuralist text. Nor is there the slightest sense in supposing that structuralism is some kind of general scientific theory from which history may be deduced or predicted. One may speak of contradictions and potentialities, resistances and susceptibilities, even of the experiential genesis of variation. But the principles of classification by which a society deals with events are themselves specific and historical; they cannot be read out directly from the given qualities of the world but must be empirically *discovered* (Lévi-Strauss 1972). And provided that the symbolic means by which a given group organizes its experience are lawful and logical, history is likewise rendered arbitrary, for the world is hardly obliged to conform to the principles by which one section of humanity conceives it. A general theory of cultural systems from which history is a deduction seems an impossibility.[35]

Of course, even if this conclusion were acceptable in principle, there would remain basic disagreements between structuralism and contemporary Marxism on the "prehistory of society." More precisely, there remain issues of the relations between structure and material action, and of the powers of their respective logics to account for cultural form. Still, one might ask if Marx himself did not see some essential distinctions between bourgeois and precapitalist formations in the mode of organization and historic functioning. For a modern Marxism to repudiate structuralism on grounds of its "embarrassment in the face of history" may be in some respects a similar embarrassment to itself. It would not be the first time that Marxism ignored Marx. If, as Pouillon says, "it is not the structuralists who put the structures in history," neither were the structuralists the first to recognize them: "Men make their own history, but they do not make it just as they please; they do not make it under circumstances chosen by themselves. . . . The tradition of all the dead generations weighs like a nightmare on the brain of the living" (Marx, n.d. [1869], p. 15).

(1963*b*). They were given support by Hocart's parallel analysis of Fiji, especially his observation: "There is a remarkable similarity between Fijian and Winnebago organization" (1970 [1936], p. 103; see also pp. 285 ff.). The Fijian analysis likewise benefited much from T. Turner's course of lectures on structuralism, Winter Quarter 1975, University of Chicago, and his study of Kayapó kinship and social organization (T. Turner, manuscript).

35. Not even biological evolutionism has such pretensions; see Monod (1972) for a parallel discussion of "chance" and "necessity" in that realm.

Marx was clearly aware of the ability of archaic societies to structure the circumstances of history. The passage from *Capital* on the permanence of Indian village communities is a classic statement of "stereotypic reproduction":

> Those small and extremely ancient Indian communities, some of which have continued down to this day, are based on possession in common of the land, on the blending of agriculture and handicrafts, and on an unalterable division of labour, which serves, whenever a new community is started, as a plan and scheme ready cut and dried. Occupying areas of from 100 up to several thousand acres, each forms a compact whole producing all it requires. . . . If the population increases, a new community is founded, on the pattern of the old one, on unoccupied land. The whole mechanism discloses a systematic division of labour; but a division like that in manufactures is impossible, since the smith and the carpenter, etc., find an unchanging market. . . . The law that regulates the division of labour in the community acts with the irresistible authority of a law of Nature, at the same time that each individual artificer, the smith, the carpenter and so on, conducts in his workshop all the operations of his handicraft in the traditional way, but independently and without recognizing any authority. The simplicity of the organization for production in these self-sufficing communities that constantly reproduce themselves in the same form, and when accidentally destroyed spring up again on the spot and with the same name—this simplicity supplies the key to the secret of the unchangeableness of Asiatic societies, an unchangeableness in such striking contrast with the constant dissolution and refounding of Asiatic States, and the never-ceasing changes of dynasty. [1967 (1867) 1:357–58]

Marx recognized the stereotypic reproduction of Asiatic communities, although by comparison with a modern anthropology his theory of it does not seem powerful.[36] By the more general views set forth in *Pre-Capitalist Economic Formations,* the relative stability of early society was the concomitant of a production for use-values—of an economy in which "man is

---

36. Nor entirely consistent with the notion of a continuous reformulation of the present by material activity in the world; "History is nothing but the succession of separate generations, each of which exploits the materials, the capital funds, the productive forces handed down to it by preceding generations, and thus, on one hand, continues the traditional activity in completely changed circumstances and, on the other, modifies the old circumstances with a completely changed activity" (Marx and Engels 1965, p. 57).

the objective of production not production the objective of man.'' Controlled by the producers in their capacity as members of the proprietary community, production was organized as the reproduction of individuals in these definite relations to kith and kin (Marx 1964, pp. 67 ff.; 1973, pp. 471 ff.). The goal was not the unlimited accumulation of an abstract "wealth," alongside the re-creation of the producers merely as "workers." For the individual it was the concrete realization, the self-objectification, of a social existence. Such ends are finite. Marx could accord the world that knew them the same kind of respect the structural anthropologist pays to the search for "closed shapes, forms and given limits," and to "satisfaction from a limited standpoint" (Marx 1973, p. 488). But Marx would differ from all later anthropologies in the idea that the ancient community which thus mediated the producers' relations to nature and to themselves was not in its own right a *social product*. It belonged rather to the order of nature: the spontaneous development of "natural" bonds of kinship or blood, producing, moreover, by instruments that came more or less naturally to hand.

On the one side, then, the classic structural causality of historical materialism is here suspended, its field of application relativized as appropriate strictly to the capitalist formations. But the social order of early cultures cannot be considered a superstructure erected on the real foundation of economic relations. For, as Marx repeatedly insists, in such forms as the organic clan community the social order is the *"presupposition"* of production, as also its final intention. At this stage, the irreducible conditions men encounter in production, conditions prior to and independent of their will, to which they thus must submit their material activity, are their "natural bonds" of blood, language, and custom. For early society, "real foundations" and "superstructures" in decisive respects exchange their places. Yet, on the other hand, the suspension of the classic causality leaves an understanding of precapitalist society as a kind of absence, at once of culture and of history. The "simplicity of the organization for production" which Marx saw as key to the immutability of the archaic community not only was an unalienated condition by comparison with bourgeois society, it specifically lacked the structural differentiations which give bourgeois society its dialectic movement: separation of the means of production from the producers, of the producers from the products, of production from the "needs" of the producers and of individuals from the collectivity. Without these discontinuities, what remains for Marx is a kind of continuity which the anthropology of tribal communities will not readily accept: a continuity of culture and nature. Marx remains true to his own appreciation of his method as a "naturalism"; in respect to the formation of culture he is a gradualist—consistent with his position on language as involving no decisive rupture in relation to practical experience (see below, pp. 139–47). For Marx, early society was the natural within the social itself. This allows him to relegate the social conditions of production to the role of preconditions—that is, fundamental and external constraints. Although in such a state society is capable of responding to natural forces, or even of negating itself in exploiting these forces, it has no truly historical movement in the sense of a socially generated self-movement. It does not know *social forces*. As Alfred Schmidt explains,

> Pre-bourgeois development had a peculiarly unhistorical character because in it the material prerequisites of labour—the instruments as well as the material—were not themselves the *product* of labour, but were found already to hand in the land, in nature, from which the active Subject as well as the community to which it belonged did not essentially differentiate themselves. Under capitalism, however, these subjective and objective conditions of production became something created by the participants of history. Relationships were no longer determined by nature but *set up* by society. . . .
>
> If the earlier modes of human intervention in nature were fundamentally modes of nature's "self-mediation," since the mediating subject (individual or community) remained a part of immediately natural existence, under capitalism the mediation of nature became something strictly historical, because social. [Schmidt 1971, pp. 178–79]

Even for Marx, then, history may be embarrassed in the face of structure. In the archaic cultures praxis beats a retreat before social relations which are essentially relations of kinship. Shall we then conclude that the debate with French structuralism implies the same cultural discontinuity as the debate with British structuralism? Do we have to deal with two different kinds of society, one that structures itself by events and another that structures events by itself? And if so, are not Marxism and anthropology destined to remain apart, each the truth of a different social order?

Two Types of Society: Two Types of Theory?

Lévi-Strauss seems content to stay on his side of the line. He takes his reason from Marx: that the class differentiations of modern ("hot") societies power a movement unknown to the egalitarian ("cold") systems of the tribal world. (The thermodynamic metaphor is an analogy to the steam engine [Lévi-Strauss in Charbonnier 1969, p. 33].) In *La Pensée Sauvage*, Lévi-Strauss illustrates the corresponding contrast in historical performance by an apparently trivial example, competitive games.

The singularity of tribal games is that they are played as rituals, with the outcome therefore ordained in advance. When soccer was adopted by the Gahuku-Gama of New Guinea, two opposing clans might compete for days on end—as long as was necessary to reach a draw. Such is the general paradigm of ritual, played out "like a favoured instance of a game, remembered from among the possible ones because it is the only one which results in a particular type of equilibrium between the two sides" (1966, p. 30). To the same effect, during the funerary rites of the Fox Indians, the living give the moiety of the deceased one last game, which the latter always win. To "win" in the Indian symbolism is to "kill"; thus, the dead are accorded the satisfaction of being still alive, while it is the living who die (ibid., p. 32). In contrast, competitive games as we know them begin from a preordained symmetry, the rules and number of players the same for both sides, but move by means of contingent events to a social disjunction. A winner and loser are produced out of differences in talent, resources, and chance. Ritual games are just the reverse: in ordering events according to a preexisting plan, they conjoin groups that were initially asymmetrical and dissociated. In ritual, Lévi-Strauss writes,

> There is an asymmetry which is postulated in advance between sacred and profane, faithful and officiating, dead and living, initiated and uninitiated, etc., and the "game" consists in making all the participants pass to the winning side by means of events, the nature and ordering of which is genuinely structural. Like science . . . the [competitive] game produces events by means of a structure; and we can therefore understand why competitive games flourish in our industrial societies. Rites and myths, on the other hand, like "bricolage" (which these same societies only tolerate as a hobby or pastime), take to pieces and reconstruct sets of events . . . and use them as so many indestructible pieces for structural patterns in which they alternately serve as ends or means. [Ibid., pp. 32–33]

Of course the professor at "a large midwestern university" who regularly attends the football games will be detached and sophisticated enough—make it the University of Michigan rather than Ohio State—to see that the analogy is overdrawn, certain similarities understressed. Anyone who dispassionately observes such a game knows that it too is a ritual, structured not merely in the beginning but also in the upshot. Even as the rules are the same for everyone, so is the outcome stipulated. Not necessarily that it is "fixed." But as seriously as the Gahuku-Gama play for a draw, the one favored instance in American football is that there should be a winner. A tie carries all the disapprobation of the incest tabu; as it was put by the well-known sociologist Duffy Daugherty, "a tie—it's like kissing your sister." Moreover the winners are entitled to certain ceremonial privileges, ranging from the band's reversing their caps to taunting the losers and tearing down the goalposts. And at the end of a season's play, a hierarchy of the teams has been effected, which offers the "champions of the West" a trip to the Rose Bowl on New Year's Day—where of course the pageantry is Californian in its exaggeration. It's not as if we didn't have a culture.

Still the difference in ritual (or games) subsists, and it is enough to support the point that there is a difference in the cultural orders. Where for the Gahuku-Gama or the Fox the social outcome is an equilibrium axiomatically produced, any disparity in abilities being subordinated to that end, we have a kind of empirical society which precipitates organization out of the play of real forces. Ours too may be a culture, but its form is constructed from events, as the system gives people license to put their means to the best advantage and certifies the result as a genuine society. Thus the nature of man seems a "perpetual and restless desire of power after power, that ceaseth only in death," and society but the collective effect, miraculously ordered out of private contention "as if by an Invisible Hand." Organization is the socialized realization of desire.

And such is not only how it appears to us, but often to our several sciences of society. My description was phrased as a clumsy disguise of academic economics, yet the problematic is common in political science, sociology—and a certain anthropology (cf. Macpherson 1962; 1973). History too is often written in utilitarian style, as if it were decided by the distribution of resources and the skill people display in manipulating them. The content of the economizing varies, but all our social sciences participate in the going conception that society is produced by enterprising action. Society is the set of relationships empirically constituted by the pursuit of private interests with the means on hand.

Perhaps this helps explain the peculiar relation to nature characteristic of Western culture. The foregoing allusion to Hobbes was also motivated. So far as I know, we are the only people who think themselves risen from savages; everyone else believes they descend from gods. This could well be a fair statement of the difference. In any case, we make both a folklore and a science of the idea, sometimes with little to distinguish between them. The development from a Hobbesian state of nature is the origin myth of Western capitalism.[37] But just as Hobbes did not conceive that the commonwealth abolished the nature of man as wolf to other men, but merely held that it permitted its expression in comparative safety, so we continue to believe in the savage within us—of which we are slightly ashamed. At an earlier period it was *Homo economicus,* with a natural propensity to truck and barter, which idea rationalized bourgeois society to itself. It took but two centuries to evolve another species, *Homo bellicosus,* or so one might name that contentious human ape popularized by a number of modern writers to account for about everything wrong at the moment. Not that the reduction to biology is unscientific; it characterizes the best of evolutionary anthropology. Yet in this respect our science may be the highest form of totemism. If totemism is, as Lévi-Strauss says, the explication of human society by the distinctions between species, then we have made an empirical science of it.

Actually, the parallel to processes of totemic thought may be a detailed one. For in the first place, as Marx observed, the biological explanation of the distinctions between species was modeled on bourgeois society; whereupon, once elaborated, the theory was turned back to explain the human world. A letter from Marx to Engels describes the initial projection from culture to nature:

> It is remarkable how Darwin recognizes among beasts and plants his English society with its division of labour, competition, opening of new markets, "inventions," and the Malthusian "struggle for existence." It is Hobbes's "bellum omnium contra omnes," and one is reminded of Hegel's *Phenomenology,* where civil society is described as a "spiritual animal kingdom," while in Darwin the animal kingdom figures as civil society. [Cited in Schmidt 1971, p. 46]

The second phase, the re-presentation of culture to itself in the form of nature, is described in a letter from Engels to P. L. Lavrov:

---

37. Contrast the native historian David Malo (1951) on the origin of the difference between Hawaiian chiefs and commoners. Commoners are the descendants of those who wandered off in pursuit of their private interests; hence, they were forgotten by the others (they lost their genealogies).

The whole Darwinist teaching of the struggle for existence is simply a transference from society to living nature of Hobbes's doctrine of "bellum omnium contra omnes" and of the bourgeois-economic doctrine of competition together with Malthus's theory of population. When this conjurer's trick has been performed . . . the same theories are transferred back again from organic nature into history and it is now claimed that their validity as eternal laws of human society has been proved. [In Schmidt 1971, p. 47]

But, correspondences of (the so-called) totemisms to one side, what seems to emerge from the encounter of historical materialism with the two anthropological structuralisms is a distinction between the West and the rest. Such is the present conjuncture: a century of human sciences converge on this distinction. Yet the result might have been anticipated, since anthropology from the beginning accepted the specificity of the "primitive" as its academic charge, although it might mean an amputation of its pertinence at least as drastic as the relativization of historical materialism. I have tried to argue here the plausibility of this "two societies—two sciences" view. *But only to deny it in a later chapter* as a kind of false consciousness: a translation of different integrations of code and praxis into a radical distinction in the nature of societies, as if the one knew no conceptual axioms, as the other knows no practical consequences. This is "false consciousness" because, I suggest, the distinction at issue legitimizes the mode of appearance of Western society as the true explanation of it. The derivation of organization from practical activity, and of consciousness from the relations of persons, ignores the constituted symbolic quality of our own institutions. Yet if it follows that the determination of consciousness by social being, as generally understood, needs some revaluation, it also follows that this remains, just as is, the best explanation of Western social science. For much of that science is the self-conception of capitalism.

The real issue for Marxism and anthropology comes down to the relation between praxis and the symbolic order. And that is an issue best explicated from the history of anthropology itself—precisely because the history of anthropology is a sustained sequitur to the contradiction of its existence as a Western science of other cultures. The contradiction is an original condition: a science of man sponsored by a society which, in a way no different from others, exclusively defined itself as humanity and its own order as culture. Still, I believe that in the anthropological event this society did learn something from others—about itself.

2

Culture and Practical Reason

Two Paradigms of Anthropological Theory

The opposition recently raised by Lévi-Strauss (1972) between ecology and structuralism—within a higher unity of naturalism, or perhaps it is a transcendental materialism—is not novel. In its main outlines it is endemic to Anglo-Saxon anthropology. This conflict between practical activity and constraints of the mind inserts itself in an original, founding contradiction, between the poles of which anthropological theory has oscillated since the nineteenth century like a prisoner pacing between the farthest walls of his cell. Many of the same premises which divide structuralism from an explanation by adaptation also differentiate Boas from Morgan, Radcliffe-Brown from Malinowski—or even different aspects of a single theoretical project, as the emphasis at once on the symbolic definition of culture and its technological determinism in the work of Leslie White. The alternatives in this venerable conflict between utilitarianism and a cultural account may be broadly phrased as follows: whether the cultural order is to be conceived as the codification of man's actual purposeful and pragmatic action; or whether, conversely, human action in the world is to be understood as mediated by the cultural design, which gives order at once to practical experience, customary practice, and the relationship between the two. The difference is not trivial, nor will it be resolved by the happy academic conclusion that the answer lies somewhere in between, or even on both sides (i.e., dialectically). For there is never a true dialogue between silence and discourse: on one side the natural laws and forces "independent of man's will" and on the other the sense that groups of men variously give to themselves and their world. The opposition therefore cannot be compromised; in Louis Dumont's term, the relation can only be an encompassment. In the end, culture in its specificity will be referred to one or the other dominant logic—the "objective" logic of practical advantage or the meaningful one in the "conceptual scheme." In the first case, culture is an instrumental system, in the second the instrumental is subject to systems of another kind.

The relevance of this parochial controversy to Marx's invocation of praxis is patent—although, as we shall see, Marx's position cannot be simply assimilated to the received empirico-materialism in anthropology. Still, it is by a moderate distinction from Marxism, "if not Marx himself," that Lévi-Strauss most succinctly states his own perspective:

> If, as I have said, the conceptual scheme governs and defines practices, it is because these, which the ethnologist studies as discrete realities placed in time and space and distinctive in their particular modes of life and forms of civilization, are not to be confused with *praxis* which—and here at least I agree with Sartre—constitutes the fundamental totality for the sciences of man. Marxism, if not Marx himself, has too commonly reasoned as though practices followed directly from *praxis*. Without questioning the undoubted primacy of infrastructures, I believe that there is always a mediator between *praxis* and practices, namely the conceptual scheme by the operation of which matter and form, neither with any independent existence, are realized as structures, that is as entities which are both empirical and intelligible. [1966, pp. 130–31]

Lévi-Strauss goes on to explicate the contrast, as if it were a matter of complementary pursuits:

> It is to this theory of superstructures, scarcely touched on by Marx, that I hope to make a contribution. The development of the study of infrastructures proper is a task which must be left to history—with the aid of demography, technology, historical geography and ethnography. It is not principally the ethnologist's concern, for ethnology is first of all psychology. [Ibid.]

The seriousness of Lévi-Strauss's criticism seems only disguised by this modest disclaimer. And perhaps he concedes too much of his science. If the conceptual scheme encompasses matter in the terms of a human existence, still it does not come upon the scene of practical action merely to add the appropriate interpretation of material facts or instrumental relations. Nor would the decoding of the scheme be confined to "superstructure." This scheme is the very *organization* of material production; analyzing it, we are in the economic base itself. Its presence there dissolves the classic antinomies of infrastructure and superstructure, the one considered "material" the other "conceptual." Of course, it does not dissolve the "material" as such. But the so-called material causes must be, *in that capacity*, the product of a symbolic system whose character it is our task to investigate; for without the mediation of this cultural scheme, no adequate relation between a given material condition and a specific cultural form can ever be specified. The general determinations of praxis are subject to the specific formulations of culture; that is, of an order that enjoys, by its own properties as a symbolic system, a fundamental autonomy.

Morgan

The issues involved in the option between the practical and meaningful logics have been fought, as I say, on a dozen battlegrounds over a hundred years of anthropological war. A reflection on that history will go a long way toward clarifying them. But I must warn that the excursion will be a history "for us"—a way of taking consciousness of ourselves in history—without any pretension to the status of a "true" diachronic account. Thus I set up the contrasts between Lewis Henry Morgan and Franz Boas as a paradigmatic opposition, without reference to other figures of the intellectual context and background whose influences were surely critical to the controversy thus personified. Again, I leave aside or consider summarily many serious thinkers of later times, both in anthropology and in kindred disciplines, whom others might justifiably consider more important and exemplary. Perhaps such cavalier treatment may be excused by likening it to a history with which anthropologists have become familiar: a version of the past as it is actually lived by one segment of the society, as the charter of its present condition (see Pouillon 1975).

I begin with Morgan—and with the further qualification that the choice is in some measure equivocal. As with every founding father, Morgan's thought tends to be more generalized than the views that have differentiated from it, containing within itself the "germs" of almost every succeeding position. This means the man may be submitted to many theoretical readings, any one of which, precisely as it becomes a charter of present contention, may be guilty of less than adequate respect for the original generality. So Morgan has been categorized by later scholarship as an "idealist" for his emphasis on the unfolding of original "germs of thought"; as a "materialist" for his grounding of social evolution on developments in the arts of subsistence; and then again, as a "philosophical dualist" for his simultaneous dependence on both. An allusion to the "natural logic of the mind" has led some to consider him a "mentalist," while others hold him guilty of "racism" for referring culture to the organism (including the famous transmission of customs "with the blood"). Without claiming to decide all the arguments, I do think it important not to be misled by a certain resemblance of Morgan's terminology to the discourse of modern structuralism, that is, the invocation of original germs of thought, unfolding in response to human wants and needs but according to the "natural logic of the mind." Mind appears in Morgan's theory as the instrument of cultural development rather than its author (cf. Terray 1972). Passive rather than active, simply rational rather than symbolic, the intelligence responds reflexively to situations it does not itself produce or organize, so that in the end a *practical logic*—biologic in the earlier stages, technologic in the later—is what is realized in cultural forms. The conceptual scheme is not the construction of human experience but its verbalization, as in the classifications of kinship, which are merely the terms of a de facto ordering of relations effected by economic or biological advantage. For Morgan, thought is recognition; conception is perception; and language, the reflection of distinctions which already have their own reason. The symbolic quality of culture does not appear in Morgan's scheme; words here are merely the names of things.

Consider the argument of *Ancient Society* concerning the development of punaluan marriage, the gens and, on these bases, the Turanian kinship terminology. Punaluan marriage was for Morgan the triumph of biology in society, a great reform over the consanguineal unions of brothers and sisters in a group which had marked a more rudimentary humanity. The critical evidence of this advance came from contrasting marriage patterns and kinship classifications of contemporaneous Hawaiians. Hawaiian kinship terminology attested to the original consanguineal state, since all men of one's own generation were "brothers," all women "sisters," and the children of both indiscriminately "sons" and "daughters." But the marriage practice, *punalua,* argued the exclusion of own sisters from the group of women shared by brothers and own brothers from the men shared by sisters. Morgan concluded that the contradiction between marriage and kinship in contemporary Hawaii recapitulated the earliest stages of emancipation from the consanguineal state. Exactly how the prohibition of true sibling marriage first came about, Morgan is not sure; he speaks of the primeval steps as "isolated cases," something on the model of chance variations, the advantages of which were slowly recognized:

> Given the consanguine family, which involved own brothers and sisters and also collateral brothers and sisters in the marriage relation, and it was only necessary to exclude the former from the group, and

retain the latter, to change the consanguine into the punaluan family. To effect the exclusion of the one class and the retention of the other was a difficult process, because it involved a radical change in the composition of the family, not to say in the ancient plan of domestic life. It also required the surrender of a privilege which savages would be slow to make. *Commencing, it may be supposed, in isolated cases, and with a slow recognition of its advantages,* it remained an experiment through immense expanses of time; introduced partially at first, then becoming general, and finally universal among the advancing tribes, still in savagery, among whom the movement originated. It affords a good illustration of the principle of natural selection. [Morgan 1963 (1877), pp. 433–34; emphasis mine]

It is important to grasp the nature of human intellection Morgan here proposes. The example of punalua is particularly apposite, for it is common stock-in-trade in Anthropology 101 to illustrate the arbitrariness of the symbol by the observation that no ape could grasp the distinction betweeen "wife" and "sister" any more than he could tell the difference between holy water and distilled.[1] Yet what Morgan is saying is just the opposite—That the difference between "husband" and "brother" or "wife" and "sister" is not a symbolic construction put upon the world, but the rational sequitur to an objective difference *in* the world; that is, between biologically superior and inferior men. It is a perception of the biological advantages ensuing from the distinction, thus a representation in social terms of a logic external to these terms. The reform marked by punalua was the first of a long series culminating in monogamy, a series in which mankind progressively extricated itself from an original promiscuity and its attendant evils of inbreeding. And this first step epitomizes Morgan's notion of the whole. It was effected by observation and experience: attention to the deleterious consequences of inmarriage—"the evils of which could not forever escape human observation" (Morgan 1963, p. 433)—and experience of the mental, hence institutional, advantage of outmarriage. "It is fair inference that the punaluan custom worked its way into general adoption through a discovery of its beneficial influence"

---

1. The use of "symbol" and "sign" in American anthropology, or at least a large segment of it, tends to be the reverse of the famous definitions of Saussure's *Course in General Linguisitics;* in the former tradition, "symbol" is truly arbitrary or unmotivated, "sign" is motivated (compare Langer 1957 or White 1960 with Saussure 1966 [1915]). As a general rule I shall follow the American usage, except where the context is clearly Saussurean.

(p. 509). Thus thought is recognition, and the mind a vehicle by which nature is realized as culture.

Morgan's further explication of the gens (clan) as a growth upon the basis of the punaluan family and a codification of its advantages carries to a higher power exactly the same conception. As matrilineal, the original gens represents the natural working out of the punaluan family over time—given the impossibility of ascertaining paternity under the existing marital conditions. The social concept of descent is once more an awareness of relationships already prevailing (p. 442). (Later in Morgan's scheme descent will become patrilineal, under the influence of the growth of "property"—Morgan's general term for the possession of strategic "wealth"—which is the juncture at which economic interest, or the effective deployment of growing means of subsistence, takes over from biological advantage as the practical determinant of social form.) Just like the punaluan family, whose function in this respect it duplicates and generalizes, the gens worked its way into acceptance by the "advantages it conferred"—namely, the improved stock that must result from the rule of exogamy:

> It was evidently a primary object of the organization to isolate a moiety of the descendants of a supposed founder, and prevent their intermarriage for reasons of kin. . . . The gens, originating probably in the ingenuity of a small band of savages, must have soon proved its utility in the production of superior men. Its nearly universal prevalence in the ancient world is the highest evidence of the advantages it conferred. [Ibid., pp. 73–74; cf. also pp. 68, 389, 442]

In turn, the Turanian kinship system reflects the organization on the basis of punalua and the gens. By its distinction between parallel and cross-kin, it puts into words the differences already established in fact. Turanian kinship is no more than the faithful articulation of the social distinctions developed by natural selection.

The theory can be summarized as follows: Men early developed certain practices, forms of behavior such as the exclusion of own brothers and sisters from group sexual unions, which proved naturally useful and advantageous. The advantages were appreciated and the behaviors formulated as modes of organization—for example, punaluan family, the gens—which were in turn subject to secondary reflection or codification in kinship terminology. The general line of force in the argument, *the orientation of logical effect,* is from natural constraint to behavioral practice, and from behavioral practice to cultural institution:

1. circumstance→practice→organization and codification (institution).

To understand any given segment in the chain of effect, it is referred to the reason in the segment preceding: as codification expresses organization, so the institutional structure as a whole is referred to practice and practice to experience in the world—such that the total sequence represents the sedimentation within culture of the logic of nature (adaptive advantage).[2]

But then, Morgan's theory is appropriate to a nonhuman culture—or else to a noncultural humanity. For just as thought is the recognition of an external significance, so the words of men are not the concept of external realities but the sign. Consisting merely of the capacity to act rationally upon experience, the intelligence Morgan understands as human is not different in kind from that of other mammalian species—especially the beaver. In his famous monograph *The American Beaver and His Works* (1868), Morgan argued vigorously for the commonality of "the thinking principle" in man and beast. The beaver's mental qualities, he wrote, are "essentially the same as those displayed by the human mind" (p. 252). The difference between these qualities and human thought, "and, inferentially, between the principles they respectively represent, is one of degree and not of kind" (ibid.). The specific resemblance consists in the ability to make "a rational use" of perceptions conveyed by the senses, to act pragmatically on experience. Hence, for Morgan the source of significance that is materialized in the species' productions, whether it be the house of African or beaver, lies in nature itself. Morgan returned repeatedly to animal psychology, always concerned to show "that all species, including the human, *receive immediate guidance from nature*" (Resek 1960, p. 51; emphasis mine).[3] His theory of knowledge was thus characterized by the

---

2. More generally, since economic interest takes over from biological advantage in later stages of Morgan's scheme, the base logic could be characterized simply as "practical advantage." From an ecological perspective, however, the difference is only between modalities of adaptive advantage. (Indeed, one metaphor running from early man through patriarchial herders and capitalism is improvement of the stock.)

3. Resek, Morgan's most penetrating biographer, makes a nice connection between the rationality attributed to animals and Morgan's own anthropological epistemology. Distrustful of both instinct and imagination, Morgan's long work on social evolution left untouched the history of ideas, even as—supreme rationalist—he could consider this work itself untouched by ideology. Morgan "never doubted that his thoughts were true reflections of reality. That he was wealthy, at times in dissent, a Whig, had little if any bearing on what he *saw* at the base of the Rocky Mountains or in an Aztec pueblo. He would have cast out the notion that subjective, irrational or subconscious factors made

assumption—to adapt Cassirer's general description—that the "real" is given "*tout fait,* in its existence as in its structure, and that for the human mind [*esprit*] it is only a matter of taking possession of that reality. That which exists and subsists 'outside' of us must be, as it were, 'transported' into consciousness, changed into something internal without, however, adding anything new in the process" (Cassirer 1933, p. 18). Morgan reduced language, then, to the act of naming the differences manifest to experience. He preferred to respect the continuity of intelligence, at the expense of the creativity of language, by holding that the beaver was merely "mute," not dumb, even as he held that the linguistic faculty of man was only rudimentary in Savagery and developed gradually through that long period. Morgan was a presymbolic anthropologist.[4]

Yet the same concept of the concept continues in many recent anthropologies of praxis. It is an implicit but decisive premise of the philosophy. The analysis must neglect the fundamental arbitrariness of the word—acknowledging perhaps that there is no inherent relation between the sound-image and the concept (idea), but supposing there is such between the concept and objective reality to which it refers.[5] Language, then, is symbolic only in the sense that it represents the world in another form, but it has itself no sense apart from the world; therefore, it is in use, if not in invention, sign behavior.

But the arbitrariness of the symbol is the indicative condition of human culture.[6] And it is not simply that the sound-combination "sheep" has no necessary connection to the animal so designated, any more than does the word "*mouton,*" but that the concept of sheep also varies in different

---

every man his own historian. The laws of nature and society were discovered in broad daylight, not in the recesses of the soul or the musing of philosophers. He attempted to prove this to others—if it needed proof—in his essays on animal psychology" (Resek 1960, pp. 151–52).

4. For a similar position on language in the work of the English evolutionary anthropologist E. B. Tylor, see Henson (1974, pp. 16–17).

5. Since neither sound-image nor idea can occur without the other, as Benveniste argued in a well-known gloss on the Saussurean text, their relation is consubtantial and absolute, and in that sense not arbitrary. The true contingency is between the concept and the word, a relation Benveniste refuses to treat, as outside the scope of linguistics (1971, pp. 43–48).

6. "So long as we regard sensations as signs of the things which are supposed to give rise to them, and perhaps endow such signs with reference to past sensations that were similar, we have not even scratched the surface of the symbol-mongering human mind" (Langer 1957, p. 43).

societies. The example is of course motivated by the celebrated one of Saussure's in which he uses the difference in meaning between *sheep* and *mouton* to illustrate the difference between linguistic value and signification. Both the French and English words refer to the same species but they do so as it were "in different terms": each, by virtue of the semantic differentiations of the respective languages, conveys a distinct conception of (and relation to) the species. The English word does not apply to the animal in its prepared, culinary state, for which there is a second term, "mutton"; but the French have not yet been able to participate in the higher distinction between the raw and the cooked:

> Modern French *mouton* can have the same signification as *sheep* but not the same value, and this for several reasons, particularly because in speaking of a piece of meat ready to be served on the table, English uses *mutton* and not *sheep*. The difference in value between *sheep* and *mouton* is due to the fact that *sheep* has beside it a second term while the French word does not.
>
> Within the same language, all words used to express related ideas limit each other reciprocally. . . . The value of just any term is accordingly determined by its environment; it is impossible to fix even the value of the word signifying "sun" without first considering its surroundings: in some languages it is not possible to say "sit in the *sun*." [Saussure 1966 (1916), pp. 115–16]

So far as the concept or meaning is concerned, a word is referrable not simply to the external world but first of all to its place in the language—that is, to other related words. By its difference from these words is constructed its own valuation of the object, and in the system of such differences is a cultural construction of reality. No language is a mere nomenclature. None stands in a simple one-to-one correspondence of its own terms with "the" objective distinctions. Each bestows a certain value on the given distinctions and thereby constitutes the objective reality in another quality, specific to that society.[7] Indeed, as a total social project, the symbolic activity is at once synthetic as well as analytic, bringing to bear on the concept the

---

7. "La représentation 'objective'—c'est là ce que je veux essayer d'expliquer—n'est pas le point de départ du processus de formation du langage, mais le but auquel ce processus conduit; elle n'est pas son *terminus a quo,* mais son *terminus ad quem.* Le langage n'entre pas dans un monde de perceptions objectives achevées, pour adjoindre seulement à des objets individuels donnés et clairement délimités les uns rapport aux autres des "noms" qui seraient des signes purement extérieurs et arbitraires; mais il est lui-même un médiateur dans la formation des objets; il est, en un sens, le médiateur par excellence,

entire cultural logic. For if, on one hand, the differences in linguistic value effect a particular *découpage* of the external world, dividing it up according to certain principles, on the other hand, the elements so segregated are regrouped by meaningful correspondences between them. Here I speak not merely of semantic distinctions but of cultural propositions. And the symbolic arbitrariness of the latter is even greater than that of the former. At least in theory there are natural limits on the semantic field of a single lexeme: no single word, for example, is likely to signify, simultaneously and *exclusively,* the two species cattle and lobster. But the same example will suggest to Americans, among whom the peculiar combination ''steak and lobster'' is a definite category of dining, that culture is not under a like constraint. There appear to be no theoretical limits assignable a priori as to what will be classed with what else in the cultural scheme. ''A relative by marriage is an elephant's hip.'' The propositional logic is marvelously varied and so, even within this one and the same world, are the cultures. [8]

In brief, by symbolic valuation and synthesis of the objective reality, we create a new kind of object, with distinct properties: culture. Language is a privileged means of this project. But for Morgan, language is no more than perception articulate. Hence the passage from nature to culture in Morgan's view is no more momentous than, say, the reduction of the *Odyssey* from the spoken form to writing. As a leading Marxist recently wrote of Kautsky, so it can be said of Morgan that for him ''human history . . . is an appendage of natural history, its law of motion merely forms of appearance of biological laws'' (Schmidt 1971, p. 47). [9]

---

l'instrument le plus important et le plus précieux pour la conquête et pour la construction d'un vrai monde d'objets'' (Cassirer 1933, p. 23).

For a fine anthropological discussion of the cultural relativity of the distinction between belief and experience, a distinction peculiar to those Western societies which undertake the anthropology of others, see Needham 1972 (especially p. 173).

8. In the same sense of a cultural construction, one may note of Saussure's sheep/mutton that this animal takes its place in the Anglo-Saxon world as fit for butchery alongside pigs and cattle, which share a parallel declension of terms for the prepared state (pork, beef), while all differ in this respect from horses and dogs. History without structure would not seem to explain the classification, since we have no Norman-inspired word for *''cheval''* by analogy to mutton, beef, and pork. In chapter 4, I discuss the logic of edibility/inedibility in the American scheme (pp. 170–79).

9. I am indebted to Professor Paul Kay for most helpful discussion of the problem of the ''arbitrariness of the sign.'' My indebtedness extends even to certain phrases which are his—as any errors or misconceptions remain mine. Among the errors I would avoid is the claim of an extreme linguistic relativism. I do not mean to suggest that thought must coincide with the grammatical distinctions of a given language. The whole idea seems to

Boas

Against this background, Boas's odyssey "from physics to ethnology" becomes significant as founding an opposition within which anthropology has cycled these many years. As George Stocking (1968) so well describes it, that was a journey of many years in which Boas passed from a monistic materialism to the discovery that "the seeing eye is the organ of tradition"; a journey of many stages in which he discovered that for man the organic does not follow from the inorganic, the subjective from the objective, the mind from the world—and, in the end, culture from nature. The first steps were taken within physics itself. In his dissertation on the color of sea-water, Boas remarked on the difficulty of determining the relative intensities of lights that differed slightly in color. Quantitative variation in the object did not evoke corresponding variation in the subject.[10] Boas was later to repeat the experience on the linguistic level, when with Northwest Coast informants he discovered that sounds considered the same by a speaker of one language might be heard as completely different by speakers of another, and vice versa, as each perceived in the discourse of the other the distinctions appropriate to his own.[11] Between times he passed naturally through a phase of Fechnerian psychophysics that had the same import: sensory experiments in threshold phenomena which not only reiterated the conclusion that objective differences in stimuli engendered no parallel differentiation of response—that the human reaction to quantity was itself qualitative—but also that the response depended on situational factors and the person's mental set. Perception in the human subject is apperception; it depends, one might say, on the mental tradition. But that itself is not decisive, not unique to man. For any given human group, the

---

imply a suspension of the symbolic powers necessary to its postulation. There is also some evidence that inner speech, which is "a distinct plane of verbal thought," has a different and more simplified structure than spoken language; nor is this yet the most profound level of a complex, and largely unknown, relation between thought and word (Vygotsky 1962).

10. "In preparing my doctor's thesis I had to use photometric methods to compare intensities of light. This led me to consider the quantitative values of sensations. In the course of my investigation I learned to recognize that there are domains of our experience in which the concepts of quantity, of measures that can be added or subtracted like those with which I was accustomed to operate, are not applicable" (Boas [1938] in Stocking 1974, p. 42).

11. "The alternation of the sounds is clearly an effect of perception through the medium of a foreign system of phonetics" (Boas 1966a[1911], p. 14; cf. Stocking 1974, pp. 72 ff.).

tradition at issue is a set of accumulated meanings: collective and historical theory which makes of their perception a conception.[12]

Allow me here a brief digression and an apparently curious comparison. It is fascinating that both Boas and Marx early in their intellectual lives came to exactly the same juncture. At a certain point both were compelled to refuse a mechanistic materialism come down to them from the Enlightenment. But they chose alternate conceivable responses, in themselves not enormously different, but enough so to lead them to fatefully different enterprises. Marx had to react to the contemplative and sensualist materialism of Feuerbach, a materialism of the hypothetical individual subject passively responding to concrete reality; but Marx's reaction was also constrained by the idealism of Hegel, which had appropriated to itself the active historical subject. The resolution, as Marx set it out in the first thesis on Feuerbach, was to appropriate the activism of idealism to remedy the defect of a materialism which conceived "the thing, reality, sensuousness . . . only in the form of the *object or of contemplation,* but not as *sensuous human activity, practice,* not subjectively" (Marx 1965, p. 661; written in 1845). "Feuerbach, not satisfied with *abstract thinking,*" Marx wrote in the fifth thesis, "wants contemplation; but he does not conceive sensuousness as practical, human-sensuous activity." Marx stressed that such praxis must be understood as social and, in its historical specificity, not as the action of an abstract and isolated individual. Yet the recognition of the social, common to Marx and Boas, was inscribed in a difference of emphasis. Marx went to practice, and to the structures of reality built up from concrete and present action, in historically specified ways, of sensuous human beings. Boas took the same problem of mechanical materialism to the Eskimo, and later to the Northwest Coast, to discover the historical specification of the acting subject. Marx's choice led to historical materialism; Boas's to culture.[13]

12. "The first impression gained from a study of the beliefs of primitive man is, that while the perceptions of his senses are excellent, his power of logical interpretation seems to be deficient. I think it can be shown that the reason for this fact is not based on any fundamental peculiarity of the mind of primitive man, but lies, rather, in the character of the traditional ideas by means of which each new perception is interpreted; in other words, in the character of the traditional ideas with which each new perception associates itself determining the conclusion reached" (Boas 1965 [1938], pp. 198–99).

13. Hence Boas's parallel rejection of "geographic" and "economic" determinism, based on a notion of culture as more than the *condition* of man's relation to nature but the *conception* thereof (e.g., 1965 [1938], pp. 175–77). All the key issues of later debate—as also those discussed in chapter 1—are here prefigured: "there is no reason

This end of Boas's journey in the structuring power of tradition seems now, in retrospect, inherent in the conditions of its beginning. Boas began by questioning the essence of Morgan's thesis, the expression of nature in culture by the mediation of a reflexive mentality. In a series of letters to his uncle in America in 1882–83, he describes the background of his Eskimo project:

> While in the beginning my intention was to regard mathematics and physics as the final goal, I was led through the study of the natural sciences to other questions which prompted me also to take up geography, and this subject captured my interest to such an extent that I finally chose it as my major study. However, the direction of my work and study was strongly influenced by my training in natural sciences, especially physics. In the course of time I became convinced that my previous materialistic *Weltanschauung*—for a physicist a very understandable one—was untenable, and I gained thus a new standpoint which revealed to me the importance of studying the interaction between the organic and inorganic, above all between the life of a people and their physical environment. Thus arose my plan to regard as my life's task the [following] investigation: How far may we consider the phenomena of organic life, and especially those of the psychic life, from a mechanistic point of view, and what conclusions can be drawn from such a consideration? [Cited in Stocking 1968, p. 138]

In a way Boas's anthropological career can be characterized as a process in which the original axiom, the human construction of experience, was transposed from the psychological level to the cultural. Stocking singles out the early (1888) paper "On Alternating Sounds" as containing the germs of that development, and so of the modern concept of culture. More than a critical or methodological exercise, Stocking writes, this paper

> foreshadows a great deal of modern anthropological thought on "culture." At least by implication, it sees cultural phenomena in terms of *the imposition of conventional meaning on the flux of experience.* It sees them as historically conditioned and transmitted by the learning process. *It sees them as determinants of our very perceptions of the external world.* And it sees them in relative rather than absolute terms.

to call other phases of culture a superstructure on an economic basis, for economic conditions always act on a pre-existing culture and are themselves dependent upon other aspects of culture" (ibid., p. 175). Time would sharpen the opposition into the material reality of symbolization vs. the symbolization of material reality—which last for Boas was neither rationality nor disguise.

Much of Boas' later work, and that of his students after him, can be viewed simply as the working out of implications present in this article. [Ibid., p. 159; emphases mine]

In fact, the paths by which Boas reached the cultural concept were diverse and sometimes circuitous (cf. Stocking 1968, pp. 195–223; 1974, pp. 1–20). One of these is of special relevance here, as it developed from direct confrontation with Morgan on the issue of general laws of social evolution. Modern anthropology tends on balance to consider this particular controversy unfortunate, for the nominalist fragmentation operated by Boas on the content of cultures to prove the diversity of developmental processes enshrined that "shreds and patches" conception of the object that American ethnology would spend decades in expiating. Indeed, Radin early and vigorously criticized the "quantitative" notion of the detached culture trait which Boas had developed out of his obsession with disproving evolutionism (Radin 1966 [1933]). Yet the negative dismemberment of culture had to generate a contradictory and synthetic result. What had rationalized for Boas the disparity of apparently similar traits, as they actually existed in various societies, were the differences in meanings and uses locally assigned. If these meanings implied dissimilar processes of development, and hence proved Morgan wrong, it was by their implication also of a total and oriented context: a *culture* that patterned the traits according to its own unique genius. Since Boas argued that the masks of society A, used to deceive the spirits, were not comparable to the masks of society B which commemorated the ancestors—and similarly that clans, totems, or moiety systems varied the world over—he had to conclude the existence of cultures: of totalities whose "dominant ideas" or patterns create this differentiation (Boas 1966*b* [1940], pp. 270–89, and passim). In a well-known article, "History and Anthropology," Lévi-Strauss observes the conceptual eventuality of the method:

Are we then compelled to carry Boasian nominalism to its limit and study each of the cases observed as so many individual entities? We should be aware, first, that the *functions* assigned to dual organization do not coincide, and, second, that the *history* of each social group demonstrates that the division into moieties stems from the most different origins. Thus, depending on the case, dual organization may be the result of the invasion of a population by an immigrant group; of fusion between two neighboring groups, for any of several reasons (economic, demographic, or ceremonial); of the crystallization, in institutional form, of empirical norms designed to insure marriage

exchanges within a given group; of the distribution within the group—
over two parts of the year, two types of activity, or two segments of
the population—of two sets of antithetical behavior, each of which is
considered equally indispensable for the maintenance of social equilibrium; and so forth. We are therefore forced to reject the concept of
dual organization as a spurious category and, if we extend this line of
reasoning to all other aspects of social life, to reject *institutions* exclusively, in favor of *societies*. [Lévi-Strauss 1963*b*, pp. 10–11]

Boas's general problematic thus differs radically from Morgan's. Where
Morgan had understood practice and its customary formulation by the logic
of objective circumstances, Boas interpolated an independent subjective
between the objective conditions and organized behavior, such that the
latter does not follow mechanically from the former. On the psychological
level, where it was first announced, the intervening term may be characterized roughly as a mental operation, generated by context and previous
experience, which in governing the perception specifies the relation between stimulus and response (fig. 7). On the cultural level, toward which
Boas's thought was in continuous development, the mediating term is the
tradition, the *Völkergedanken* or the dominant pattern, which orders at
once the relation to nature, the existing institutions, and their interaction
(fig. 8).

The similarity of both formulas to Lévi-Strauss's is unmistakable
(above, pp. 56–57). Indeed the terms of Lévi-Strauss's statement of his
position—in opposition to a certain Marxism—perfectly describe Boas as
well, even to the specification of the tertium quid between praxis and
practices as a "conceptual scheme" (or code). Adopting these terms, the
theoretical contrast between Boas and Morgan might be generally set out as
shown in figure 9.

Of course "conceptual scheme" has a different quality in these two
perspectives. For Boas it is the encoding, while for Morgan it is the
codification, of distinctions external to itself. For Boas the significance of
the object is the property of thought, whereas for Morgan thought is the
representation of objective significance. If in Morgan's conception, then,
thought and language function as sign, Boas's is essentially a problematic
of the symbolic. Indeed the structure of the symbolic as Boas developed it
would account for empiricist-rationalist views of the kind Morgan entertained: that is, as a characteristic form of cultural self-reflection, a post-
factum appeal to the reasonableness of practices whose true logic is in-
explicit and whose true sources are unknown.

Boas argued that the formation of a culture, as a process of rendering experience meaningful, necessarily proceeds on a theory—of nature, of man, of man's being in nature. This theory, however, remains unformulated by the human group that lives it. Language is a privileged example of this unconscious process, but other customs, practices, beliefs, and prohibitions are just as much grounded in unreflected thought and ideas beyond recall. All are based on the categorization of experience, the appropriation of percept by concept, just as in the word stems or syntax of a given language experience is not simply represented—it is classified. And as every classification must have its principle, each language is "arbitrary" at

Figure 7

(2) Psychological level

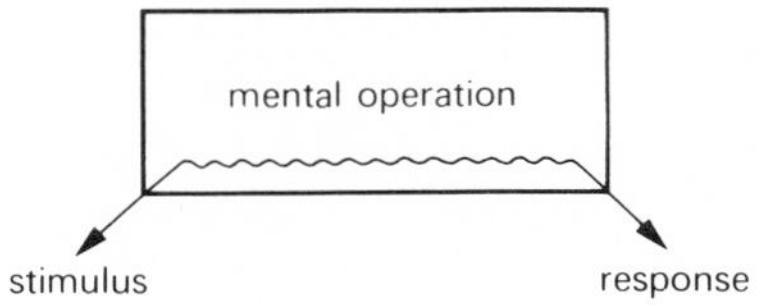

mental operation

stimulus   response

Figure 8

(3) Cultural level

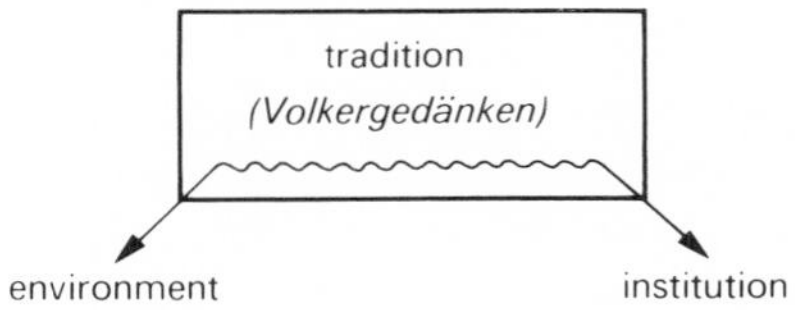

tradition
(Volkergedänken)

environment   institution

Figure 9

(4) Boas:

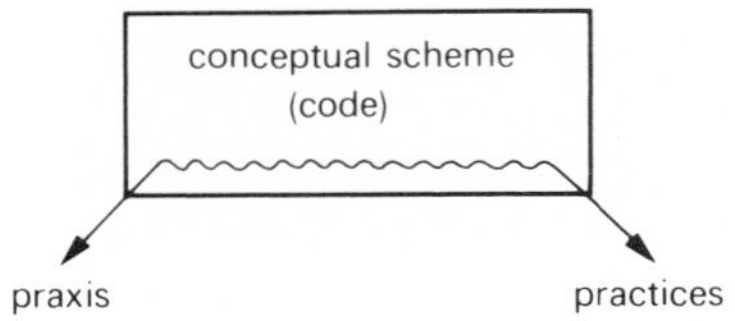

conceptual scheme
(code)

praxis   practices

(5) Morgan: praxis ——▶ practices ——▶ conceptual scheme (code)

once from the perspective of any other language and in relation to the real, grouping under a single significance a range of things or events that in the other may be separately conceived and denoted. Boas explains:

> Languages differ not only in the character of their constituent phonetic elements and sound clusters, but also in the groups of ideas that find expression in fixed phonetic groups. . . . Since the total range of personal experience which language serves is infinitely varied and its whole scope must be expressed by a limited number of word-stems, an extended classification of experiences must necessarily underlie all articulate speech.
>
> This coincides with a fundamental trait of human thought. In our actual experience no two sense-impressions or emotional states are identical. We classify them, according to their similarities, in wider or narrower groups, the limits of which may be determined from a variety of points of view. . . .
>
> In various cultures these classifications may be founded on fundamentally distinct principles. . . . For instance: it has been observed that colors are classified in quite distinct groups according to their similarities without any accompanying difference in the ability to distinguish shades of color. . . . The importance of the fact that in speech and thought the word calls forth a different picture, according to the classification of green [with] yellow or green [with] blue as one group can hardly be exaggerated. [Boas 1965 (1938), pp. 189–90; see also Boas 1966a (1911)][14]

Boas further argued—in an observation now classic—that although language and other customs are both organized by an unreflected logic, there is a difference between them in that the classifications of the former do not normally rise to consciousness, whereas the categories of culture do, and are typically subject to secondary reinterpretation (1966a, p. 63). Essentially the difference arises from the mode of reproduction. Embedded in unconscious rules, the categories of language are automatically reproduced

---

14. Boas's explanation of degrees of generalization and differentiation, especially in vocabulary, were often vaguely functionalist, appealing to preoccupying "interests" or "needs" of the people. But he emphasized that a people's categories (hence the interests and needs) cannot be understood by invocation of rational processes, that is, as based either on conscious reasoning or on practical utility (1965 [1938], p. 204–25). At the same time, Boas refused to acknowledge de facto practice as the only basis of terminological categories; it might as easily work the other way round, the behavior reflecting the classification—a position from which he taxed Morganian theories of kinship terminology (e.g., 1966a [1911], pp. 68–69).

in speech. But the continuity of custom is always vulnerable to disruption, if only by the comparison with other ways or in the socialization of the young. Custom, therefore, becomes an object of contemplation as well as a source thereof, and to a conventional reason which remains unexpressed we give a conventional expression which seems only reasonable. The cultural logic reappears then in mystified form—as ideology. No longer as a principle of classification but in satisfaction of a demand for justification. No longer, then, as arbitrary in relation to an objective reality but as motivated by the cultural reality.

The implications of this understanding for the anthropological project are still unresolved; in some respects they are not yet realized. On one hand, how much of what we take as essential institutions and beliefs should be analyzed as folk etymology? Conversely, it no longer seems possible to share Boas's optimism concerning anthropological categories, that by some sustained positivist operation opposite to the formation of the ideas and customs to which they refer, they could indeed be "derived from, consistent with, and in a sense internal to, the phenomena themselves" (Stocking 1974, p. 4). In any event, the commentary on Morgan's rationalist analysis implied by the notion of secondary consciousness would not be difficult to develop. If "the origin of customs of primitive man must not be looked for in rational processes," as Boas wrote (1965 [1938], p. 215), still the origin of certain rational processes might be looked for in custom. The reasonableness of institutions, and above all their utility, is the principled way we explain ourselves to ourselves. Rationality is our rationalization. Boas gives the telling example of the incest tabu, which once we were content to ascribe to religious reasons, but now "a utilitarian concept, the fear of unhealthy offspring due to the intermarriage of close relations, is brought forward as the reason for our feelings" (1965 [1938], p. 208).[15]

The point is that when we render the conventional as the useful, it also

---

15. The famous case is the origin of table manners: "The example of table manners gives also a fairly good instance of secondary explanation. It is not customary to bring the knife to the mouth, and very readily the feeling arises, that the knife is not used in this manner because in eating thus one would easily cut the lips. The lateness of the invention of the fork, and the fact that in many countries dull knives are used and that a similar danger exists of pricking the tongue or the lips with the sharp-pointed steel fork which is commonly used in Europe, show readily that this explanation is only a secondary rationalistic attempt to explain a custom that otherwise would remain unexplained" (Boas 1965 [1938], p. 65).

becomes for us "natural," in the double sense of inherent in nature and normal in culture. Hence Morgan, who made of this contradiction an ethnological theory—the status of which might be then described as the appropriation of the meaningful realities of other peoples' lives by the secondary rationalizations of our own.

Anthropological Varieties of Practical Reason

First announced in the work of Morgan and Boas, the founding disagreement over the nature of the anthropological object continues to assert itself even today across all manner of other theoretical controversies. This is not to underestimate the portent of such famous antinomies as "history/ science," "culture/society," "diachrony/synchrony." But if these oppositions succeeded in generating a development from one theoretical moment to the next, it was only to reproduce at each stage the unresolved contradiction at the base. In the upshot, the later perspectives which appear to mark theoretical ruptures find themselves internally at odds along the same lines that separate the Morganian view from the Boasian. One functionalism is this way distinguished from another, as also one historicism from another, and a moiety of functionalists or evolutionists finds an unlikely ally in the tribe of the other. Is it so paradoxical to group certain theoretical emphases of Lévi-Strauss and Leslie White? (see below, p. 103) The agreement on principles between the archevolutionist Morgan and the archfunctionalist Malinowski is much more complete.

Malinowski and "Neofunctionalism"

Even more explicitly than Morgan, Malinowski considered culture the instrumental realization of biological necessities: constructed out of practical action and interest, as guided by a kind of superrationality—to which language offers only the interest of a technical support (cf. Leach 1957). We must take our stand, Malinowski wrote, on two axioms: "First and foremost, that every culture must satisfy the biological system of needs, such as those dictated by metabolism, reproduction, the physiological conditions of temperature." And second, "that every cultural achievement that implies the use of artifacts and symbolism is an instrumental enhancement of human anatomy, and refers directly or indirectly to the satisfaction of a bodily need" (Malinowski 1960 [1944], p. 171). To borrow a phrase from the French sociologist Baudrillard, it is as if culture were a sustained metaphor on the biological functions of digestion. In the last analysis, culture is referable to practical-organic utility. Simple or complex, it is "a vast apparatus, partly material, partly human and partly spiritual, by which man is able to cope with the concrete, specific problems that face him" (Malinowski 1960 [1944], p. 36).

It would merely rehearse the commonplace to make a point-for-point concordance of the Morganian text with the Malinowskian. Because he is so explicit, Malinowski becomes much more interesting for certain theoretical implications of the praxis argument which are only hinted in Morgan, although truly contained there and in many subsequent versions, up to the most recent "neofunctionalist" ecology. I discuss several of these implications, which might be summarily entitled "the ethnographic hubris," "diminishing returns to functionalist explanation," "terror," "ecology fetishism," "utilitarian dualism," and "the disappearance of culture." The first has to do with the particular subject/object relation involved in Malinowski's pragmatic emphasis, one that contrasts radically with a Boasian relativism.

The overriding sense of Malinowski's project was to reduce all manner of seemingly bizarre customs, from the Australian *Intichiuma* to Trobriand totemism, to practical (read biological) values. Clearly Malinowski was guided by a peculiar sympathy for the aborigines (cf. Jarvie 1969, pp. 2–3). He would show that the reason underlying "the apparently senseless antics of what we then called 'savages'" (Richards 1957, p. 18) was something any European could understand: material advantage. It was in fact an inversion of Boasian relativism, if informed by the same toleration. Underneath, the Intichiuma is profitable; so the Australian aborigine is our brother:

> From the first . . . an interest in the usefulness of the apprently sense-less antics of what we called "savages" was paramount in [Malinow-ski's] work. His first published article set out to show that the *Inti-chiuma* ceremonies of the Australian aborigines, with their wild dances, their painted bodies and their symbolically carved shields, actually perform a function in their economic life. . . . After his field trip to the Trobriands he published his first major article on the economic life of the islanders, which showed the same determination to prove that what seemed to the European to be useless ceremonial exchanges of goods actually played an important part in their economic organization. [Richards 1957, p. 18][16]

16. As Malinowski's project is popularly described: from the bizarre to the bazaar. Leach's article (1957) on Malinowski's epistemology has an excellent analysis of this process

There is more ot this than the obvious implication that if the interpretation proves acceptable to the European, it suggests more about him than about the "savages"—most generally that the anthropologist's "etic" is his own society's "emic." Something is to be said about the subject/object relation implied by the compulsion to make a practical "sense" out of an exotic custom that is both intricate and not prima facie a matter of practical necessity. It raises the anthropologist to the divinity of a constituting subject, from whom emanates the design of the culture. Rather than submit himself to the comprehension of a structure with an independent and authentic existence, he understands that structure by his comprehension of its purpose—and so makes its existence depend on him.

For Malinowski it was an announced point of ethnographic method "to grasp the native's point of view, his relation to life, to realize *his* vision of his world" (1950 [1922], p. 25). This was a fundamental tenet of his "radical empiricism," as Leach calls it. But clearly there is a contradiction between such empiricism and the compulsion to resolve strange customs to utilitarian notions. "Empiricism" must then consist of the radical application of a theory, that is, of practical interest and personal calculation, which holds that the apparently peculiar ways the people are acting have no particular claims, in their own terms, on our attention. Kroeber once asked, obviously with Malinowski in mind: "Why does a Yurok not eat in a canoe while it floats on the ocean?" To such questions "there is no obvious answer of the sort of answer there is to why an arrow is feathered or what use a fish net has" (Kroeber 1948, p. 307). Malinowski, this criticism implied, refuses to concede to any opacity in the cultural system, let alone attempt to understand its inherent logic. Whole areas of culture thus escape a functionalist explication, since they make no apparent practical sense. Leach points this out for witchcraft: "It is in accord with Malinowski's dogma that reasonableness is natural to mankind that witchcraft beliefs—being neither sensible nor rational—were never effectively incorporated into the Functionalist scheme" (Leach 1957, pp. 128–29; cf. Nadel 1957).

There were many other domains of Trobriand life—kinship, magic, polity—of which Malinowski left an incomplete and unsystematic account

---

of "making sense." Malinowski wrote: "as a matter of fact, we shall be able to show that some realities which seem very strange at first sight [cannibalism, couvade, mummification, etc.] are essentially cognate to very universal and fundamentally human cultural elements; and this very recognition will admit of the explanation, that is, the description in familiar terms of exotic customs" (1960 [1944], p. 41).

because of some of the same theoretical scruples. Texts and the people's statements he held rather at a discount as mere formulations of the ideal, by comparison with the real pragmatic motives that governed men's relations to such rules and to each other (cf. Malinowski 1966 [1926]). In all this, Malinowski inverted not only the premises of a Boasian anthropology, but the original relationship of the anthropologist to the people. True that Boas would end with no more understanding of Kwakiutl kinship than Malinowski had of the Trobriand system. In fact, Boas was a lot more incoherent—out of a decent respect for the unintelligibiltiy of the Indian. Boas thought the facts would "speak for themselves." Nowadays this is commonly taken as the sign of a naive empiricism. But what was intended in the first place was a submission to the culture in itself, a commitment to finding the order in the facts rather than putting the facts in order (cf. Smith 1959). Boas's empiricist naivety was the delusion that the order would reveal itself *just as presented,* across the texts of a thousand salmon recipes, without benefit of any understanding on his part.[17] Here was a totally different relation to the object. The anthropologist was reduced to the status of a recording device: not even his own intelligence was permitted to come into play. But for Malinowski, the "savage" was pure negativity. He did not exist; Malinowski would create him: "I hear the word 'Kiriwina' . . . I get ready; little gray, pinkish huts: It is I who will describe or create them" (Malinowski 1967, p. 140).

Utilitarian functionalism is a functional blindness to the content and internal relations of the cultural object. The content is appreciated only for its instrumental effect, and its internal consistency is thus mystified as its external utility. Functionalist explanation is a kind of bargain made with the ethnographic reality in which content is exchanged for an "understanding" of it. But a theory ought to be judged as much by the ignorance it demands as by the "knowledge" it affords. There is an enormous disparity between the richness and complexity of cultural phenomena such as the Intichiuma and the anthropologist's simple notions of their economic virtues. Only the most infinitesimal fraction of that rich reality, and nothing of its specific content, is accounted for by its func-

17. Radin succinctly put the Boasian principle—"No one has the right to obliterate the exact form in which his information was received"—although Radin in the same work soundly criticizes the master's temptation to cut up the culture into traits for diffusionist treatment, among other imperfections of historicist method (1966 [1933]). For an excellent discussion of Boas's attitude of circumspection toward the phenomenon in itself, however, see his article "The Study of Geography" (in Boas 1966b [1940]).

tion.[18] When Malinowski set out to show that ''the Intichiuma ceremonies of the Australian aborigines, with their wild dances, their painted bodies and their symbolically carved shields actually performed a function in their economic life''—namely, that they stimulated production in anticipation of the rites (Malinowski 1912)—what in fact do we learn of these wild dances, painted bodies, and a thousand other properties of the Intichiuma?

Such conceptual impoverishment is the functionalist mode of theoretical production. It is only exacerbated when the function is sought on the biological level—as is often true not only of Malinowski but of more recent versions of ecological anthropology (cf. Vayda 1965, p. 196; Vayda and Rappaport 1967). For the further removed the cultural fact from the sphere of utility to which it is referred—the organic, the economic, the social—the fewer and more mediated must be the relations between this fact and the phenomena of that sphere; and consequently the fewer and less specific are the functional constraints on the nature of the custom under consideration. So the less determinate will be the explanation by functional virtues; or, conversely, the greater will be the range of alternative cultural practices that could equally (or even better) serve the same purpose. There must be many ways of stimulating production other than staging an Intichiuma ceremony. Indeed, the explanation rather defeats its objective of rendering custom reasonable; for that is a bizarre way of going about one's business. To satisfy ourselves on the indeterminacy of any such explanation, it is only necessary to turn the argument around: it is advantageous to increase production—therefore the Intichiuma? Malinowski's functionalist understanding would have been more powerful if, à la Radcliffe-Brown, he had referred the ceremony to the level of social fact. The prevailing relations between totemic clans, men and women, initiated and uninitiated would go a long way toward making the wild dances and painted shields intelligible. Less is said when economic advantages are adduced. And still less would have been gained had Malinowski carried through his project to the biological level. Then the cultural content, whose specificity consists in its meaning, is lost altogether in a discourse of ''needs'' empty of signification.

One is tempted to formulate a general rule of diminishing returns to functionalist explanation: the more distant and distinct the cultural practice

18. I am indebted to Frithjof Bergmann on this point, and to Raymond C. Kelly for a first formulation of ''the law of diminishing returns to functionalist explanation'' which follows from it.

from the register of its purported function, the less this function will specify the phenomenon. The rule might be conceived as a working expression of the "relative autonomy" of different cultural domains (ceremony/economy), and notably of the irreducibility of the cultural to constituent levels of phenomenal integration (superorganic/organic). In the latter regard, the general source of inadequacy in explanations by natural function relates precisely to the valuational activity of symboling: again, the arbitrary nature of the sign, which engages the objective only selectively, thus submits the natural to a specific logic of culture. Lucien Sebag argues it well:

> par définition toute réfraction d'une réalité à travers un langage implique une perte d'information, ce qui est abandoné pouvant à son tour devenir objet d'un traitement du même ordre. L'activité linguistique apparaît donc comme un effort permanent pour soumettre à un ensemble de formes un donné qui outrepasse toujours leurs limites. Mais ce n'est pas là le propre du seul langage; c'est la culture tout entière qui se laisse définir de la même manière, la relation du donné naturel met ceci en pleine lumière: qu'il s'agisse de la sexualité, des rythmes du développement corporel, de la gamme des sensations ou des affects, chaque société apparaît comme soumettant à un principe d'organisation qui n'est jamais le seul concevable, une réalité qui se prête a une multiplicité de transformations. On comprend de ce fait pourquoi l'explication naturaliste est toujours insuffisante; car l'être du besoin dévoilé en deçà des diverses modulations culturelles ne peut jamais nous donner que l'esquisse de la forme même de la culture, jamais de son contenu; or c'est ce dernier qui doi être compris. [Sebag 1964, pp. 166–67].

It is the content which must be understood. That is our object. Yet functionalist practice, as we have seen, consists of taking the cultural properties merely as the appearance. The cultural concrete-real becomes an abstract-apparent, simply a form of behavior assumed by the more fundamental forces of economy or biology. Sartre speaks in an analogous context of a "bath of sulfuric acid." Moreover, as the supposedly essential forces are in truth abstract—*human* survival, *human* needs, and so on—the abstraction of the symbolic pertaining to the object has been complemented by the symbolization of an abstraction belonging to the anthropologist. Sartre's thrust was aimed at a certain fashionable Marxism, content to neglect the authentic logic of a "superstructural fact," such as a work of art or an act of politics, and of the specific determinations of its author, in favor of the general determinations of class and production. From this vantage the poetry of a Valéry is dismissed as a species of "bourgeois idealism." Sartre's criticism seems point-for-point appropriate to classic functionalist practice:

Marxist formalism is a project of elimination. The method is identical with the terror in its inflexible refusal to *differentiate;* its goal is total assimilation at the least possible effort. The aim is not to integrate what is different as such, while preserving for it a relative autonomy, but rather to suppress it. . . . Specific determinations awaken in the theory the same suspicions as persons do in reality. For the majority of Marxists, to think is to claim to totalize and, under this pretext, to replace particularity by a universal. It is a claim to lead us back to the concrete [the material] and thereby present us with fundamental but abstract determinations. . . . The Marxist would believe that he was wasting his time if, for example, he tried to understand the originality of a bourgeois thought. In his eyes the only thing that matters is to show that the thought is a mode of idealism. . . . The Marxist is therefore impelled to take as an appearance the real content of a behavior or of a thought and, when he dissolves the particular in the Universal, he has the satisfaction of believing that he is reducing appearance to truth. [Sartre 1963, pp. 48–49]

In the same way, Malinowski repeatedly dissolved the symbolic order in the acid truth of instrumental reason. Whatever the cultural domain at issue, its examination could begin only once it was rid of symbolic consistency. Whether it was kinship or totemism, myth or magic, the belief in spirits or the disposition of the dead, even the analysis of language itself, Malinowski's first step was to deny any internal logic, any meaningful structure, to the phenomenon as such (see, for example, the analyses throughout *Magic, Science and Religion* [1954]). It follows that human intellection, "speculation" as Malinowski deemed it, could have no constitutive role. Custom originates in practice, in life—in the playing out not of thought, but of emotion and desire, instinct and need. From this perspective, "the savage" could be allowed little interest in nature that was not dictated by hunger, nor any conception beyond the rationalization of such desire. Hence Malinowski's famous dictum on the mentality displayed in totemic classifications: "The road from the wilderness to the savage's belly and consequently to his mind is very short, and for him the world is an indiscriminate background against which stand out the useful, primarily the edible, species of plants and animals" (1954, p. 44). Likewise, "there is little room for symbolism in his ideas and tales" (ibid., p. 97). As for myth, it is "not an idle rhapsody . . . but a hard-working, extremely important cultural force" (ibid., p. 97):

Studied alive myth . . . is not symbolic, but a direct expression of its subject matter; it is not an explanation in satisfaction of a scientific interest, but a narrative resurrection of a primeval reality, told in satisfaction of deep religious wants, moral cravings, social submissions, even practical requirements [ibid., p. 101]. . . . We can certainly discard all explanatory as well as symbolic interpretations of these myths of origin. The personages and beings are what they appear to be on the surface, and not symbols of hidden realities. As to any explanatory function of these myths, there is no problem which they cover, no curiosity which they satisfy, no theory which they contain. [Ibid., p. 126]

This too was Malinowski's celebrated approach to language. *Pace* Boas, language contains no theory: it contains nothing and is nothing but a verbal gesture, "a 'grip' on things," whose meaning consists in the effects induced upon the hearers. "Words are part of action and they are equivalent to actions" (Malinowski 1965 [1935] 2:9). And as words are action, meaning is the reaction evoked; the former is the stimulus, the latter the response; one is the instrument, the other its product:

The meaning of a single utterance, which in such cases is often reduced to one word, can be defined as the change produced by the sound in the behavior of people. It is the manner in which a sound appropriately uttered is correlated with spatial and temporal elements and with human bodily movements which constitutes its meaning; and this is due to cultural responses produced by drill, or "conditioning" or education. A word is a conditioning stimulus of human action and it becomes, as it were, a "grip" on things outside the reach of the speaker but within that of the hearers. [Ibid., p. 59][19]

It is also entailed that meaning is limited to experience by association: that is, to an original and indexical reference which remains the basic concept of the utterance through its subsequent reproductions. Rather than

19. Malinowski developed this instrumental-pragmatic view of language in a number of writings. For example, in the article on "Culture" in the *Encyclopedia of the Social Sciences:* "The meaning of a word is not mysteriously contained in it but is rather an active effect of the sound uttered within the context of situation. The utterance of sound is a significant act indispensable in all forms of human concerted action. It is a type of behavior strictly comparable to the handling of a tool, the wielding of a weapon, the performance of a ritual or the concluding of a contract. The use of words is in all these forms of human activity an indispensable correlate of manual and bodily behavior" (Malinowski 1931, p. 622; cf. Malinowski 1949 [1923]; 1964 [1936]). For a critical account of Malinowski's theories of language, see Henson (1974).

classifying experience, language for Malinowski is itself divided by experience. One word is differentiated from another as the real-world context in which the first occurs is perceptibly distinguishable from the context of the second. "Language in its structure mirrors the real categories derived from practical attitudes of the child and of primitive or natural man to the surrounding world" (Malinowski 1949 [1923], pp. 327–28). This sort of ultimate refusal of the symbolic, of the word as category, led Malinowski into some choice *bévues*. One was "the doctrine of homonyms": since each empirically distinct reference of a given word constitutes a distinct meaning, Malinowski was obliged to conclude that the "word" in question is really a number of different ones, an accidental set of homonyms.[20] If such were the case, of course, neither words nor communication as we know them could exist, inasmuch as the contexts of two different uses of the same word are never the same; hence each such sound is a different "unit" from every other—which is to say that there are no words but only an infinitude of fugitive contextual signals. Similar difficulties are posed by the fact that two people can never experience the same reality in exactly the same way, if they are in any way different themselves. Again, as "ultimately all meaning of words is derived from bodily experience," Malinowski would insist that even the most abstract concepts, such as those of science, really derive from commonplace or infantile praxis. "Even the pure mathematician, dealing with the most useless and arrogant branch of his learning, the theory of numbers, has probably had some experience of counting his pennies and shillings or his boots and buns" (1965 [1935] 2:58). Malinowski here ignores the fact that the system of numbers must have antedated the counting, but this is the kind of error he always makes in his ontogenetic arguments (as of classificatory kinship practice), confusing the way the individual is socialized into the system with the explanation—indeed the "origin"—of the system (cf. Malinowski 1930).[21] Finally, Malinowski's concept of meaning is unable

20. "In order to define a sound, we must discover, by careful scrutiny of verbal contexts in how many distinguishable meanings it is used. Meaning is not something which abides within a sound [i.e, not the Saussurean two sides of the paper]; it exists in the sound's relation to the context. Hence if the word is used in a different context it cannot have the same meaning; it ceases to be the same word and becomes two or more semantically distinguishable units" (Malinowski 1965 [1935] 2:72; cf. Leach 1957, pp. 130–32).

21. Ricoeur (1970, pp. 197–219) gives a brilliant general critique of the notion of word as pure praxis (including the imperative word), that applies throughout to Malinowski. In particular regard to mathematics, Ricoeur writes: "It is because man has expressed space in geometry, instead of living and experiencing it in actual measurements, that

to account for his own ethnographic project of making functional sense of exotic custom. For inasmuch as the ostensible form of these customs is strange or even nonfunctional, Malinowski cannot be guided by experience in his interpretation; or at least he must selectively categorize and valorize the people's rational attitudes over their unreasonable behavior by a principle not given with the ethnographic encounter. Malinowski held that the word does not embody any idea, that its meaning is external, in its empirical "effects." A sound ethnography, then, generated from a prolonged socialization in Trobriand life, should be just what a Trobriander would have written. But if Malinowski is to "create them," he must organize his ethnographic experience by his concepts. And this he does by his own admission, if in contradiction to his notion that the word contains no idea:

> There is no such thing as a description completely devoid of theory. Whether you reconstruct historic scenes, carry out a field investigation in a savage tribe or a civilized community . . . every statement and every argument has to be made in words, that is, in concepts. Each concept, in turn, is the result of a theory which declares that some facts are relevant and others adventitious, that some factors determine the course of events and others are merely accidental by-play; that things happen the way they do because personalities, masses, and natural agencies of the environment produced them. [Malinowski 1960 (1944) p. 7]

Ricoeur observes that in the strongest case of the word as praxis, the "imperative word," the "effect" requires the presence of symbolizing beings in a symbolized context, as the "understanding" includes at once a project and a system of valuations which differentiate the world and men's actions in it.[22] One may make the same point in another way. It is easy to

---

mathematics has been possible and, through it, mathematical physics and the techniques resulting from successive industrial revolutions. It is striking that Plato contributed to the construction of Euclidean geometry through his work of denominating such concepts as line, surface, equality, and the similarity of figures, etc., which strictly forbade all recourse and all allusion to manipulations, to physical transformations of figures. This asceticism of mathematical language, to which we owe, in the last analysis, all our machines since the dawn of the mechanical age, would have been impossible without the logical heroism of a Parmenides denying the entirety of the world of becoming and of *praxis* in the name of the self-identity of significations. It is to this denial of movement and work that we owe the achievements of Euclid, of Galileo, modern mechanism, and all our devices and apparatus. For within these, all our knowledge is contracted, all the words which at first did not attempt to transform the world" (ibid., pp. 201–2).

22. "The word, we said, does not 'make' anything, at most it incites to action . . . but if it incites to action this is because it *signifies* what is to be done and because the exigency

see in Malinowski's understanding of language as *work* and of meaning as
the response *produced* in the hearer, the same reduction of human subject
to manipulated object that informs his ethnographic technique. The Alter in
this conception is merely a means to an end, a raw material to be worked
upon like any other. But again, as Ricoeur insists, the sequel to a remark in
the behavior of another is not the same kind of relation as the effect of a
tool on the shape of an object; it is not "produced" as a material good is
produced (1970, p. 203). Not merely because the Other is an intentional
being like myself. More decisively because the communication implies a
community, and therefore the bringing to bear on the "effect" of all those
common conceptions of men and things which, ordering their interrela-
tions, determine the specific "influence" of the word.

Malinowski's elimination of symbol and system from cultural practices,
this cannibalism of form by function, constitutes an epistemology for the
elimination of culture itself as the proper anthropological object. Without
distinctive properties in its own right, culture has no title to analysis as a
thing-in-itself. Its study degenerates into one or another of two commonplace naturalisms: the economism of the rationalizing individual (human
nature); or the ecologism of selective advantage (external nature).
Malinowski, of course, cannot be held responsible for inventing either
problematic, or for developing either to the full, but the first is definitely
embedded in his work as the second is there prefigured. The economism or
utilitarianism develops from his distinction between cultural norm and
subjective attitude, and from the submission, in his view, of the "ideal" to
a pragmatic self-interest—which installs the latter as the true operator of
social life.

Malinowski could "see things as the natives saw them" provided, as it
were, they agreed to see things his way. They would have to incline to an
analysis which valued practical action over cultural norm, and again with
regard to the action, the subjective affect over the ostensible form. By
Malinowski's notions, the rules were one thing but the actions another and
truer one—the former mere talk to the latter's "reality," the norms having

---

signified to another is 'understood' by him and 'followed' by him. . . . The word articu-
lates in phrases, verbs and nouns, objectives, complements, plurals, etc., and because
of this we are able to master our action by a sort of 'phrasing' of our gestures. . . . The
meaning of this phrasing is not a transformation of things or of ourselves, is not a
production in the literal sense, but a signification, and every signification designates
emptily what work will fulfill in the sense in which one fulfills a plan, a wish, a
purpose . . . it is through this void of significations, which designate without making
something, that the word connects and structures action" (ibid., p. 204).

some lesser claim to existence and analysis than the behavior motivated by an enlightened self-interest. Still the act—the "wild dances," the exchanges of kula ornaments that could not be possessed—remains peculiar in observable properties, and to privilege it over the rule in the name of rational interest would require a second distinction: between that outward, incongruous form and the practical attitudes the people bring to it. The truest data of ethnography consist not in facts of cultural order but in the way that order is subjectively lived, the famous "imponderabilia of everyday life." Anthropologists are too frequently taken in, Malinowski insists, by the natives' retailing of "legal fictions" such as the solidarity of the clan, rules of clan exogamy, and the like, which represent only the "intellectual, overt, fully conventionalized aspect of the native attitude." But "the natural, impulsive code of conduct, the evasions, the compromises and non-legal usages are revealed only to the field worker who observes life directly, registers facts, lives at such close quarters with his 'material' as to understand not only their language and their statements, but also the hidden motives of behaviour, and the hardly ever formulated spontaneous line of conduct" (Malinowski 1966 [1926], pp. 120–21). The importance of this "natural, impulsive code" is that in the end it prevails over the conventional: in the end, the cultural form submits to the "spontaneous" praxis. "The true problem is not to study how human life submits to rules—it simply does not: the real problem is how the rules become adapted to life" (ibid., p. 127).[23]

By thus separating the cultural order from the human subject as fiction is separated from real life, Malinowski introduces a type of ontological schizophrenia into ethnology—which happens to be the normal social science thought of our time. Human social life is taken to be divided against

---

23. Fortes acutely describes the opposition between "ideal" norm and "real" practice in Malinowski's work, and documents its transposition into a contrast of form and sentiment, which left no possibility of understnading kinship, for example, as a system in its own right: "What is significant is the emphasis on *practice* (the activity; the behaviour; the concrete mutual services; the exhibited self-interest, ambition, and vanity; the facts of mother love and paternal affection; in short the actions and feelings and thoughts of individuals in social situations, as directly observed by the ethnographer and as admitted by the actors) as the *'reality'* of social life, as against *'ideal,'* or *'theory,'* the merely verbal formulation (Fortes 1957, p. 160)... the facts of social relationship and social grouping are, in his scheme, merely facts of custom and motive broadly on a par with, for instance, magical beliefs, and springing in the last resort from such universal human instincts as those of parenthood or such common human sentiments as vanity and ambition. So we have nowhere a connected analysis of Trobriand local organization, kinship, and political structure" (p. 164).

itself, composed of two different kinds of object standing in relations of counterposition and competition. On one hand, there are the conventional rules and forms which amount to "the culture" of the situation. They alone have the right to that status, as they alone are described by specifically cultural properties: matrilineal descent, clan exogamy, mortuary rituals, affinal payments of valuables, yam production, classificatory kinship. In principle they might also be comprehended that way; that is, by a logic at once of significance and action, developed from the symbolic attributes— as the valuation of goods and the division of labor, for example, may be related to kinship classifications or marriage practices. But the identification of the cultural attributes as the "norm" or the "ideal" vis-à-vis "real life" must condemn such an effort as metaphysical. Culture is instead subordinated to another logic—which as it does not preserve the symbolic properties cannot either give an account of them.[24] Opposed to the culture norm, on the other hand, is the "actual behavior" of the people. And this, as specifically human, must be described and understood in terms drawn from another universe of discourse: the people's needs, drives, motives, desires, feelings, and sentiments. At this point, in a sort of basic inversion of Durkheimian principles, although still in agreement with the premise that "man is double," Malinowski displaces the social dynamic onto the natural level, seeking to account for it by forces emanating from the organism itself. We have to deal with the struggle of the individual subject to achieve his own ends in the face of constraining cultural conventions. Meaningful analysis thus gives way to manipulative rationality, to the formal analysis of means-ends relations based on an eternal teleology of human satisfactions. From this alternate vantage, culture appears simply as a *medium* or an *environment* of the constituting dynamic of human purpose. It is a medium in the sense of a set of means at the disposition of the subject, through which he achieves his self-appointed ends. And it is an environment, not merely as a set of constraints external to the individual, but as something upon which he works his intentions and in so doing orders the properties of this milieu.[25] So conceived, the interaction between

---

24. Sorokin correctly characterizes the procedure as "the fallacy of logical inadequacy"— cited with approval by Parsons and described thus: "It is to explain a body of fact with properties clearly differentiating it from others, in terms of a schema applicable to the others in the same way" (Parsons 1968 [1937] 1:354). The same fallacy applies to ecologism as well as economism (utilitarianism), as we shall see in a moment.

25. "The problems set by man's nutritive, reproductive, and hygenic needs must be solved. They are solved by the construction of a new, secondary, or artificial *environment*. This

"life" and "culture" is necessarily unequal: a relation of subject to object, active to passive, constituting to constituted. Behaving with a mind singular toward their own best interests, the people accordingly formulate and reformulate their cultural order (cf. Firth 1963). But the efficacy of culture as a meaningful order is accordingly suspended. Culture is reduced to an epiphenomenon of purposeful "decision-making processes" (as they say).

That familiar phrase of course is not Malinowski's, but it makes an appropriate connection with the current social science wisdom. The axiomatic adoption of the problematic of the calculating subject, rationally ordering the social world according to desires equally axiomatic, this utilitarianism is an instinctive consciousness we have of others as of ourselves. Many of those who might criticize Malinowski's functionalism are nevertheless satisfied with its essential counterposition of personal interests and social order (e.g., Jarvie 1967, p. 77; Kuper 1973, p. 49; or even Wolf 1964). It is true that Malinowski was the first among anthropologists to deny the generality of an "economic man" (1921; 1950 [1922]). But was this not simply to give the same concept an even greater scope? "In the pages of Argonauts and its successors," Leach has written, "the 'savage' ceases to be a marionette . . . . He is a live human being operating a bizarre system of social organization through the exercise of natural choices about alternate means to alternate ends" (1957, p. 127). In the same vein, Bateson judged that Malinowski's functionalist method "is probably sound and in its careful investigation might give a coherent system of anthropology allied to systems of economics based upon 'calculating man' " (1958, p. 27). For, as Malinowski himself reported, "Whenever the native can evade his obligation without the loss of prestige, or without the prospective loss of gain, he does so, exactly as a civilized businessman would do" (1966 [1926], p. 30). The perspective at issue remains the home-bred economizing of the marketplace, here transposed from the analysis of bourgeois economy to the explication of human society. The analytic place then left to society has been brilliantly described by Dumont:

---

environment, which is neither more nor less than culture itself, has to be permanently reproduced, maintained and managed" (Malinowski 1960 [1944], p. 37; emphasis mine). "We also indicated that culture, as the handiwork of man and as the *medium* through which he achieves his ends—a medium which allows him to live, to establish a standard of safety, comfort and prosperity; a medium which gives him power and allows him to create goods and values beyond his animal, organic endowments—that culture, in all this and through all this, must be understood as *a means to an end,* that is, instrumentally or functionally" (ibid., pp. 67–68; emphases mine).

In modern society . . . the Human Being is regarded as the indivisible, "elementary" man, both a biological being and a thinking subject. Each particular man in a sense incarnates the whole of mankind. He is the measure of all things (in a full and novel sense). The kingdom of ends coincides with each man's legitimate ends, so the values are turned upside down. What is still called "society" is the means, the life of each man is the end. Ontologically, the society no longer exists, it is no more than an irreducible datum, which must in no way thwart the demands of liberty and equality. Of course, the above is a description of values, a view of mind. . . . A society as conceived by individualism has never existed anywhere for the reason we have given, namely, that the individual lives on social ideas. [Dumont 1970, p. 9–10; for other important discussions of utilitarianism (economism, individualism) see Dumont 1965; Macpherson 1962; Parsons 1968 [1937]; Polanyi 1944]

The economistic separation of normative structure from pragmatic action, if it does not altogether banish culture from the anthropological purview, does impoverish it to the status of a secondary concern. Only adumbrated by Malinowski, these effects appear much more clearly in an "ecological anthropology" which does homage to its intellectual sources by styling itself also as "functionalist" or "neofunctionalist" (cf. Collins and Vayda 1969). Yet as Marx said truly, the anatomy of man is the key to the anatomy of the ape. The more developed economic system makes an explicit differentiation of categories that remain combined, ambiguous, or only virtual in the less-developed one. In the same way, the implications foreshadowed in a given intellectual perspective become explicit only in more evolved versions of it. The new ecological functionalism demonstrates that the effect of Malinowski's resolution of cultural content to biological function, particularly of the symbolic to the instrumental, is a final solution to the culture problem. For it becomes explicit that culture does not warrant any special understanding, that is, as distinct from a biological explanation. In this event, culture disappears.

As in Malinowski's functionalism, this process depends on the theoretical appropriation of cultural qualities as organic effects: translation that not only dissolves the cultural specifications but allows them to reappear in a more scientific (i.e., quantifiable) form. Rappaport explains:

While the questions are asked about cultural phenomena, they are answered in terms of the effects of culturally informed behavior on biological systems: organisms, populations and ecosystems. The distinctive characteristic of ecological anthropology is not simply that it

takes environmental factors into consideration in its attempts to elucidate cultural phenomena, but that it gives biological meaning to the
key terms—adaptation, homeostasis, adequate functioning,
survival—of its formulations. [1971, p. 243]

The theoretical practice might be called "ecology fetishism." Nothing
cultural is what it seems; everything is mystified as a natural fact which has
the ostensible virtue of being basic and exact although it is essentially
abstract. Marriage becomes "an interchange of genetic materials," as
hunting is "an interchange of energy with the environment," corn, beans,
and squash are an "unbalanced diet," society a "population" of human
organisms, and cannibalism a "subsistence activity." ("In examining
cannibalism, we are operating from the premise that all activities which
make food available for group members, food which they then actually
consume, are 'subsistence activities' and that they can then be compared
individually and/or taken together as constituent activities in an overall
behavioral repertory called 'food-getting pattern'"—Dornstreich and
Morren 1974, p. 3). The same way of thinking as applied to the discovery
of sanitary values in dietary tabus Douglas (1966) has called "medical
materialism." It is only a particular anthropological or ecological version
of the exchange of meaningful content for functional truth that Sartre
described as the vulgar Marxism.[26] This petty metaphysical commerce in

26. As for Marx himself, far from being implicated, it was he who gave such fetishism its
most general criticism and explanation: "The apparent stupidity of merging all the manifold relationships of people in the *one* relation of usefulness, this apparently metaphysical abstraction arises from the fact that, in modern bourgeois society, all relations are
subordinated in practice to the one abstract monetary-commercial relation. This theory
came to the fore with Hobbes and Locke. . . . In Holbach, all the activity of individuals
in the mutual intercourse, e.g., speech, love, etc., is depicted as a relation of utility and
utilisation. Hence the actual relations that are presupposed here are speech, love, the
definite manifestations of definitie qualities of individuals. Now these relations are supposed not to have the meaning *peculiar* to them but to be the expression and manifestation of some third relation introduced in their place, the *relation of utility or utilisation*. . . . All this is actually the case with the bourgeois. For him only *one* relation is
valid on its own account—the relation of exploitation; all other relations have validity
for him only insofar as he can include them under this one relation, and even where he
encounters relations which cannot be directly subordinated to the relation of exploitation, he does at least subordinate them to it in imagination. The material expression of
this use is money, the representative of the value of all things, people and social relations. Incidentally, one sees at a glance that the category of 'utilization' is first of all
subtracted from the actual relations of intercourse which I have with other people (but
by no means from reflection and mere will) and then these relations are made out to be
the reality of the category that has been abstracted from themselves, a wholly metaphysical method of procedure" (Marx and Engels 1965, pp. 460–61).

ethnographic details would hold no interest were it not for its avowed intention of engrossing the concept of culture.

Malinowski opposed "culture" to behavior; for ecology, it *is* "behavior." It may be learned behavior, but it is not by that characteristic worthy of different treatment than the "species-specific behavior" of any other group of organisms. Think of it simply as a "cultural repertoire" (Collins and Vayda 1969, p. 155). Thus understood, the phenomenon as such does not distinguish man from any other species, nor anthropology from biology. As "behavior"—or even more abstractly, "bodily movements"—culture can be studied in the same way as the actions of any animal, that is, as good for the species or bad for it under the selective conditions as naturally constituted:

> Attention to cultural ideas, values or concepts cannot, however, be said to be a *sine qua non* of the analysis of ecosystems including man. One may choose rather to place emphasis upon the *actual physical behavior or bodily movements through which man directly effects alterations in his environment.* . . . Indeed, a possible approach, suggested by Simpson . . . among others, is *to regard human culture simply as the behavior or part of the behavior of a particular species of primates.* By so regarding it we are enabled to study and interpret it as we do the behavior of any other species: for example, with respect not only to its interaction with environmental variables but also to the effect of this interaction upon natural selection. The fact that human behavior is complex, varied, variable, and, to a considerable extent, population-specific may make observation and description formidable tasks, but it does not mean that basically different principles must be used in the study of human behavior and the study of behavior in other animal species. [Vayda 1965, p. 4; emphasis mine]

The ecological functionalism puts culture in double jeopardy. It is threatened with liquidation because it cannot be specified as such by natural reasons, and because consideration of its specific quality would invite in a reason of another nature. The crisis then becomes ontological in its proportions. Culture is exchanged for "behavior." Its concrete qualities are only the appearance of "bodily movements" whose wisdom is their biological effect. Ontology thus recapitulates methodology. And anthropology loses its object. The properties of culture having been ignored in the practice of its explanation, it is presumed that these properties have no autonomy or value as such—which is a rationalization of the fact that the explanation cannot account for them:

It would seem that a unified science of ecology has definite contributions to make toward the realization of anthropological goals and does
not entail any appreciable sacrifice of traditional anthropological interests. It may, however, entail a somewhat different sacrifice, i.e., of
the notion of the autonomy of a science of culture. [Vayda and Rappaport 1967, p. 497]

This sacrifice of the autonomy of culture (and cultural science) would be
the consequence of its subordination within a larger system of natural
constraint. Insofar as the latter is conceived as a cybernetic order, as is
common in ecological studies, including culture in a "unified science"
would also entail displacing the property of "mind" from humanity to the
ecosystem. As a self-regulating set of thermodynamic relations, responsive
to "information" or significant alteration of its components, the ecosystem
as a whole is now the site of a "mental activity" which must logically (in
the interest of the exclusive authority of the Behemoth) be denied any of its
parts. As Bateson explains such systems: "we can assert that *any* ongoing
ensemble of events and objects which has the appropriate complexity of
causal circuits and the appropriate energy relations will show mental
characteristics. It will *compare,* that is, be responsive to difference. . . . It
will 'process information' and will inevitably be self-corrective either toward homeostatic optima or toward the maximization of certain variables"
(1972, p. 315). Clearly, if any of the components of this self-regulatory
system were able to impose its own project on the totality, then the latter
would become a mere chain of consequences, governed only negatively by
the limits of possible functioning. Hence to preserve systematicity, mind
can be a property only of the whole: "in no system which shows mental
characteristics can any part have unilaterial control over the whole. In other
words, *the mental characteristics of the system are immanent, not in some
part, but in the system as a whole"* (ibid., p. 316).

Within the ecosystem, the interactional node or subsystem encompassing man and his immediate environs would be characterized by feedback
relations as reciprocal and equal as those between any other elements of the
circuit, notwithstanding that the man-nature transaction is mediated by
culture. Culture here is merely the self-mediation of nature. It is merely the
human mode of response, and hence systematically governed, inasmuch as
man is but a functional variable of the whole—a reactive component in
mutual determination with environmental variables, themselves as much
subject to his object as vice versa. One of Bateson's favorite illustrations is
the interaction of man and tree in woodchopping:

Consider a man felling a tree with an axe. Each stroke of the axe is modified or corrected, according to the shape of the cut face of the tree left by the previous stroke. The self-corrective (*i.e.,* mental) process is brought about by a total system, tree-eyes-brain-muscles-axe-stroke-tree; and it is this total system that has the characteristics of immanent mind. [Ibid., p. 317]

The problem is that men never merely "chop wood" as such. They cut logs for canoes, carve the figures of gods on war clubs, or even chopfirewood, but they always enter into relations with the wood in a specific way, a cultural way, in terms of a meaningful project whose finality governs the terms of the reciprocal interaction between man and tree. If the purpose is a canoe, the response to a change in the tree is different than if the aim is getting firewood. The response to the last stroke depends on an objective that is not given to the process as a natural process; that stroke and every one before it back to the initial cut depend on the meaningful intent. The determinate interaction of tree-eyes-brain-etc. has been stipulated by a symbolic order; it is a paradigmatic example of nature harnessed to the service of culture. The cybernetic alternative envisioned in ecosystem theory for its part is an ultimate ecology fetishism, most appropriate to its own cultural context of industrial and bureaucratic capitalism, whose project likewise consists in reducing both men and things to their functional specifications as elements of a self-determining productive process.[27]

G. P. Murdock

The end of the "terror" will be death to the noble culture. In George Peter Murdock, anthropology may have already found its Robespierre. Murdock took the apparently fitting occasion of the Huxley Memorial Lecture of 1971 to announce culture's demise. It is interesting to see how he finally

27. "In fact, in the production process of capital . . . labour is a totality . . . whose individual component parts are alien to one another, so that the overall process as a totality is *not* the *work* of the individual worker, and is furthermore the work of the different workers together only to the extent they are [forcibly] combined, and do not [voluntarily] enter into the combination with one another. The combination of this labour appears just as subservient to and led by an alien will and an alien intelligence—having its *animating unity* elsewhere—as its material unity appears subordinate to the *objective unity* of the *machinery*, of fixed capital, which, as *animated monster*, objectifies the scientific idea, and is in fact the coordinator, does not in any way relate to the individual worker as his instrument; but rather he himself exists as an animated individual punctuation mark, as its living isolated accessory" (Marx 1973 [1857–58], p. 470).

got to this point of methodological self-awareness. For the central argument of Murdock's *Social Structure* (1949) had already repeated in all essentials the Morganian understanding of the relationships between practical circumstance, utilitarian action, and cultural order. Murdock might be the first to take issue with Morgan on matters of methodology and details of interpretation, but his comprehension of social structure is in the direct line of praxis theory. For Murdock, the formation of "consanguineal kin groups"—and by consequence the classification of kinsmen—amounts to the recognition of de facto arrangements on the ground, that is, of the relationships precipitated by residential practices, which in turn respond to practical exigencies. Residential practice is thus the dynamic key. Determining the actual composition of social groupings, it plays a role in Murdock's scheme analogous to that played by exogamous unions in the first stages of Morgan's: the medium by which objective or natural constraint is reified in cultural form. Kinship relations are constituted by reflexive awareness of the group composition thus established. They are the articulate expressions of residential arrangements, and residential arrangements in turn reflect the "fundamental life conditions":

> The conditions of existence of any society are always undergoing change—sometimes rapidly, sometimes slowly—in consequence of natural events such as famines and epidemics, of social events such as wars and revolutions, of biological influences such as increasing population density, of internal adaptations such as technological inventions, and of external contacts which may stimulate cultural borrowing. Many changes in fundamental life conditions may exert pressure in the direction of modifying the existing rule of residence. So diverse are the causal factors in social change, and so few are the alternatives in residence rules, that nearly any society, whatever its level of culture and existing forms of social organization, can probably encounter particular concatenations of circumstances that will favor the development of any one of the alternative rules of residence. [Murdock 1949, p. 203]

So, for example,

> Patrilocal residence seems to be promoted by any change in culture of the conditions of social life which significantly enhances the status, importance, and influence of men in relation to the opposite sex. Particularly influential is any modification in the basic economy whereby masculine activities in the sex division of labor come to yield the principal means of subsistence. [Ibid., p. 206]

Such residential practices generate specific alignments of kinsmen,[28] the "recognition" of which—recognition which may be withheld—establishes kinship groups such as lineages and the customary classifications of persons:

> Unilocal residence does not produce lineages or sibs directly. It merely favors the development of extended families and exogamous demes with their characteristic unlinear alignment of kinsmen, and either of these may lead to the recognition of non-localized kin groups. What matrilocal or patrilocal residence accomplishes is to assemble in spatial proximity to one another a group of unilinearly related kinsmen of the same sex, together with their spouses. [Ibid., p. 210]

Murdock resumes the whole argument in a just-so story of the development of a patrilocal-patrilineal system out of a dual organization of matrilineal clans. The example is capital on several accounts, perhaps not least that Murdock is compelled to couch his explanation as a myth of origin. At the same time, Morgan's own method clearly comes through, not only in general but in the details of the growth of patriliny out of matriliny (although of course Murdock does not hold that this was a universal sequence of evolution). As the story goes, some factor appears in the matrilineal setting which "places a premium on patrilocal residence," such as the introduction of cattle (Morgan's own "factor"), slaves, or shell money, accompanied by the notion that prestige is enhanced by polygyny (ibid., p. 217). Now one man after another, "as he acquires wealth,"[29] is able by the offer of bride-price to persuade other men to allow their daughters to remove to his own home. And one man after another begins to leave some of his property to his own sons, rather than to his sister's sons as matriliny enjoins. So, "bit by bit," ties with "patrilineal kin" are strengthened at the expense of "matrilineal," until the people finally discover they have been speaking patriliny without knowing it:

> Almost before the population of the village realizes that anything particularly significant has happened, they discover that the houses on one side of the street are now occupied by patrilineally related males with their wives and children, and that a similar group lives across the way.

---

28. Murdock here gives himself "kinship" as a natural-genealogical fact, in exactly the manner that Schneider has recently exposed and criticized (Schneider 1968; 1972).

29. Murdock, like Morgan, takes "wealth" as a natural category, in something of the same way as he assumes "kinship" or "patrilineal kin" as a genealogical category.

Patrilocal residence has become firmly established, patrilineal inheritance is accepted, and the former matri-clans have been transformed into incipient patri-clans. The situation is ripe for the development of patrilineal descent, and this may occur quite rapidly if there are patrilineal societies in the neighborhood to serve as models. [Ibid., p. 216]

Murdock's basic position may be illustrated another way, from a classic contretemps with Leach in which Murdock's own conception of the relation between the order lived and the order thought emerges clearly out of the misunderstanding. In a way Murdock's mistake was a true one, for he recognized in Leach's privileging of individual choice over jural rule a deviation from the structural-functional paradigm similar to his own practice.[30] With respect to the Sinhalese village of Pul Eliya, Leach had said, "social structures are sometimes best regarded as the statistical outcome of multiple individual choices rather than a direct reflection of jural rules" (1960, p. 124). For Murdock, then, it was only logical to agree with Leach—by inverting the dictum to the effect that jural rules are best regarded as the outcome of a statistical trend in individual choice (Murdock 1960, p. 9). That was what he had been saying at least since 1949.

And in 1971 the logical conclusion dawned upon him. That year, before the assembled anthropologists of Great Britain and Ireland, in an event whose theoretical insignificance was matched only by its solemnity, Murdock renounced his adherence to the concepts of "culture" and "social system." Such, as he said, are merely "illusory conceptual abstractions" from "the very real phenomena" of individuals interacting with each other and with their environment in the pursuit of their own best interests. Murdock had finally become conscious of the theory in his practice. This new conception of culture was not more than an "illusory conceptual abstraction" from the method he had been using all along:

30. Although Leach has been greatly influenced by French structuralist techniques, even as he was trained in the traditions of Radcliffe-Brown, he is of course capable of a Malinowskian disagreement with both, specifically on the interposition of practical interest between circumstance and the social order. This is explicitly so in *Pul Eliya,* to which the example above refers, but it is also the case in *Political Systems of Highland Burma,* insofar as he understands the imposition of one or another alternative code (*gumsa/gumlao*) as a choice dictated by political advantage. Thus the theoretical necessity to assume a natural propensity to compete for prestige, different only in content from the economizing premise of classical economics, and to allow it the role of a general moving force in human affairs (1954, p. 10).

It now seems to me distressingly obvious that culture, social system, and all comparable supra-individual concepts, such as collective representation, group mind, and social organism, are illusory conceptual abstractions inferred from observations of the very real phenomena of individuals interacting with one another and with their natural environments. The circumstances of their interaction often lead to similarities in the behaviour of different individuals which we tend to reify under the name of culture, and they cause individuals to relate themselves to others in repetitive ways which we tend to reify as structures or systems. But culture and social structure are actually mere epiphenomena—derivative products of the social interaction of pluralities of individuals. [Murdock 1972, p. 19]

But one ought not to deduce that such derivation of ontology from methodology amounts to an exception, at least for the social sciences, of our general thesis that concept does not follow from practice. The seeming empirical status of the proposition that culture is the "epiphenomenon" of another reality is itself an illusion. What was harbored all along in the method, and surfaces here as the true source of the proposition, is bourgeois society. Hence Murdock merely produces for anthropology the same kind of solipsistic reduction Max Weber attempted for sociology, with the same suspension of the collective or the objectivized in favor of individual intentions. Or consider the notion Murdock would latterly put in the place of the so-called culture, namely, Frederik Barth's "decision-making approach to the study of social phenomena," an approach which "focuses on the events of social life rather than on its morphological or statistical features and views social behavior from the point of view of the decisions made by individuals in 'the allocation of time and resources' from among the alternatives available to them" (ibid., pp. 22–23). The anatomy of man and ape: Murdock's latest paradigm is an evolved form of that embedded in Malinowski's functionalism—albeit the crossing of phylogenetic lines here is complex, since, as Kuper says of Barth's model, "Radcliffe-Brown's view of social structure as a network of real dyadic relationships has become, ironically, the salvation of Malinowski's manipulative man" (1973, p. 230). But the "manipulative man" reveals the common ancestry of all such utilitarian theories. The general idea of social life here advanced is the particular behavior of the parties in the marketplace. Now all of culture is understood as the organized effect of individual businesslike economizing. Culture is Business on the scale of Society. Murdock's concept of culture is no lesson from anthropological experience: the anthropological concept was already a cultural experience.

And more, this conclusion from "experience" that culture does not exist is an illusion doubly compounded. For it takes as the model of all social life not the reality of bourgeois society but the self-conception of that society. It credits the appearance of Western culture as its truth, thus conspiring in the illusion that it really is the socialized product of practical activity by ignoring the symbolic constitution of the practical activity. Social science elevates to a statement of theoretical principle what bourgeois society puts out as an operative ideology. Culture is then threatened with a neglect in anthropology that is matched only by the consciousness of it in society.

It is some consolation that in the line of praxis theory initiated by Julian Steward this neglect has become the source of a certain regret.

Julian Steward

Steward's founding perspective on "cultural ecology" is in general terms the same as Morgan's decultured problematic, and in the details of the paradigmatic article on patrilineal bands (1936) it is exactly Murdock's idea of social structure. Thus it would not be worthwhile to make an exposition here were it not for the paradoxical context in which Steward, and later Murphy (1970), places his cultural ecology—as an opposition to the biological. The paradox is instructive. Its unraveling will show how the mystification of the cultural logic as the a priori of economic action establishes the practical logic as the determinant of cultural form.

In preamble to the main ecological argument on "primitive bands," Steward in one way or another allows himself the main technical and social conditions of hunters and gatherers—referring some of these to economic advantage, others to human nature, and still others simply to empirical fact. Territorial "ownership" is understandable on the basis that "any animal may secure food and water more efficiently in terrain which it habitually utilizes"; family groups, on the basis of "a chronic sex excitability" in the human species; and the band of families, on the grounds that "In practically all human groups several families cooperate. . . . This provides a kind of subsistence insurance" (Steward 1936, p. 332). The principal relations of production—the division of labor by sex—are assumed by virtue of their empirical generality among hunters. So also is the simple technology given, not only as a set of tools in themselves but as a self-evident set of intentions, the provision of "subsistence." This technology is deployed in areas of limited food resources; hence, hunters are able to achieve only small band aggregates, on the order of twenty to fifty persons, and have low population densities.

Given these conditions, the argument proceeds to determine the ecological basis of various band forms, "patrilineal," "matrilineal," and "composite." As in Murdock's analysis, the critical link between environment and social structure is residential practice. Steward concentrates on the most widespread band type, the patrilineal, which he understands as the formalization of patrilocal residence. In the first version of the study (1936), patrilocality is explained by innate male dominance and the economic importance of men in hunting cultures (p. 333). In a later version, patrilocality is referred particularly to its economic advantages in areas of dispersed but fixed animal resources: "an environment in which the principal food is game that is nonmigratory and scattered, which makes it advantageous for men to remain in the general territory of their birth" (i.e., since they already know the territory) (1955, p. 135). With patrilocality thus established on the grounds of its economic advantage, the structure of the band follows as recognition and articulation—in a way by now familiar to us. Patrilocal residence must aggregate "patrilineal" relatives. Therefore the incest tabu is imposed at the band level, and the group is organized as an exogamous patrilineage. To sum up the argument in general terms: economic effectiveness in the given set of technical and environmental circumstances requires certain social practices and relations (patrilocal residence) which are in turn formulated and codified as a social structure (patrilineal band). Pure Morgan.[31]

The proposition is also pure praxis. For it is specifically the "behavior patterns of *work*," as "required" by the ecological context, that are realized in cultural form. Murphy explains Steward's perspective:

> The environment *per se* is not the critical factor, for the "behavior patterns" *required* in its exploitation using certain "economic devices" are the key elements. These behavior patterns are work, and the "economic devices" technology. Quite simply, the theory of cultural ecology is concerned with the process of work, its organization, its cycles and rhythms and its situational modalities [1970, p. 155].
> ... *Patterns of work are directly derivative from the tools and resources* to which they are applied, and these two factors serve to

31. The paradigm, praxis → practice → structure, is generalized by Steward in the form of "three fundamental procedures of cultural ecology": "First, the inter-relationship of exploitative or productive technology and the environment must be analyzed. ... Second, the behavior patterns involved in the exploitation of a particular area by means of a particular technology must be analyzed. ... The third procedure is to acertain the extent to which the behavior patterns entailed in exploiting the environment affect other aspects of culture" (1955, pp. 40–41).

limit the human activities to which they are related [p. 156]. . . . *And it is from the analysis of activity, rather than of institutions and values, that the theory is derived.*

These activities are those pertaining to the work cycle and from them emerges the structure of Shoshone society [p. 156]. . . .

The point I wish to stress is that the realm of social action involved in material production, i.e., work, underlies the entire Shoshone social system. Resources are the object of work and therein lies their importance for an understanding of society and culture. . . . As objects of work, they have certain unmodifiable characteristics to which labor must be adjusted if they are to be accessible to exploitation. Tools derive their central position in the analysis of society as instruments and mediators of work. The use of tools *requires* certain modes of *behavior,* and the application of these instruments to materials induces further behavioral adjustments [p. 157]. . . .

The theory and method of cultural ecology is not a kind of environmental determinism, nor is it even centrally concerned with the environment. It is a cultural theory, without being "culturalogical" or "superorganic." Further, it is an action theory, in the sense that this term has been used in sociology. While recognizing that behavior is in good part regulated by norms, *it also sees the norms as arising in the first place from social action and being a crystallization of behavior* that, in turn, maintains these behavior patterns [p. 163] . . . tools and resources *require* [Murphy's italics] some kinds of behaviors if they are to be successfully integrated, and these requirements, the work process, make further demands on the general social structure. [P. 163; all emphases mine except where otherwise noted][32]

Murphy goes on to make an eloquent defense of this "cultural ecology," as against the biological reductions of the "new ecology" (of which

32. Murphy's own interesting theoretical work (1971) turns on the same dualism of action and norm, society and culture, and the irreconcilable premises that activity generates ideas and perception is culturally ordered, often deceptively (e.g., pp. 34–35, 55, 90–91, 100–101). The contradictions of a dialectical interplay then become contradictions of Murphy's own, with activity prior to idea, which is the precondition of activity, the two propositions themselves related by an aleatory negativity: e.g., "I have argued that although ideas are generated by action, they are not merely a reflection of that activity or a restatement of it in symbolic and ideal form. Rather, ideas, including ones that are normative in a society, may deny behavioral reality, they may reinterpret it according to other frameworks of meaning, they may simplify and distort it, or they may be in open and conscious conflict with social action. This does not mean that the normative system is unrelated to conduct, for ideas are the precondition of activity" (p. 158).

Vayda, Sweet, and Leeds are cited as avatars).[33] But the defense is not without contradiction, and in the final analysis it is difficult to distinguish the two positions except for differences of sentiment.

According to Murphy, Steward understood society as a distinctive mode of integration, and as such not subordinated to nature. Ordered by ideas and activities, society enjoys a relative autonomy. But to put the contradiction in a nutshell, the ideas are ideas about activities, while the reason in the activities is practical effectiveness under the circumstances, so that the principle of cultural order remains the natural one of adaptive advantage. As Murphy himself observes (in the passage just cited), Steward's theory rests on the activity of work "rather than institutions or values." These institutions and values, therefore, do not organize the human interconnection with nature, but come on the scene *post festum,* as a crystallization of the relationships established in the work situation. On the other hand, the patterns of work are "directly derived from the tools and resources"; they are such as are "required" for effective integration of the two in the process of production (cf. Steward 1938, pp. 260–61). Everything thus comes down to the notion of "requirement"; and the "requirement" in question is the purely objective one of dealing successfully with the environment. Murphy's own conclusions about the relations of culture to nature are true, but they are unfortunately not pertinent to Stewardian ecology:

> Higher order phenomena arrange lower order phenomena to their purposes, though they may not change their properties. Correspondingly, human social systems reach out and embrace ecosystems rather than the reverse proposition, and culture reorders nature and makes appendages of the parts of it that are relevant to the human situation. [1970, p. 169]

Exactly so. But all of Steward's philosophy runs to just the opposite effect. The cultural morphology is rendered intelligible on precisely the same basis as the wings of a bird or the gills of a fish. Culture does not

33. "The 'new ecology' as I must call it to distinguish it from Steward's cultural ecology, is concerned with the systematic fit and coherence between culture and environment, and this search for connectedness and order in the relationship causes the distinctions between the two to blur and disappear. . . . The connections between a social system and its environment may indeed be ordered but this hardly erases the boundaries between the two. . . . The distinctiveness and autonomy of the social system is derived from the fact that its integration lies in the realm of ideas and social activities, as these are adjusted to produce a coherent and ordered way of life. It is related to nature but its modalities lie beyond nature" (Murphy, 1970, p. 164).

reorder nature by its own purposes—because, for Steward, all purpose but the practical disappears at the moment of production. Ecological wisdom consists in forgetting the cultural ordering of nature at every decisive point. The interaction of technology with the environment according to determinate relations of production—on which is erected a cultural morphology—is taken by Steward for an instrumental fact. Hence the order that is transmitted through action into structure is the eco-logic of effective adaptation.

Steward's problematic is a design for the neglect in theoretical principle of ecology as a cultural system. Partly this is a matter of omission, failure to develop in concept what is recognized in fact. Steward is well aware that the particular character of technology stipulates the character of the environment—that is, gives significance to resources by a criterion of cultural relevance. But in Steward's mode of argument this is a given, along with the relations of family and of production (division of labor by sex: men hunting, women gathering). The cultural ordering of nature is thus disguised as the premise to a naturalistic ordering of culture. Indeed, the entire intentionality of the productive process is neglected in the assumption that this is a "subsistence" economy, condemned by the poverty of technical means to whatever meager existence can be squeezed out.

Such naturalization of the hunter-gatherer economy is, of course, the received anthropological wisdom.[34] And it plays directly into an "ecological" explanation of the total culture. For in ignoring the historical character of the economic objectives, both in quality and in quantity, both the particular goods that are sought and the intensity of the process, it misses out on the cultural organization of the relation to culture.[35] Not even hunters are engaged in a mere subsistence economy. Every such group distinguishes the edible from the inedible, and not only for the population

34. "A man who spends his whole life following animals just to kill them to eat, or moving from berry patch to another, is really living just like an animal himself" (Braidwood 1957, p. 122; cf. Sahlins 1972, chap. 1; Lee and DeVore 1968).

35. Specifically missing is the cultural intentionality embodied in the code of desirable objects. As Baudrillard explains, properly speaking an "object of consumption [hence of production] does not exist any more than a phoneme has an absolute meaning in linguistics. This object does not take meaning either in a specific relation with the subject . . . or in an operative relation to the world (the object-utensil); it only takes on meaning through its difference from other objects, according to a hierarchial code" (1972, p. 61). Such being the case, there are "no needs save those of which the system has need," and it is not that consumption is a function of production, but that *"com-summativité"* is a structural mode of production (ibid., p. 89).

as a whole but for specific classes of age, sex, and ritual condition as these are locally defined. Moreover, a host of examples from Australian aborigines are enough to show that different types of intergroup exchange have corresponding implications for the intensity and social patterns of work. The Australians are even capable of a concrete totemism, in which neighboring groups specialize in producing different utilitarian objects for trade from materials that are equally available to all, in this way duplicating on the economic plane the increase rites and the interdependence of groups imagined in the totemic system. In brief, what Steward neglects is the organization of work as a symbolic process operating both in the relations of production and in the finalities. The activity of production is instead culturally deconstituted, to make way for the constitution of culture by the activity of production.

The real issue posed for anthropology by all such practical reason is the existence of culture. The utility theories have gone through many changes of costume, but always play out the same denouement: the elimination of culture as the distinctive object of the discipline. One sees through the variety of these theories two main types, proceeding along two different routes to this common end. One type is naturalistic or ecological—as it were, objective—while the second is utilitarian in the classic sense, or economistic, invoking the familiar means-ends calculus of the rational human subject.

Naturalism understands culture as the human mode of adaptation. Culture in this view is an instrumental order, conceived (according to the particular ecological school) as engaged in reproducing itself as culture or in maintaining the human population within limits of biological viability. In either event, the praxology is "objective" in the sense that explanation consists of determining the material or biological virtues of given cultural traits; there is no theoretical demand that the actors calculate directly in adaptive utilities—on the contrary, the most triumphant "eurekas!" will be reserved for demonstrations that they do so *malgré eux*. The disappearing act performed on culture consists of its absorption, one way or another, within nature. Either cultural practice is a behavioral mode of appearance of the laws of natural selection, just like any "species-specific behavior," or else it is subsumed within a more general ecosystem which alone and as a totality enjoys the powers of self-regulation or "mind" and whose constraints are realized in cultural forms.

Rather than a pragmatics of cultural forms, the subjective utilitarianism is by contrast concerned with the purposeful activity of individuals in pursuit of their own interests and their own satisfactions. One might say that this second type of pragmatic theory presupposes a universal Economic Man, if with a relativized set of preferences, that is, man proceeding rationally toward goals which, however, vary from society to society. The relativization is thus an accommodation to cultural variation, but also its appropriation as premise by an explanation that purports to account for it as consequence. In this praxology, culture is taken as an environment or means at the disposition of the ''manipulating individual,'' and also as a sedimented resultant of his self-interested machinations. The characteristic resolution of culture is thus solipsistic in form. Only the actors (and their interests taken a priori as *theirs*) are real; culture is the epiphenomenon of their intentions.

All these types of practical reason have also in common an impoverished conception of human symboling. For all of them, the cultural scheme is the *sign* of other ''realities,'' hence in the end obeisant in its own arrangement to other laws and logics. None of them has been able to exploit fully the anthropological discovery that the creation of meaning is the distinguishing and constituting quality of men—the ''human essence'' of an older discourse—such that by processes of differential valuation and signification, relations among men, as well as between themselves and nature, are organized.

Cultural Reason

In the opening paragraphs of this chapter, I described the relation between practical and cultural accounts as a repetitive and cyclical opposition from which anthropology has been unable to escape these past hundred years. Still, just as in American society, where what is most fundamentally conventional is also deemed the most natural, the struggle for recognition of the cultural perspective began at a disadvantage, and might be better described as an attempt to liberate anthropology from the prison house of naturalism. This attempt has gone on in Europe as well as America, and it has been marked not merely by a greater anthropological consciousness of the symbolic but by its increasing penetration into the analysis of the practical.

On the American side, Boas's concept of culture as a meaning-structure interposed between circumstance and custom had been sustained by his own students. It went through various developments, notably Ruth Benedict's idea of an orienting logic that gathered up the shreds and patches left lying about by Lowie and stitched them into consistent patterns of culture. In Benedict's conception, order came from the infusion of comparable meanings and attitudes through all the practices of the culture. This was not a differential code, of course, but a global *opératoire,* organizing the environment, social relations and, above all, history: a selective screen which reduced the potential chaos of cultural borrowing (diffusion) by a criterion of acceptance and an assignment of significance (Benedict 1961 [1934]).

In the work of another well-known American, Leslie White, the Boasian paradigm lives alongside the Morganian, without, however, achieving a unity of the theoretical opposites. This ambivalence in White's philosophy may not be idiosyncratic; it is a fair judgment that the practical reason and the symbolic cohabit without much remark or scandal in most anthropological theory. For White, ideas are on the one hand the reflex of the technological base, either directly or as mediated by the social relations likewise so determined. Here White elaborates directly on the epistemology in Morgan. Men's ideas of the world can only derive from the way they experience it, and their experience must depend on the way they are technically articulated to it:

> Ideological, or philosophical, systems are organizations of beliefs in which human experience finds its interpretation. But experience and interpretations thereof are powerfully conditioned by technologies. There is a type of philosophy proper to every type of technology. The interpretation of a system of experience in which a *coup de poing* is a characteristic feature will, as it must, reflect this kind of experience. It would not be improper to speak of a *coup de poing* type of philosophy as well as of technology. . . . One type of technology will find expression in the philosophy of totemism, another in astrology or quantum mechanics. [White 1949, pp. 365–66]

As ideas follow from the technical conditions of perception, the evolution of philosophy is essentially resolved by White into the successive stages of false consciousness and true, the transition between them effected by a brief period of metaphysics. With increasingly effective means of dealing with the world technologically, an earlier supernaturalism, representing the anthropomorphic conceit of a fundamental ignorance, must needs give way to a scientific philosophy based on objective knowledge.

On the other hand, there is White's own insistence upon the uniqueness of "symbolic behavior," that is, a system of meanings specifically not bound to physical reality. Hence the way the world is "experienced" is no simple sensory process such as might follow directly from tehnologically exposing reality to view. The human power of bestowing meaning—of experiencing as meaning—constructs another kind of world:

> Man differs from the apes, and indeed all other living creatures so far as we know, in that he is capable of symbolic behavior. With words man creates a new world, a world of ideas and philosophies. In this world man lives just as truly as in the physical world of his senses. Indeed, man feels that the essential quality of his existence consists in his occupancy of this world of symbols and ideas—or, as he sometimes calls it, the world of the mind or spirit. This world of ideas comes to have a continuity and a permanence that the external world of the senses can never have. It is not made up of the present only but of a past and a future as well. Temporarily, it is not a succession of disconnected episodes, but a continuum extending to infinity in both directions, from eternity to eternity. [White 1942, p. 372]

But then from this symbolist perspective,—as opposed to the positivist and utilitarian consciousness through technological disclosure—the tool is itself an idea. It is "not merely a material object, or even a sensory image as it may be to an ape. It is also an idea" (White 1942, p. 373). If a stone ax generates a given type of philosophy, nevertheless the ax itself is a concept whose meaning and use, as is true of all concepts, are fixed not by its objective properties but by the system of relationships between symbols. Thus the technological determination of culture in White's evolutionary theory lives side by side with the cultural determination of technology in his symbolic theory:

> An axe has a subjective component; it would be meaningless without a concept and attitude. On the other hand, a concept or an attitude would be meaningless without overt expression, in behavior or speech (which is a form of behavior). Every cultural element, every cultural trait, therefore, has a subjective and an objective aspect. But conceptions, attitudes, and sentiments—phenomena that have their locus in the human organism—may be considered for purposes of scientific interpretation in an extrasomatic context, i.e., in terms of their relation to other symboled things and events rather than in terms of their relationship to human organism. . . . [Thus an axe may be considered in terms of its relationship] to other symboled things and events such as arrows, hoes, and customs regulating the division of labor in society. [White 1959a, p. 236][36]

---

36. In this article, White unnecessarily gives culture a contextual definition; namely, "symbolates" viewed in the context of other "symbolates," which puts the burden of the determination on the anthropologist—even as the locus of the symbolic remains in the

As against the fundamentally practical and technological paradigm which connects him with Morgan, White is thus capable of a symbolic perspective—which puts him in unlikely company. Allow me to juxtapose a passage previously cited from Lévi-Strauss with a text from White's presidential address to the anthropology section of the AAAS:

Lévi-Strauss

If, as I have said, the conceptual scheme governs and defines practices, it is because these, which the ethnologist studies as discrete realities placed in time and space and distinctive in their particular modes of life and forms of civilization, are not to be confused with *praxis* which . . . constitutes the fundamental totality for the sciences of man. . . . Without questioning the undoubted primacy of infrastructures, I believe that *there is always a mediator between praxis and practices, namely the conceptual scheme by the operation of which matter and form, neither with any independent existence are realized as structure,* that is as entities which are both empirical and intelligible. [1966, p. 130; emphasis mine]

White

Thus [with symbols] man built a new world in which to live. To be sure, he still trod the earth, felt the wind against his cheek, or heard it sigh among the pines; he drank from streams, slept beneath the stars, and awoke to greet the sun. But it was not the same sun! Nothing was the same any more. Everything was "bathed in celestial light"; and there were "intimations of immortality" on every hand. Water was not merely something to quench thirst; it could bestow the life everlasting. *Between man and nature hung the veil of culture, and he could see nothing save through this medium.* He still used his senses. He chipped stone, chased deer, mated and begat offspring. *But permeating everything was the essence of words: the meanings and values that lay beyond the senses. And these meanings and values guided him—in addition to his senses—and often took precedence over them.* [1958 ms; emphasis mine][37]

_____

human subject—and ignores the real process by which human productions are reified or "objectivized," i.e., become "extrasomatic." See Berger and Luckmann (1967) for a recent discussion of "objectivation," tied, however, to just-so origins in praxis.

37. The comparison is admittedly mildly disingenuous, for the final sentence of White's paragraph is a proposition which Lévi-Strauss would not endorse, although it is *le propre* of Boasianism: "Man had become the irrational animal."

It seems that wherever one turns in American anthropology one meets, if not precisely this ambivalence of White's, some incompleteness in the appropriation of the cultural object by meaning. The impressive ethnoscience developed by Goodenough, Lounsbury, Conklin, and others, especially out of the linguistic legacy of the Boas school, has been shackled by a positivist concept of culture as behavioral competence or ethnography, therefore of meaning as referential significance and of analysis as translation—in terms of an apparently objective code whose "objectivity" encodes a theory. Or to take examples of a very different kind (if equally impressive in intellectual quality), the efforts of Geertz or Schneider, each in their own way, have likewise turned on a specific limitation of the symbolic, as is built into the distinction between action and ideology, society and culture. This particular distinction has been more characteristically European, and more immediately the tenet of British than of American social anthropology. Since its implications reach back to Durkheim, then on again to the modern French structuralism—which also incorporates the Boasian tradition through Lévi-Strauss—it has seemed to me most valuable to give the most attention to the playing out of the relation between utilitarianism and culture in this tradition. I begin with Durkheim.

Although the hero of a certain later "functionalism," Durkheim developed his own position on society in contradistinction to just the kind of economism and radical individualism we have seen embedded in Malinowski's project (cf. Parsons 1968 [1937]; Lukes 1972). Durkheim chose Spencer as his particular sociological antagonist on these issues, most notably in *The Division of Labor* (1949 [1893]). Hence, parallel to the contrast between Morgan and Boas one might formulate a paradigmatic comparison of Spencer and Durkheim, the latter debate centering on utilitarianism proper or economistic action, thus on the opposition of individual and society, where the former concerned the material logic of production and thereby the global opposition of culture and nature. For several reasons, however, the exercise on Spencer and Durkheim would not be as useful. One is the large residual resemblance between Spencer's "superorganic" and Durkheim's "society." More important, Durkheim framed his concept of the social in a general confrontation with classical political economy, not just with Spencer, so that it is most effectively understood as a broad critique of the self-conception of capitalism parading as a theory of society. It was a general objection to the adoption of the rationalistic formula of the economizing individual as the model of *social* production, a model that would place society in the status of predicate to presupposed human needs and purposes. As against such voluntarism and intentionalism, Durkheim posed the social fact. The overwhelming properties and powers he accorded it in relation to the individual represent a direct contraversion of the liberal economist's idea of society as the public outcome of private interest.

So the celebrated admonition of *The Rules of the Sociological Method* to "treat social facts as things" was something more than a lesson in positivist reification. To stress the facticity of the social fact was precisely to remove it from individual production: "For everything that is real has a definite nature that asserts control, that must be taken into account and is never completely overcome, even when we succeed in neutralizing it" (1950*a* [1895], pp. lv–lvi). All the affirmative features of sociality in Durkheim's scheme are in the same way negatives of individuality. It is not merely that the social fact is collective. Besides, it is *conscience* as opposed to desire, conventional as opposed to spontaneous; and rather than originating in wants, which are internal, it imposes itself as constraints, which are external. "Indeed, the most important characteristic of a 'thing' is the impossibility of its modification by a simple effort of the will" (ibid., p. 28). Similarly, the true source of Durkheim's strictures on psychology lay in his attack on economy. As he saw it, the real origin of reductionism was the ideology of calculating man:

> In fact, if society is only a system of means instituted by men to attain certain ends, these ends can only be individual, for only individuals could have existed before society. From the individual, then, have emanated the needs and desires determining the formation of societies; and, if it is from him that all comes, it is necessarily by him that all must be explained. Moreover, there are in societies only individual consciousnesses; in these, then, is found the source of all social evolution.
>
> Hence, sociological laws can be only a corollary of the more general laws of psychology. [Ibid., pp. 97–98]

From early on, as Lukes observes, Durkheim took the position that political economy was a stage in the development of social science that had to be overcome. Forced to conceive that "there is nothing real in society except the individual," such a science would offer no theoretical room for sociology. And as for this eternal individual from whom society had been abstracted, Durkheim could only hold him in the same kind of contempt as had Marx. This "individual" was himself abstract. Deprived of all coordinates of time, place, and history, all that remained was "the sad portrait of the pure egoist" (Durkheim [1888], cited in Lukes 1972, p. 80).

Neither Malinowski nor Weber: Durkheim refused to conceive society as the external object of human manipulation or to trade it off for the sole reality of the intentional subject. How then Radcliffe-Brown? Surely the same considerations would prevent Durkheim from indulging in the thinly disguised utilitarianism of a sociological functionalism. Not even his enthusiasm for "solidarity" ever permitted him to suppose in principle that the function of a custom, or its role in the satisfaction of the *besoins sociaux,* could provide an account of its specific nature.[38] Nevertheless, the lineaments of Radcliffe-Brown's functionalism show forth in Durkheim's ontology. Negating the political economy, Durkheim was forced to reproduce at the level of society, viewed as a kind of supersubject, the same economism he refused as constituting at the level of the individual. One can follow this union of opposites very well in an early paper (1887) on German moral science, where Durkheim champions the social perspectives of the economic historians G. Schmoller and A. Wagner against the liberals of the "Manchester school." For the latter, Durkheim writes,

> political economy consists of the satisfaction of the needs of the individual and especially of his material needs. In this conception, the individual thus exists as the unique end of economic relations; by him and for him everything is done. As for society, it is a figment of thought, a metaphysical entity that the scholar can and must ignore. What goes by that name is only the collection of all individual activities; it is a whole no greater than the sum of its parts. . . . One sees that basically the liberal economists are unknowing disciples of Rousseau, whom they mistakenly repudiate. True, they recognize that the state of isolation is not ideal, but like Rousseau they see nothing in the social tie but a superficial rapprochement, determined by the conjunction of individual interests. [Durkheim 1887, p. 37. But see his later essay (1965) on Rousseau for a changed opinion.]

But then, the argument against the individual being is exactly the existence of a *social being*—and against the ordering power of individual need, it is the *social need.* The denial that a given practice, for example, economic, stems from individual desire takes the form of an insistence on its social utility:

> For [Wagner and Schmoller], on the contrary, society is a true being, without doubt nothing outside the individuals who compose it, but

---

38. "To show in what respect a fact is useful is not to explain why it is true nor why it is what it is. For the uses it serves presuppose the specific properties which characterize it, but do not create it. The need we have of things cannot determine that they be such and such and, by consequence, it is not this need that can take them out of nothing and give them existence" (Durkheim 1950*b* [1895], p. 90; cf. pp. 94–95, 109–11; and 1965, pp. 42–44).

which nevertheless has its own nature and personality. These expressions of the current tongue—collective consciousness, collective mind, the body of the nation—do not have a mere verbal value but express facts that are eminently concrete. It is wrong to say that the whole is equal to the sum of its parts. By the simple fact that the parts have definite relations with each other, are arranged in a certain way, something new results from the assemblage: a composite being, surely, but one with special properties and which may even under special circumstances become conscious of itself. . . . As . . . the social being has needs of its own and among them the need of material things, it institutes and organizes in order to satisfy these needs an economic activity which is not that of this or that individual or that of the majority of the citizens, but of the nation in its entirety. [Ibid., pp. 37–38]

Society thus has its own ends, which are not those of the individual, and it is by the first, not the second, that social activity may be understood. "In order for a fact to be sociological, it must interest not only all the individuals taken separately, but the society itself. The army, industry, the family have social functions inasmuch as they have as their objective the one to defend, the other to nourish society, the third to assure its removal and continuity." (Durkheim 1886, p. 66) In the event, the utilitarian teleology could not be avoided. The whole means-ends paradigm was built into the conception of the social fact, inasmuch as this fact was determined by *opposition* to individual need. Only now, the *life of society* was the relevant finality. But, in addition, precisely as it had been defined as exterior and by contradistinction to individual welfare, this idea of social survival had a number of permanent effects on the idea of the social object. One was the view that society was continuously menaced from within by a war of each against all and was constructed to avoid that danger: a concept that profoundly inspired many of the works of the *Année Sociologique* group, as it also stood behind Radcliffe-Brown's concern for "coaptation" and the jural order generally (cf. Sahlins 1972, chap. 4). It may be that this notion of subterranean strife and the functional problems it presents to society remain the most important legacy bestowed on social science by capitalist ideology. More obviously, the emphasis on the life of society as opposed to individual purpose provided logical rationale for the appropriation of the entire organic metaphor as the basic idea of social constitution. The tradition of society as an organism was of course maintained by Radcliffe-Brown, and with it the division of social anthropology or sociology into the life-science branches of morphology, physiology, and evolution. It required only the proposition that the "social function" of an institution, or its contribution to social continuity, is also its *"raison d'être''* (Radcliffe-Brown 1950, p. 62) to complete in one movement a reversal of Durkheim's dictum to the contrary—and the transfer of utilitarianism from the individual to the supersubject that Durkheim's own initial line of argument had made inescapable.

Durkheim's concept of symboling, including the well-known ''sociological epistemology,'' ultimately fell victim to the same kind of dualism—as it likewise became in the hands of anthropological followers another form of instrumental logic. Lukes and others have argued, against the objections of Lévi-Strauss to the derivation of collective representation from social morphology, that Durkheim had become increasingly aware of the autonomy and universality of meaning. Perhaps this is another case of the difference between being aware of a fact and knowing its right theoretical place. The texts that might be persuasively cited on both sides of the issue amount to only one of the set of paradoxes in the master's understanding of the relation of thought to the world. Another is the problem (much like Malinowski's) of the difference between the sociologist's way of knowing and the way knowledge is constituted in childhood and society—processes so distinct in Durkheim's conception as to leave him unable to encompass his own positivist program. For that program held that social facts, precisely because they were ''things,'' could only be penetrated from outside as guided by perception and without preconception. Yet Durkheim never believed that either our own knowledge as members of society or, a fortiori, the social facts had the same type of genesis. The dilemma so posed might be exemplified by two brief passages from the *Rules*. On one hand, Durkheim writes that ''all education is a continuous effort to impose on the child ways of seeing, feeling, and acting which he could not have arrived at spontaneously'' (1950*a* [1895], p. 6). Yet some pages later he says: ''Moralists think it necessary to determine with precision the essence of the ideas of law and ethics, and not the nature of ethics and law. They have not yet arrived at the very simple truth that, as our ideas (*représentations*) of physical things are derived from these things themselves and express them more or less exactly, so [as scholars] our ideas of ethics must be derived from the observable manifestation of the rules that are functioning under our eyes'' (ibid., p. 23). Durkheim held simultaneously to a mediated and an unmediated relation of subject and object. If the latter conformed to the scientific project, the first was the fate of man in society. The contradiction, however, was actually more complex and not without a certain resolution. For in the mediated case, society alternately confronted man as a supersubject whose own concepts of the world dominated and replaced his individual sensibilities and then as an object, the direct experience of which accounted empirically for that process of conceptual imposition. As the locus of this antagonistic dualism between society and sensibility, man was "double" in Durkheim's view, and the duality of his being corresponded to an opposition between (individual) perception and (social) conception as well as between egoistic gratification and collective morality.[39]

I note these dialectic convolutions because they help explain both the virtues and the limitations of Durkheim's problematic as culture theory. These virtues are only partially documented by the influence of Durkheim's concept of the social fact on Saussure's formulation of the distinction between *langue* and *parole* (Doroszewski 1933). In *Primitive Classification* (with Mauss) and *The Elementary Forms of the Religious Life,* Durkheim had himself developed a notion of the sign, particularly as concerns the "categories" of class, number, space, time, cause, and the like, that was in several essentials very close to Saussure's. A paradox again from the point of view of the arbitrary character of the sign, since for Durkheim the categories represented the de facto social morphology—on which more will be said later. Yet as concepts emanating from the social totality, they specifically transcend individual experience. Rather than articulating such experience, they amount to a metalanguage by which it is organized.[40] And since the categories are not the particulars of experience but rather general ideas of the particulars (such as make an experience a particular), they specifically do not reflect perception but appropriate it within a relative cultural system.[41] Finally, Durkheim recognizes the arbitrary charac-

39. In a late paper (1914), sequel to the *Elementary Forms,* Durkheim wrote: "Our intelligence, like our activity, presents two very different forms: on the one hand, are sensations and sensory tendencies; on the other, conceptual thought and moral activity. Each of these two parts of ourselves represents a separate pole of our being, and these two poles are not only distinct from one another but are opposed to one another. Our sensory appetites are necessarily egoistic: they have our individuality and it alone as their object. When we satisfy our hunger, our thirst and so on, without bringing any other tendency into play, it is ourselves, and ourselves alone, that we satisfy. [Conceptual thought] and moral activity are, on the contrary, distinguished by the fact that the rules of conduct to which they conform can be universalized. Therefore, by definition, they pursue impersonal ends. Morality begins with disinterest, with attachment to something other than ourselves" (1960 [1914], p. 327; cf. 1951, and Lukes 1972, pp. 23–24).

40. "In fact, there are scarcely any words among those which we usually employ whose meaning does not pass, to a greater or less extent, the limits of our personal experience. Very frequently a term expresses things which we have never perceived or experiences we have never had or of which we have never been the witnesses" (Durkheim 1947 [1912], p. 434).

41. "Thinking by concepts is not merely seeing reality on its most general side, but it is projecting a light upon the sensation which illuminates it, penetrates it and transforms it. Conceiving something is both learning its essential elements better and also locating it in

ter of the sign directly, as a logical consequence of the distinction between the individual fact and the social—exactly because individual sensation is only a fleeting fact which as social beings we have the means and the liberty to represent in other terms:

> A sensation or an image always relies upon a determinate object, or upon a collection of objects of the same sort, and expresses the momentary condition of a particular consciousness; it is essentially individual and subjective. We therefore have considerable liberty in dealing with the representations of such an origin. It is true that when our sensations are actual, they impose themselves upon us *in fact*. But *by right* we are free to conceive them otherwise than they really are, or to represent them to ourselves as occurring in a different order from that in which they are really produced. In regard to them nothing is forced upon us except as considerations of another sort [namely social considerations] intervene. [Durkheim 1947 (1912), p. 14][42]

It must follow that for Durkheim the social fact, above all the collective consciousness, is no simple recognition of material circumstance. Opposition to this reduction would carry Durkheim, at least momentarily, beyond his own sociological reflectionism. From the determination of the meaningful scheme by the social morphology, he moved to a determination of the social morphology as meaningful—and of the meaningful syntax as sui generis. "The ideal society," he insisted, "is not outside of the real society; it is part of it. . . . For a society is not made up merely of the mass of individuals who compose it, the ground which they occupy, the things which they use and the movements which they perform, but above all is the

---

its place; for each civilization has its organized system of concepts which also characterizes it" (ibid., p. 435).

42. Elsewhere Durkheim writes of the alienation involved in such appropriation of individual experience with a regret something like Marx's in the *1844 Manuscripts:* "We understand only when we think in concepts. But sensory reality is not made to enter the framework of the concepts spontaneously and by itself. It resists, and, in order to make it conform, we have to do some violence to it, we have to submit it to all sorts of laborious operations that alter it so that the mind can assimilate it. However, we never completely succeed in mastering our sensations and in translating them completely into intelligible terms. They take on a conceptual form only by losing that which is most concrete in them, that which causes them to speak to our sensory being and to involve it in action; and, in so doing, they become something fixed and dead. Therefore, we cannot understand things without partially renouncing a feeling for their life, and we cannot feel that life without renouncing the understanding of it. Doubtless, we sometimes dream of a science that would adequately express all of reality; but this is an ideal that we can approach ceaselessly, not one that is possible for us to attain" (Durkheim 1960 [1914], p. 329).

idea which it forms of itself" (1914 [1912], p. 422). In disagreement with the going historical materialism, Durkheim counterposed a "whole world of sentiments, ideas and images which, once born, obey laws all their own. They attract each other, repel each other, unite, divide themselves, and multiply, though these combinations are not commanded and necessitated by the condition of the underlying reality" (ibid., p. 424; compare, however, the earlier remarks on Labriola, in Lukes 1972, p. 231). Note that even within the sociological epistemology a fundamental twist appeared in the relation of society and nature that could lead away from all reflectionism. Society, Durkheim was wont to say, comprises the "molds" within which are formed the human experience. Consequently, the world as known to man was a social world—precisely *not* a reflection, but *inside* society. The history of the world was the narrative of the tribe's existence, just as geographic space might be laid out from the central point of a village. And the objects of this social existence were not merely classed isomorphically with man, in correspondence with the categories of men, they were thereby given a place within the human groups. ("For the Australian, things themselves, everything which is in the universe, are a part of the tribe; they are constituent elements of it and, so to speak, regular members of it, just like men they have a determinate place in the general scheme of organization of the society" [Durkheim 1947 (1912), p. 141].) If, as Durkheim put it, the universe does not exist except insofar as it is thought, then it has been encompassed within an even greater order; so that it can no longer itself be thought to act simply from outside, in a purely natural way. And in that theoretical event, the opposition to Marxism was overdrawn. Just as Durkheim would accord with Marx on the recognition that "man is not an abstract being, squatting outside the world," so they must come together on the corollary proposition of a socialized or humanized nature. Lukács's description does for both: "Nature is a social category. That is to say, whatever is held to be natural at any given stage of social development, however this nature is related to man, and whatever form his involvement with it takes, i.e., nature's form, its content, and its objectivity are all socially conditioned" (1971, p. 234).

This concept of the social appropriation of nature, of the natural order as a moral order, continues to inform the best structural anthropology, British or French. It was essential to Radcliffe-Brown's early work on Andamanese belief and ceremonial, as well as his studies of totemism, taboo, and religion in general. It has been central also to the ethnographic enterprises of Evans-Pritchard and his students, as well as to more recent analyses of classification by Douglas, Leach, Bulmer, or Tambiah. Moreover, one recognizes in this problem-matrix of British social anthropology the same general view of the relation of custom to nature that distinguished Boas from Morgan. If the British functionalism reproduced a certain kind of economism, even magnified it by the transposition of a utilitarian teleology to the social supersubject, it would by the same movement avoid the vulgar naturalism or ecologism. Evans-Pritchard's *The Nuer* (1940) makes the whole argument in its construction, bridging the contrast between the general determinations of ecology and the specificity of the lineage system by famous passages on the social constitution of time and space. But then, Evans-Pritchard had already developed the essentials of a true cultural ecology in his work on Zande witchcraft (1937). Why, he asked there, do essentially rational people like the Azande, who know very well that their garden was lost to trampling elephants or their house to fire, nevertheless blame their neighbors and kinsmen and take appropriate magical actions of defense or retaliation? The answer he came to was that the *social* effect does not follow from the natural cause. Although it may be the property of fire to burn a house, it is not the property of fire to burn *your* house. Or again, the answer might be taken specifically to the cultural level; it is not in the nature of fire to burn a *house;* fire only burns wood. Once incorporated into the human realm, the action of nature is no longer a mere empirical fact but a social meaning. And between the property of fire to burn wood and a man's loss of his property, there is no commensurate relation. Nor is there a commensurate response. By no natural logic is magical action against a specific type of person sequitur to the process of combustion. A natural fact encompassed by the cultural order, if it does not surrender its physical properties, no longer dictates their consequences. The particular cultural "result" is no direct predicate of the natural cause. In a critical sense it is the other way round.

Durkheim's sociological epistemology had its limits as a theory of meaning, however, limits which seem to be reproduced even in the best modern work. I do not speak of the sentimentality in Durkheim's explanation of Australian totemism, the derivation of logical form from indistinct affect for which Lévi-Strauss reproached him—a problem also posed by the role Durkheim and Mauss (1963 [1901–2]) assigned to "confusion" in the generation of conceptual categories. It was rather the fatal differentiation of social morphology and collective representation—recreated by modern writers as society (or social system) versus culture (or ideology)—which arbitrarily limited the scope of the symbolic and left the field open to the usual functionalist dualism. "Society," Durkheim had written, "supposes a self-conscious organization which is nothing other than a classification" (1947 [1912], p. 443). The difficulty was that Durkheim derived the categories that society "supposes" from its already-achieved constitution, so leaving the form of society itself unaccounted for—except as it was "natural." Thus the dualism of social structure and cultural content, which moreover continually menaced the latter with a functional reduction to the utilitarian models and purposes of the former.

In Durkheim's view, we have seen, men's fundamental notions—of class, time, number, and the like—were given not innately or transcendentally but in the very organization and action of social life:

> The first logical categories were social categories; the first classes of things were classes of men, into which things were integrated. It was because men were grouped, and thought of themselves in the form of groups, that in their ideas they grouped other things, and in the beginning the two modes of grouping were merged to the point of being indistinct. Moieties were the first genera; clans, the first species. Things were thought to be integral parts of society, and it was their place in society which determined their place in nature. [Durkheim and Mauss 1963 (1901–2), pp. 82–83; cf. Durkheim 1947 (1912), pp. 431–47]

Yet moieties are themselves categorizations (of men), hence represent the mental operations of which they are presumed to be the original model. Rodney Needham cogently put the objection:

> the notion of space has first to exist before social groups can be perceived to exhibit in their disposition any spatial relations which may then be applied to the universe; the categories of quantity have to exist in order that an individual mind shall ever recognize the one, the many, and the totality of the divisions of his society; the notion of class necessarily precedes the apprehension that social groups, in concordance with which natural phenomena are classed, are themselves classified. In other words, the social "model" must itself be perceived to possess the characteristics which make it useful in classifying other things, but this cannot be done without the very categories which Durkheim and Mauss derive from the model (1963, p. xxvii).[43]

43. Durkheim had drawn criticism in the same vein from the contemporary philosopher D. Parodi, who objected to the idea that our categories of understanding and logic should derive in the first place from "la manière dont telle tribu avait orienté ses tentes." He

Durkheim formulated a sociological theory of symbolization, but not a symbolic theory of society. Society was not seen as constituted by the symbolic process; rather, the reverse alone appeared true. What then of the underpinning of the categories, society itself? The problem of its nature became particularly acute on the epistemological level, for Durkheim had to face the question of how categories derived from a particular social formation could prove adequate to understanding the world. The answer in one sense was highly satisfactory, as it reconciled (*tout à coup*) all the paradoxes of Durkheim's superorganicism—by combining them, as it were, into a superparadox that future generations would have to wrestle with. The answer to how categories modeled on society could apply to nature was that society itself was natural:

> But if the categories originally only translate social states, does it not follow that they can be applied to the rest of nature only as metaphors? . . .
> But when we interpret a sociological theory of knowledge in this way, we forget that even if society is a specific reality it is not an empire within an empire; it is a part of nature, and indeed its highest representation. The social realm is a natural realm which differs from the others only by a greater complexity. . . . That is why ideas which have been elaborated on the model of social things can aid us in thinking of another department of nature [note the exact inverse of Lévi-Strauss's idea of "the so-called totemism"]. It is at least true that if these ideas play the role of symbols when they are thus turned aside from their original signification, they are well-founded symbols. If a sort of artificiality enters into them from the mere fact they are constructed concepts, it is an artificiality which follows nature very closely and which is constantly approaching it still more closely. [Durkheim 1947 (1912), pp. 18–19]

It is not important to dwell on this recuperation of society by nature, or the naturalization of the sign and the other contradictions to his own best sociological understanding that Durkheim presents here. Suffice it to indicate certain consequences of the distinction between social structure and

---

wrote: "Il semble manifeste au contraire, au point qu'on ose à peine le faire remarquer, que la simple existence de cérémonies ou de travaux réguliers, que la simple distinction des clans et des tribus et de leur place respective dans le camp, présupposent les categories logiques et ne sont possibles que grâce à l'intervention préalable des idées de temps, d'espace, de causalité" (1919, p. 155n). I should like to thank M. Mark Francillon for drawing my attention to this passage and work.

mental concept as realized in a later anthropology. For the same incomplete appreciation of the symbol, that is, as merely the representation of social realities, continues to haunt the structural-functionalism developed by Radcliffe-Brown and others on a Durkheimian base.[44] The ''symbolic'' has been for the most part taken in the secondary and derivative sense of an ideal modality of the social fact, an articulate expression of society, having the function of support for relationships themselves formed by real-political or real-economic processes. Thus incorporated in the received dualism, the symbolic order becomes the ideology of social relations rather than their quality. The same effect is given by the arbitrary differentiation of ''culture'' from ''social system'' in the British school, as if social relations were not also composed and organized by meaning. Indeed, to the extent that meaning is taken as the mere ''cultural content'' of relationships whose formal structure is the true concern, the symbolic is merely a variable or accidental condition of the anthropological object instead of its defining property. Even the most valuable work on the conceptualization of nature, Mary Douglas's, for example, is inclined to trade off the semantic value of the categories for their social effects. More precisely, the one tends to be identified with the other—meaningful content with social value (in Radcliffe-Brown's sense)—by a tradition that ''takes for granted that human thought serves human interests and therefore carries in itself at any given moment the social configurations of that time and place'' (Douglas 1973*b*, p. 11). The effect is a one-sided view of meaning as social diacritics, and of the total cultural order as a utilitarian project.

Acknowledging the epistemological doctrines of *The Elementary Forms*

---

44. In a quasi-Whorfian way, Jameson accounts for the representational reflex in Anglo-American social science to the preference for the term ''symbol'' as opposed to the French use of ''sign'' and the corollary tendency to relate terms to other terms in a semiotic system whose principles of differentiation would thus order objective reference. The difference of analytic predilections does seem real, even if the explanation is not entirely convincing (given normal French usage of *signe*): ''the force of the Anglo-American terminology, of the word 'symbol,' was to direct our attention towards the relationship between words and their objects or referents in the real world. Indeed, the very word 'symbol' implies that the relationship between word and thing is not an arbitrary one at all, that there is some basic fitness in the initial situation. It follows that for such a viewpoint the most basic task of linguistic investigation consists in a one-to-one, sentence-by-sentence search for referents . . . . Saussure, on the other hand, is deflected by his very terminology from the whole question of the ultimate referents of the linguistic sign. The lines of flight of his system are lateral, from one sign to another, rather than frontal, from word to theory, a movement already absorbed and interiorized in the sign itself as the movement from the signifier to the signified'' (Jameson 1972, pp. 31–32).

of the Religious Life, Douglas sets up a worship of Terminus, god of boundary stones. For her, the ordering of nature is an objectification, or else an expression in the rules for treating objects, of the differentiation of human groups. Meaning is accordingly sacrificed for social marking. And the cultural codes of persons and objects, like the correspondences between them, are consumed in abstract implications of inclusion and exclusion. For in the total theoretical project, the symbol is no more than a sign: not generative of significance by virtue of its place in a system of symbols but empirically motivated by existing social realities—which themselves, like the "human interests" presumed to constitute them, are allowed to escape any meaningful explication.[45] But then, the symbolic logic could not be expected to be any more systematic than "the devious ways people use logic to deal with one another" (Douglas 1973*a*, p. 41). On the side both of objects and of social relations, this symbolic reduction involves a progressive emptying of the semiotic code and disregard for its structure in favor of purely formal properties of distinction and categorization. It is only partly that a discussion of meaning with an eye singular to social diacritics gives one the analytic liberty to consider what is symbolically variable and problematic—say a tripartite division of species between land, sky, and water—as nonetheless a priori and normal. More important is that, in a way parallel to the Malinowskian dualism, the "cultural" has no necessary logic in itself, as its true order is a reflex of the groups and relations developed in social practice. Before their enlistment for the purposes of group differentiation, the elements of an object-code such as food differences have only the coherence of an "ambient stream of symbols" (Douglas 1971, p. 69). Yet after this process by which they are selected out of the "cultural environment" and so given classification and interrelation, they are really no better off semantically, since their meaning is no more than the governing social intention. "If food is treated as a code," Douglas writes, "the messages it encodes will be found in the pattern of social

---

45. "If you were God, could you devise a better plan? If you wanted to choose a people for yourself, reveal to them a monotheistic vision and give them a concept of holiness that they will know in their very bones, what would you do? Promise their descendants a fertile land and beset it with enemy empires. By itself that would be almost enough. A politically escalating chain would insure the increasing hostility of their neighbours. Their mistrust of outsiders would ever be validated more completely. Faithful to your sanctuary and your law, it would be self-evident to them that no image of an animal, even a calf, even a golden one, could portray their god [i.e., inasmuch as a human group that conceives itself as a distinct species must see the rest of the world as so composed, and would be no more able to accept a beneficent deity in extrahuman form than they could welcome a gentile son-in-law]" (Douglas 1973*a*, p. 40).

relations being expressed. The message is about different degrees of
hierarchy, inclusion and exclusion, boundaries and transactions across the
boundaries. . . . Food categories therefore encode social events'' (ibid., p.
61). In the same way, it is not the contrastive features of liminal species
that might command attention, thus opening into a discussion of the way
the world is culturally constructed in relation to men, but only more
abstractly whether the species is regarded benevolently, malevolently, or
with ambivalence, since this can be likened to the relations between
groups—provided one is prepared to define such relations with the same
degree of indeterminacy. And note that to lend itself to this impoverishment, the social too must suffer a structural decomposition. A fair example
is Douglas's attempt to correlate the regard for anomalous species with
types of marriage exchange, insofar as various rules—as of generalized
exchange, Crow-Omaha exclusions, or father's brother's daughter
marriage—would situate the intercalary person, that is, the affine. Douglas
achieves such a correlation between regard for the affine and relations to
interstitial species, but only by a double operation on the structure of
exchange that resolves it (sometimes falsely) into a coefficient of integration between groups. First, Douglas chooses to ignore the specific and
well-known armatures of intergroup relations, the several forms of intergroup order, as are generated by rules of elementary and complex marital
exchange. Second, she translates these determinate rules and forms into
implications of social distance, again not by considering the rules but by
invoking de facto practices which allow her to ignore them. She reasons,
for example, that since one can marry classificatory members of the preferred kinship category, the elementary structures (including the Lele form
of generalized exchange) allow for no less radical an incorporation of
strangers than would Crow-Omaha prohibitions (which interdict repeated
intermarriage with the same lines).[46] In sum, Douglas's analysis of ''how

---

46. In a similar vein, Douglas is not always careful in her cross-cultural studies to compare
''groups'' or processes of differentiation of the same order. So the social exclusiveness of
the Israelites as a people is compared with relations between Karam or Lele lines,
although the implication of father's brother's daughter marriage among the Jews, taken
by Douglas as an indication of disdain for the outsider, would equally divide minimal
lineage from minimal lineage within the same Israelite tribe (cf. Douglas 1973a). Again,
there is the question posed to the purported connection between affines and anomalous
species by the studies Douglas chooses to ignore: Leach (1964) on Kachin and Tambiah
(1967) on Thai peasants. In these instances, the affinal category is identifiable with a
normally constituted set of animals, on a logic of degree of distance from the household,
hence domesticity of the species. Conversely, the anomalous species in Polynesia are
often specifically identified with own ancestral lines, as in the Hawaiian *aumakua* (cf.
Kamakau 1964).

meanings are constituted'' (1973*a*, p. 31) tends to become a *sociability fetishism*, similar to the ecological by its substitution of abstract social effects for specific conceptual forms, the latter treated as mere appearances of the former, with the similar result of dissolving definite structural logics into inchoate functional interests.

This is not to gainsay Douglas's fine sense for the human construction of experience. Still less is it to deny the critical importance of correspondences set up in human societies between categories of persons and categories of things, or between the respective differentiations of these taxonomies. I mean only to suggest the limitations of an analysis that aims to collapse the conceptual structure of an object code into a functional message, as though cultural things were merely substantialized versions of social solidarities, the latter here assumed both as privileged and as practical.[47] So in the end, the true logic of the social-cultural whole is utilitarian. Such is the result of adherence to the fateful Durkheimian separation of social morphology from collective representation.

Lévi-Strauss's refusal to grant that distinction ontological status, on the other hand—his appropriation of the social by the symbolic—was a decisive step in the development of a cultural theory.[48] It is true that this did not entirely disengage Lévi-Strauss's work from functionalist concerns (cf.

47. Another way of thinking about these limitations is to observe that Douglas is trafficking mainly in motivated relations between *symbols,* so that to define the meaning of one by the logical connection to the other (the motivation) will necessarily permit most of the cultural content to evaporate. Douglas is actually concerned with the functioning of already symbolic elements (affinal relationships, lineages, concepts of animals, food tabus, etc.) as *signs* for one another—using ''symbol'' and ''sign'' now in the usual Anglo-American sense. (Indeed most anthropological studies addressed to the ''symbolic'' are similarly preoccupied with this second-order sign function rather than with the constitution of symbolic form and meaning.) Yet as Roland Barthes points out, an important characteristic of the motivated sign (French, *symbol*), by contrast to the unmotivated, is that in the first there is no conceptual adequacy between signifier and signified: the concept ''outruns'' the physical sign, for example, as Christianity is greater than the cross (1970 [1964], p. 38). It is easy to see, then, that when both signifier and signified in a motivated sign relation are unmotivated symbols in their own right, this inadequacy is doubly compounded. For given the logical relation between them, each of the elements, say food tabus and exclusive social groups, may act alternately as the signifier or the signified of the other. Yet each remains, beside the sign of the other, a symbol in its own domain, whose concept also depends on differential relations within that domain. Consequently, one can hardly exhaust the meaning of either by the (fractional) analogy to the other. The semiotic analysis of food practices must far transcend the reference to social groups, as much as vice versa.

48. ''Lévi-Strauss scored because he did not look at cultural facts as somehow expressions of social forces; rather both were analyzed within a single frame of reference'' (Kuper 1973, p. 223).

Boon and Schneider 1974), but it did at least give such concern much less room to operate by precluding all simple reflectionism in the relation between society and ideology. It is also true that Lévi-Strauss, in carrying the Durkheimian enterprise to a consistent conclusion by including social relations within the general system of collective representations, arrives in the process at a higher naturalism. One may even remark an apparent closure of the theoretical circle: from Morgan's insistence that the growth of institutions was predetermined and limited by "the natural logic of the human mind" to a structuralist analysis whose coda is composed by a similar phrase (Lévi-Strauss 1971; 1972). But the course has been more a spiral than a circle, since all the appropriation of the symbolic intervenes en route; and, as we have seen, it would be an error to equate Lévi-Strauss's invocation of the mind with Morgan's "thinking principle," which could do no more than react rationally to pragmatic values inherent in experience. "Never can man be said to be immediately confronted with nature in the way that vulgar materialism and empirical sensualism conceive it," Lévi-Strauss writes. His appeal to *"l'esprit humain,"* then, would not short-circuit the symbolic, but rather would draw the consequences of its ubiquity. The argument proceeds on the simple premise that inasmuch as the human world is symbolically constituted, any similarities in the operations by which different groups construct or transform their cultural design can be attributed to the way the mind itself is constructed. By the same premise, "similarities" here cannot intend the content of that design, but only the mode of ordering. It is never a question of specific meanings, which each group works out by its own lights, but the way meanings are systematically related, which in such forms as "binary opposition" may be observed to be general. Nor, consequently, is it ever a question of "biological reductionism," a charge that a discussion of culture in the context of mind might otherwise invite. No particular custom will ever be accounted for by the nature of the human mind, for the double reason that in its cultural particularity it stands to mind as a difference does to a constant and a practice to a matrix. The human nature to which Lévi-Strauss appeals consists not in an assemblage of substantial and fixed structures, but in "the matrices from which structures belonging to the same ensemble are engendered" (1971, p. 561).[49] Thus the cultural ob-

49. In this passage of *L'Homme Nu,* Lévi-Strauss turns a phrase from Piaget—based, it seems to me, on a structuralism deficient in cultural understanding (Piaget 1971)—into a clear critique of various biological reductionisms. Piaget had noted in effect that in reality every form is a content relative to its encompassing form, as every content is a form of the

ject, in its symbolic integrity, remains entirely and exclusively within the scope of meaningful interpretation. Only the commonalities of structuring can be referred to the mind, specifically including the senses and sensory transmission, which appear to operate by such similar principles as binary contrast (cf. Lévi-Strauss 1972). Beyond that lies the highest naturalism, in which Lévi-Strauss joins Marx and Durkheim by his own method of uniting mind and nature, namely, that insofar as nature uses in its own construction the same kind of processes—for example, the genetic code, the stereochemistry of odors—as the mind employs to comprehend it, there is between them an ultimate complicity which is the condition of the possibility of understanding.[50]

It would seem, however, that the main problem of "reductionism" besetting modern structuralism has consisted in a mode of discourse which, by giving mind all the powers of "law" and "limitation," has rather placed culture in a position of submission and dependence. The whole vocabulary of "underlying" laws of the mind accords all force of constraint to the mental side, to which the cultural can only respond, as if the first were the active element and the latter only passive. Perhaps it could be better said that the structures of mind are not so much the imperatives of

---

contents it encompasses. The project of reductionism, Lévi-Strauss goes on, is to explain a type of order by referring it to a content which is not of the same nature and acts upon it from the outside: "An authentic structuralism, on the contrary, seeks above all to grasp (*saisir*) the intrinsic properties of certain types of orders. *These properties express nothing which is outside of themselves* [emphasis mine]. But if one is compelled to refer them to something external, it shall be necessary to turn toward the cerebral organization, conceived as a network of which the most diverse ideologies, translating this or that property into the terms of a particular structure, reveal in their own fashion the modes of interconnection" (1971, p. 561).

50. "For nature appears more and more made up of structural properties undoubtedly richer although not different in kind from the structural codes in which the nervous system translates them, and from the structural properties elaborated by the understanding in order to go back, as much as it can do so, to the original structures of reality. It is not being mentalist or idealist to acknowledge that the mind is only able to understand the world around us because the mind is itself part and product of this same world. Therefore the mind, when trying to understand it, only applies operations which do not differ in kind from those going on in the natural world itself" (Lévi-Strauss 1972, p. 14). Lévi-Strauss sees this perspective as "the only kind of materialism consistent with the way science is developing" (ibid.). And it is indeed entirely consistent with the vision of Marx: "History itself is a *real* part of *natural history*—of nature's coming to be man. Natural science will in time subsume under itself the science of man, just as the science of man will subsume under itself natural science: there will be *one* science" (Marx 1961 [1844], p. 111).

See pp. 197–203 below for some attempt at a substantial integration of cultural and perceptual structures.

culture as its implements. They compose a set of organizational possibilities at the disposition of the human cultural project, project, however, that governs their engagement according to its nature, just as it governs their investment with diverse meaningful content. How else to account for the presence in culture of universal structures that are nevertheless not universally present? And at another level, how else to deal, other than by the invocation of a superorganism, with such contradictions in terms as "collective consciousness," "collective representation," or "objectified thought," which attribute to an entity that is social a function that we know to be individual? To answer all questions of this kind, it will be necessary to situate the human mental equipment as the instrument rather than as the determinant of culture.

We have moved, in fact, very far from Morgan's "thinking principle." But it remains to make the specific critique of the Morganian position contained within the structuralist perspective. This critique I would illustrate from the remarkable work of Lucien Sebag, *Marxisme et structuralisme*, wherein one recognizes a thesis that is also essentially Boasian. Here the seeing eye is taken in its cultural particularity. It is impossible to derive the cultural directly from experience or event, insofar as practice unfolds in a world already symbolized; so the experience, even as it encounters a reality external to the language by which it is understood, is constructed as a human reality by the concept of it (cf. Berger and Luckmann 1967). The thesis is no more than an immediate deduction from the nature of symbolic thought. Meaning is always arbitrary in relation to the physical properties of the object signified; hence the concept refers in the first place to a code of distinctions proper to the culture in question. Sebag develops the idea in the context of the going Marxist alternative, which, he objects,

> rapporte la totalité des significations au sujet sans fournir cependant les moyens de thématiser effectivement cette constitution de sens.
> C'est vers cette thématisation que tendent les distinctions que nous avons reprises après d'autres; elles excluent la possibilité d'une genèse historique ou logique de la société dans son ensemble à partir de la praxis constitutive des individus et des groupes, car cette praxis se développe dans un univers déjà symbolisé et aucun surgissement premier de cette symbolisation n'est concevable. [1964, p. 142]

But his comments on the experience of nature are also directly relevant to the conventional anthropology of praxis:

L'interférence entre nature et culture ne provient pas alors de leur mise en relation extrinsèque mais d'une culturalisation de la réalité naturelle. La nature devient culture non pas en raison de l'existence d'un système d'équivalences qui ferait correspondre à chaque unité d'un domaine une unité empruntée à un autre domaine,[51] mais à travers l'intégration d'un certain nombre d'éléments naturels à un type d'ordre qui caractérise la culture. Or cette caractéristique est propre à tout système symbolique et plus profondément à tout discours dès que le message qu'il véhicule suppose une codification supplémentaire par rapport à celle de la langue; elle peut se laisser définir comme suit: utilisation d'une matière puisée en un autre registre que celui où fonctionne le système, matière qui peut être naturelle (couleurs, sons, gestes, etc.) ou culturelle (celle fournie par des systèmes sémiologiques déjà construits); application à cette matière qui est par elle-même ordonnée, d'un principe d'organisation qui lui soit transcendant.

   L'arbitraire du signe, résultat de l'association de deux plans distincts du réel, se trouve redoublé par l'intégration de chaque unité signifiante (intégration qui est la loi même de cette association) dans un système différencié qui seul permet la surgie de l'effet de sens. [Ibid., pp. 107–8]

The resonances of Boas's first trip to the Eskimo clearly sound through. More than a practical or "economic" interest in the environment, society brings to bear meanings developed by the entire cultural order. For men, there can be no practical interest or significance in the objects of consumption such as is characteristic of animals, whose relation to the objective is precisely confined to the things as they are:

   La fécondité de la géographie humaine n'est jamais sans doute aussi grande quand que lorsqu'elle a la possibilité d'étudier comment à partir de conditions naturelles globalement identiques, certaines sociétés du même type organisent l'espace, le cycle d'activités productives, le découpage du terroir, les rythmes d'utilisation du sol, etc. Les déterminismes envisagés sont alors d'un autre ordre que ceux qu'impose le milieu, chaque société aurait pu faire le même choix que la voisine et ne l'a pas fait pour des raisons qui sont le signe de ses visées essentielles.

   On voit alors en quel sens la notion d'infrastructure peut retrouver

---

51. Compare Rappaport (1967), who finds concealed in the "cognized environment" and the ritual practices of the society the greater biological wisdom of adaptation. The distinctions of nature thus reappear in cultural translation, the latter only means of compelling adherence to the former (cf. Friedman 1974).

un sens relatif: il s'agit toujours de la limite de l'esprit, de ce qui est irréductible à un certain niveau de fonctionnement de la société. L'élevage de telle sorte d'animaux, la pratique de tel type de culture sont le produit d'un travail permanent d'intellect qui s'exerce sur un certain milieu naturel; la fabrication d'instruments, le travail de la terre, l'utilisation ordonnée et régulière de l'univers animal supposent une masse d'observations, de recherches, d'analyses qui ne peuvent en aucun cas être menées à bien de manière fragmentaire; elles ne prennent forme qu'à travers la méditation d'un système de pensée bien plus vaste qui dépasse le plan téchnologique ou simplement économique. En ce sens ces derniers n'ont pas plus un caractère naturel que n'importe quel autre aspect de la culture d'une société. [Sebag 1964, p. 216]

By bringing the latest structuralism into confrontation with Morgan and Boas, I have tried to show the continuity of anthropology's struggle with its own naturalism—which is also to say with its own inherited cultural nature. But what possible bearing this parochial controversy can have for Marxism would require another whole chapter: the next.

3

Anthropology and Two Marxisms

Problems of Historical Materialism

On first reflection, this debate between practical reason and an anthropological theory of culture seems to have no direct implication for Marx. Or at least, Marx is not implicated. The materialist conception of history is surely no functional reductionism; it does not conceive society as a modality of biological processes (Social Darwinism). This view has been known to Marxism, but not to Marx (cf. Schmidt 1971, p. 47). Nor was Marx's a naive sensuous materialism which understood thought and consciousness as the simple reflex of perception. This too has been a position of famous Marxists, but not of Marx (cf. Lenin 1972 [1920]; Cornforth 1971 [1963]; Avineri 1971, pp. 65–67; Schmidt 1971, pp. 51 ff.). Again, Marx's was no crass economism of the enterprising individual, counterposed to a social environment which he manipulates to his own best interests. For Marx, "the individual is *the social being*": man is man only as a member of society—just as that hypostasized economizing "individual" by whom Western society figures itself to itself is the alienated product of that society, its ideological self-conception.[1] With regard to all these ideas, Marx would have to say again that if such were Marxism, he was no Marxist. His own naturalism, as is often noted, was a synthesis of the activism of Hegel, minus the idealism, and the materialism of Feuerbach, minus the contemplative reflectionism. Habermas put it neatly: " 'The

---

1. "What is to be avoided above all is the re-establishing of 'Society' as an abstraction *vis-à-vis* the individual. The individual is *the social being*. His life, even if it may not appear in the direct form of *communal* life carried out together with others—is therefore an expression and confirmation of *social life*. . . .

"Man, much as he may therefore be a *particular* individual (and it is precisely his particularity which makes him an individual, and a real *individual* social being), is just as much the *totality*—the ideal totality—the subjective existence of thought and experienced society present for itself" (Marx 1961 [1844], p. 105; cf. 1973 [1857–58], pp. 83 ff).

126

active side' that idealism has developed in opposition to materialism, is to be comprehended materialistically'' (1971, pp. 26–27; cf. Livergood 1967). Man makes himself, including his consciousness, by practical activity in the world—activity, however, which even in its most solitary movements literally bespeaks (as it uses language) the presence of others. Transforming the world by the necessity of producing in it, man is transformed in his own self and in his relationship to others.[2] This dialectic originates in production, for in the process of satisfying his needs, man produces new needs; even as, in acting with the means and resources on hand, he alters the material conditions of his activity. Altering his conditions and objectives, he must then alter his conceptions, insofar as these follow from the consciousness of his being as objectified in the alterations produced, as well as from the relations to others entertained in that production. By developing new productive forces and corresponding relations of production, man develops an historical nature which determines for him the character of living nature and the spiritual as well as the political character of society. Nature, then, is "humanized nature," relative in its effects as in its conception to the constitution of society. "But *nature* . . . taken abstractly, for itself—nature fixed in isolation from man—is *nothing* for man" (Marx 1961 [1844], p. 169). The relation of society to objective circumstances is mediated by an historical subject. In a most fundamental way, therefore, Marx's position on culture and nature—his appreciation of human culture as an intervention in physical nature—runs parallel to a later anthropological understanding.[3]

Yet the paradigm was never fully symbolic. One way of seeing this incompleteness is to note that by determining the concept (the idea, the category) as a representation of concrete experience, as the actuality of the world as worked-upon, Marx generates meaning by a property specifically opposite to its symbolic quality; that is, as "stimulus free." The experiential process by which, in Marx's view, the concept comes into being is just

---

2. "Labour is, in the first place, a process in which both man and Nature participate, and in which man of his own accord starts, regulates, and controls the material reactions between himself and Nature. He opposes himself to Nature as one of her own forces, setting in motion arms and legs, head and hands, the natural forces of his body, in order to appropriate Nature's productions in a form adapted to his own wants. By thus acting on the external world and changing it, he at the same time changes his own nature" (Marx 1967 [1867], 1:177).

3. "Nature must be expressed in symbols; nature is known through symbols which are themselves a construction upon experience, a product of mind, an artifice or conventional product, therefore the reverse of natural" (Douglas 1973a, p. 11; cf. Lévi-Strauss 1966).

the reverse of what characterizes its existence as meaning—that it is not bound to any concrete objective situation. When Marx turned in his later work to the analysis of society and history per se, when he developed his materialistic conception of history, this theory of knowledge could become a serious defect. For meaning would then turn into a variety of naming, and cultural concepts would be referred on one hand to a logic of instrumental effectiveness and on the other to a pragmatics of material self-interest (class ideology). Hence there was a second moment in Marx's theory, the moment of historical materialism, intergrading with the first in his work but distinguishable from it in the way praxis theory within anthropology is distinguished from a cultural account. Now culture makes its appearance in the mediation between men and nature only to be dissolved by it, naturalistically—in the famous "metabolism" of the process.

The cultural order of production, that is to say, was in decisive respects naturalized, to generate the superstructures as culturalized forms of a natural order. Marx of course had never supposed that nature, however variable the human relation to it, thereby lost its autonomy. Nature remains refractory, irreducible, in-itself. But the specifically anthropological problem of materialist theory was that the human side of the relation also tended to be placed in nature—somewhat at the expense of culture. The historical variability of the cultural order was the problem to be explained, and in the attempt it was in a double sense transferred from the subject of explanation to the predicate. For one thing, history was abstracted from the human subject. At critical theoretical moments, man appears in essence: as a creature of *needs* and under the self-evident necessity of acting *purposively* in nature with the material means on hand. At the same time, the economic wherewithal is now taken as a "given"—a given state of the productive forces: positivist abstraction of the existing cultural construct which has the function of rendering it neutral and inert. The cultural organization becomes precisely the "means" of a natural-material project of need satisfaction. Hence the second transfer of culture to the status of predicate. Social order and thought are sequitur to the practical teleology of production, translating in their own fashion "the objective logic of the work situation" (Schmidt 1971, p. 30). Thus the action of production, naturalized, at once escapes a symbolic determination and dialectically overcomes it, to itself determine the symbolic system. The infrastructure responds to the greater wisdom of things-in-themselves, and Marx's anthropology comes after production but not *in* it.

The rest of this chapter elaborates these points in greater detail, but virtually everything has been said. [4]

Cultural and Natural Moments in Materialist Theory

The simple realization of objective nature in human culture—whether the realization be direct or mystified, the nature external or human (biological)—was from the beginning an impossibility in Marx's thought. The *Paris Manuscripts* already make any such mechanistic materialism an impossibility. As a self-conscious and intentional being, man becomes an object of his own understanding, knows himself, in the natural objects transformed by his activity; so he knows nature as a transformed or "humanized nature":

> But man is not merely a natural being: he is a *human* natural being. That is to say, he is a being for himself. Therefore he is a *species being,* and has to confirm and manifest himself as such both in his being and in his knowing. Therefore, *human* objects are not natural objects as they immediately present themselves, and neither is *human sense* as it immediately *is*—as it is objectively—*human* sensibility, human objectivity. Neither nature objectively nor nature subjectively is directly given in a form adequate to the *human* being. [1961 (1844), p. 158]

The cultural concept in this problematic is not as such semiotic, yet the import is largely the same as that of a truly cultural anthropology. For Marx as for Boas (if by virtue of different intellectual biographies), the nature known to any human group is a historical concept. [5] Boas came to

4. Throughout this chapter I concentrate on the similarities and differences between Marx and recent anthropology that have been raised in the preceding summary. Because of the vast scholarly disagreement on the relation of Engels's thought to Marx's, I leave aside, for the most part, Engels's glosses on the materialist conception of history. Nor do I provide a general assessment of Marx's ethnological studies or their relation to the present state of anthropological knowledge—for various views on which see Firth 1972; Krader 1972; 1973*a, b;* and Harris 1968, pp. 217–49, among others.

5. "Just as in Marx's view there is no purely immanent succession of ideas such as 'intellectual history' might investigate, so also pure historically unmodified nature does not exist as an object of natural-scientific knowledge. Nature, the sphere of the regular and the general, is in each case related both in extent and composition to the aims of men organized in society, aims which arise from a definite historical structure. The *historical practice* of men, their bodily activity, is the progressively more effective connecting link between the two apparently separate areas of reality" (Schmidt 1971, p. 50).

the conclusion that the seeing eye is the organ of tradition; but only after Marx had written that "the *forming* of the five senses is a labour of the entire history of the world down to the present" (1961 [1844], p. 108). Lévi-Strauss might characterize "savage thought" as a type that "does not distinguish the moment of observation and that of interpretation" (1966, p. 223); but only after Marx had written of a coming society—which like the "primitive" will know how to live without private property—in which the senses "become directly in their practice *theoreticians*" (1961 [1844], p. 107). Even in the course of that development the senses were theoreticians—if only of a deficient and one-sided nature: "the dealer in minerals sees only the mercantile value but not the beauty and the unique nature of the mineral; he has no minerological sense" (ibid., p. 109). Marx would thus insist that external nature is socially relative, dependent on the achieved state and purposes of society. The historical modes and objectives of dealing with it provide the frame by which nature is constituted for man. Habermas comments:

> While epistemologically we must presuppose nature as existing in itself, we ourselves have access to nature only within the historical dimension disclosed by the labor process. Here nature in human form mediates itself with objective nature, the ground and environment of the human world. "Nature in itself" is therefore an abstraction, which is a requisite of our thought: but we always encounter nature within the horizon of the world-historical self-formative process of mankind. [Habermas 1971, p. 34][6]

Marx had taken leave of a certain kind of "contemplative materialism"—based on the notion of an abstract individual passively reflecting an unchanging world—for an epistemology grounded in practice, and a practice situated in history. Knowledge of the world is gained by action in it, especially by transformation of it impelled by necessity (i.e., production). (The subject-object interaction would be something like C. S. Peirce's "secondness": one knows the door by the resistance it offers to our efforts; one gains self-knowledge by the force required to move the door.) Correspondingly, the human and natural worlds must change in men's consciousness with successive (and dialectical) changes in

---

6. In citing Habermas here, I choose but one of several excellent discussions of these points of Marxist theory which have appeared in recent years; among them are Avineri 1971; Bernstein 1971; Kolakowski 1969; McLellan 1970, 1971a, b; Mészáros 1972; Ollman 1971; Schaff 1970; Schmidt 1971; and Wellmer 1971, to cite only a small sample.

their worldly activity. Feuerbach, Marx wrote in a well-known passage of *The German Ideology*,

> does not see how the sensuous world around him is, not a thing given
> from all eternity, ever the same, but the product of industry and of the
> state of society; and, indeed, in that sense it is an historical product,
> the result of the activity of a whole succession of generations, each
> standing on the shoulders of the preceding one, developing its industry
> and its intercourse, modifying its social organization according to the
> changed needs. Even the objects of the simplest "sensuous certainty"
> are only given him through social development, industry and commer-
> cial intercourse. [Marx and Engels 1965, p. 57]

I stress not merely the social specification of nature but also of "need" and purpose, hence *social specification of the technological function*. No more than nature taken by itself exists for man does technology disclose its concept by its objective form. Marx continued to hold this position in later economic works, arguing it there in two important ways—for one, in a quarrel with economists over the eternal qualities of bourgeois categories. Marx observed that the economic categories by which technology is apprehended—in the society concerned and by its unreflecting "vulgar economists"—are a language constituted independently of the technical object as such. These categories represent not properties of the object, but the way it is used in a given historical instance: the integration of technical means by a determinate system of social relations. This was part of a broad understanding on Marx's part to the effect that the conscious categories are manifest forms (modes of appearance) of their own subject matter; indeed the entire cultural superstructure figures in the production of economic categories.[7]

Marx's disengagement of the economic categories from the technologic properties was motivated by his general argument against determination by the concept—that is, against idealism. But in the event, he would also prove the converse: that neither can the technology as such be held responsible for the categories, since there is no specific correspondence or adequacy between the two. The most famous example of the discontinuity was Marx's demystification of the notion of "capital" as the stock of

7. "For example, the simplest economic category, say e.g. exchange-value, presupposes population, moreover a population producing in specific relations; as well as a certain kind of family, or commune, or state, etc. It can never exist other than as an abstract, one-sided relation within an already given, concrete, living whole" (Marx 1973 [1857–58], p. 101; cf. p. 297).

material-productive means, since "capital" is only a particular historical form in which the means may exist:

> A Negro is a Negro. Only under certain conditions does he become a slave. A cotton-spinning machine is a machine for spinning cotton. Only under certain circumstances does it become *capital*. Torn away from these conditions it is as little capital as gold by itself is money, or sugar is the price of sugar. [Marx 1933 (1849), p. 28; 1967, 3:814 f.]

But just as "capital" is not machinery, so "machinery" can be nothing social apart from its integration in a given system. "Machinery is no more an economic category," Marx observed, "than the ox which drives the plough. The application of machinery in the present day is one of the conditions of our present economic system, but the way in which machinery is utilised is totally distinct from the machinery itself" (Marx to Annenkov 28 December 1846, in Marx and Engels 1936). The implications of this disjunction between the productive means and the social conception of them deserve to be emphasized, if only because of the apparent contradiction by other equally famous dicta of historical materialism (see below pp. 158–59). In the present case, however, Marx is standing on the position that the social order (including relations of production) is not determined by the nature of the technological means. Society is not specified by technology, nor can the former be thought an "expression" of the latter. In important respects it is the other way round. And this subordination of technology to culture, it we may so speak, can be integrated in a more comprehensive Marxian argument—nowadays often insisted upon—of the mediations of the base by the superstructure. "For if economics is the 'ultimate determinant,'" as Mészáros reminds us (1972, p. 115), "it is also a 'determined determinant': it does not exist outside the always concrete, historically changing complex of concrete mediations, including the most 'spiritual' ones."

The concrete *objectives* of production are likewise a general specification of the social-historical order. This is a second argument from Marx's economic studies that speaks to the encompassment of the material infrastructure. The argument is that one cannot determine the nature of what is produced—which is to say the character of use-values—simply from the nature of human needs or the fact that production satisfies them. For such "human" needs are abstract and ahistorical. But, "Our wants and pleasures," Marx observes, "have their origin in society; we therefore measure them in relation to society; we do not measure them in relation to the objects which serve for their gratification. Since they are of a social nature, they are of a relative nature'' (1933 [1849], p. 33). It follows that tools respond in their use to a social intention:

> In the labour-process, therefore, men's activity, with the help of the instruments of labour, effects an alteration, designed from the commencement, in the material worked upon. The process disappears in the product; the latter is a use-value, Nature's material adapted by a change of form to the wants of man. [Marx 1967 (1867), p. 180]

Indeed, since it is not simply the reproduction of a human physical existence but the reproduction of "a definite *mode of life*" (Marx and Engels 1965, p. 32), the entire production system is a domain of cultural intentionality.

In the first moment of the materialist theory, the ethnologist of the twentieth century finds himself on familiar ground. He recognizes in the materialist conception of history a mediation between culture and nature not respected, for example, in Morgan's discussion of the early stages of society—despite Marx's admiration for that discussion. He recognizes in Marx's conception a consciousness born of the structure of society, an historical given under which the material interaction proceeds. One can also see that Marx's refusal of the interrelated reductions of knowledge to nature, society to technology, and production to need would logically have as a positive imprint the invention of the symbolic, for it is left to account for a structure of persons and things that cannot be referred to their physical nature. And finally, the same would be true of Marx's escape from all the other well-laid traps of utilitarianism, including ecological "populationism" as well as economistic individualism.

As for the latter, the sociological Robinsonades by which theorists have sought to derive social order out of the pursuit of individual interests, Marx's criticism goes to the anthropological heart. It is not just that this calculating "individual," figured as disengaged from and acting upon society, is himself a relative, historical figure; the same is true of his renowned "interests." Opposed by theory to the social outcome as private is opposed to public and premise to consequence, these interests are in fact produced by the social process to which they are supposed to stand as the a priori:

> Private interest is itself already a socially determined interest, which can be achieved only within the conditions laid down by society and by the means provided by society and with the means provided by society; hence it is bound to the reproduction of these conditions and means. It is the interest of private persons; but its content, as well as

the form and means of its realization, is given by social conditions independent of all. [Marx 1973 (1857–58), p. 156]

Nor should the "individuals" taken in the abstract aggregate of "the population" be allowed the theoretical status usually granted that notion by an utilitarian anthropology, that is, "population" as a *quantity* mechanically affecting the form of society, or as a *finality* whose biological survival is the secret wisdom of the social forms. Adopting a position more nearly congruent with that of Fortes than that of Worsley, Marx insists that "the population" can only be understood to act or react as an *organization:*

> The population is an abstraction if I leave out, for example, the classes of which it is composed. These classes in turn are an empty phrase if I am not familiar with the elements on which they rest, e.g., wage labour, capital, etc. These latter in turn presuppose exchange, division of labour, prices, etc. For example, capital is nothing without wage labour, without value, money, price etc. Thus, if I were to begin with the population this would be a chaotic conception of the whole. [Ibid., p. 100]

In all these respects—and without further inquiry into the world-constituting function of practice—the modern ethnologist must recognize in Marx an anthropological brother.

But there is a second moment or aspect to materialist theory. It proves incorrect to suppose that Marx's concept of the historical mediation between men and nature amounts to an interposed cultural logic, as in the Boasian perspective. The true mediation is the rational and material logic of effective production brought to bear by reason in the service of her own intentions, whatever the historical character of these intentions. At this moment the promise of a cultural anthropology seems undone. Marx's paradigm is metamorphosed into the reverse of the cultural. Now organization grows out of behavior, and the language of men is the voice of their concrete experience. The cultural concept appears as the consequence rather than the structure of productive activity. Use-values—those desires and pleasures which spring from society—lose out to the objective means of their achievement. And "history" is accordingly dissolved by the acid logic of practicality, to exchange its theoretical position of sedimented being for a transcended past and a fugitive becoming. The decisive grounding of historical materialism in work, and of work in its material specifications, robs the theory of its cultural properties and leaves it to the same fate

as the anthropological materialism. The practical experience of men is
untranscendable, and from it they construct a world. Their thought and
social relations in general follow from "the behavioral system of instrumental action."

The major dimensions of this suspension of culture in materialist theory,
of its submission to a worldly logic beyond itself, can be illustrated from
The German Ideology. There will be occasion to detail repercussions in
other works, but this one is a good place to begin because successive
passages of the commentary on Feuerbach read like salvos against the
Boasian-symbolic position. Here organization is understood as a codification of empirical experience, "evolving out of the life-process of definite
individuals"—just the way, it might be said, that our society appears to us,
but explicitly not the way it is conceptually ordered. For opposed to that
conception is a harder "reality":

> The fact is, therefore, that definite individuals who are productively
> active in a definite way enter into these definite social and political
> relations. Empirical observation must in each separate instance bring
> out empirically, and without any mystification and speculation, the
> connection of the social and political structure with production. *The
> social structure and the State are continually evolving out of the life-
> process of definite individuals, but of individuals, not as they may
> appear in their own or other people's imagination, but as they really
> are;* i.e., as they operate, produce materially, hence they work under
> definite material limits, presuppositions and conditions independent of
> their will. [Marx and Engels 1965, p. 36; emphasis mine]

Experience, then, is not organized as a symbolic situation. Language
itself is reduced to another discourse, not merely nonsymbolic but mute:
the irreducible rationality of praxis. Out of this "language of real life"
comes the talk of men, which from the beginning can only be the articulation of a silent code existing beyond itself:

> The production of ideas, of conceptions, of consciousness, is at first
> directly interwoven with the material activity and the material inter-
> course of men, *the language of real life*. Conceiving, thinking, the
> mental intercourse of men, appear at this stage as the direct efflux of
> their material behaviour. The same applies to mental production as
> expressed in the language of politics, laws, morality, religion, meta-
> physics, etc., of a people. Men are the products of their concep-
> tions, ideas, etc.,—real active men, as they are conditioned by a
> definite development of their productive forces and of the intercourse

corresponding to these, up to its furthest forms. Consciousness can never be anything else than conscious existence, and the existence of men is their actual life-process. [Ibid., p. 37]

But this displacement of the conceptual order from production is the production of a disorder in men's conceptions. As Marx proceeds, the symbolic order is eliminated from production to reappear as "phantoms" formed in the brains of men, "sublimates of their material life-process." Moreover, without any internal logic, any system *in them,* conceptions have neither independence nor history; which is also to say that the meaningful scheme has no impetus in itself but only the reflected force of the necessary means and relations of production.

> In direct contrast to German philosophy which descends from heaven to earth, here we ascend from earth to heaven. That is to say, we do not set out from what men say, imagine, conceive, nor from men as narrated, thought of, imagined, conceived, in order to arrive at men in the flesh. We set out from real, active men, and on the basis of their real life-process we demonstrate the development of ideological reflexes and echoes of this life process. The phantoms formed in the human brain are also, necessarily, sublimates of their material life-process, which is empirically verifiable and bound to material premises. Morality, religion, metaphysics, all the rest of ideology and their corresponding forms of consciousness, can no longer retain the semblance of independence. They have no history, no development; but men, developing their material production and their material intercourse, alter, along with this their real existence, their thinking and the products of their thinking. Life is determined not by consciousness, but consciousness by life. [Ibid., p. 37–38]

I do not propose here to enter the lists of the controversy raging among Marxologists over the "young Marx," humanist, versus the "mature Marx," scientist. The problem is that of the supposed break (*"coupure"*) of 1844–45, just before *The German Ideology,* when Marx purportedly turned away from Hegel and a concern for human alienation in favor of the concrete analysis of history and bourgeois society, definitely abandoning in the process the received "anthropology," the explication from the starting point of the human subject (Althusser 1970 [1965]; Althusser and Balibar 1970 [1968]). Clearly, as many Marx scholars have maintained, there are continuities as well as discontinuities. To take an example pertinent to the problem at hand, when Marx turned to economic and historical study, the "idealist" enemy necessarily changed: from Hegel's Absolute Spirit to

the ideological categories by which a society—and its economists—
becomes conscious of its action. But just as the issue was the same,
the derivation of the world from the concept, so would the criticism
of the one continue to do service for the other, namely, that the "idea"
always grows out of real life experience, out of practice in the real
world—even as the source of this criticism lay in Hegelian idealism in the
first place. In a letter to Engels commenting on a work of economic
history, Marx produces an epistemology of the logical categories—worthy,
moreover, of comparison with the Durkheimian—which epitomizes this
complex dialectic:

> But what would old Hegel say in the next world if he heard that the
> general [*Allegemeine*] in German and Norse means nothing but the
> common land [*Gemeinland*], and the particular, *das Sundre, Be-
> sondre*, nothing but the separate property divided off from the com-
> mon land? Here are the logical categories coming damn well out of
> "our intercourse" [relations of production] after all. [25 March 1868
> in Marx and Engels 1936, pp. 236–37]

And, finally, in the context of the concrete analysis of social order, Marx's
pragmatic notion of meaning would be positivized and functionalized. The
categories as well as relations of production embody the instrumental logic
of a given state of the productive forces, a logic that also has a secondary
reincarnation as the functional ideology maintaining a given type of class
domination. This combined play of continuity and discontinuity helps account for what I have called "cultural and natural moments" in Marx's
theory and, more important, for the evident contradiction between the
social constitution of the material logic, which follows from Marx's permanent conception of a humanized nature, and his material constitution of
the social logic—which became the dominant notion of the "historical
materialism."[8]

8. Wellmer (1971) has an excellent discussion of the functionalization of the concept resulting from its insertion in the frame of institutional-historical analysis. Particularly important
are his observations of "the functionalization of forms of social consciousness in regard to
forms of domination," which itself rests on a reduction of the history of forms of domination to the history of material production: "Marx has to deduce the various forms of
domination directly from the various forms of productive labor, because the *sole logic* of
history which can still be permitted in a materialistic reference-system which reduces the
dialectics of morality to that of production is the logic of the progressive technological
self-objectification of men. According to this logic, the forms of social intercourse can be
apprehended, so to speak, only as secondary productive forces, whose function is to make
possible the application and development of the primary forces" (ibid., p. 92; emphasis
mine).

To complete this preliminary documentation of the "second moment" of materialist theory, I cite *in extenso* Marx's comments to Annenkov on Proudhon's *Philosophy of Misery*. The evident contrast with the cultural moment will also document the anthropological disappointment:

> What is society, whatever its form may be? The product of men's reciprocal activity. Are men free to choose this or that form of society by themselves? By no means. Assume a particular state of development in the productive forces of man and you will get a particular form of commerce and consumption. Assume particular stages of development in production, commerce and consumption and you will have a corresponding social order, a corresponding organization of the family and of the ranks and classes, in a word a corresponding civil society. . . .
>
> It is superfluous to add that men are not free to choose their *productive forces*—which are the basis of all history—for every productive force is an acquired force, the product of former activity. . . .
>
> Hence it necessarily follows: the social history of man is never anything but the history of their individual development whether they are conscious of it or not. Their material relations are the basis of all their relations. These material relations are only the necessary forms in which their material and individual activity is realised.

When their commerce no longer corresponds to their social forms, Marx goes on to say, they change these forms,

> in order that they may not be deprived of the result attained, and forfeit the fruits of civilization. . . . Thus the economic forms in which men produce, consume, exchange, are *transitory and historical*. When new productive forces are won men change their method of production and with the method of production all the economic relations which are merely the necessary conditions of this particular method of production. . . .
>
> Thus M. Proudhon, mainly because he lacks the historical knowledge, has not perceived that as men develop their productive forces, that is, as they live, they develop certain relations with one another and that the nature of these relations must necessarily change with the growth of the productive forces. . . .
>
> Monsieur Proudhon has very well grasped the fact that men produce cloth, linen, silks, and it is a great merit on his part to have grasped this small amount. What he has not grasped is that these men, according to their powers, also produce the *social relations* amid which they prepare cloth and linen. Still less has he understood that men, who

fashion their social relations in accordance with their material method of production, also fashion *ideas* and *categories,* that is to say the abstract, ideal expression of these same social relations. [Marx to Annenkov, 28 December 1846 in Marx and Engels 1930, p. 7–14]

As against Hegelian idealism, Marx had made a claim for man: that it is not the Spirit which becomes conscious of itself as existence but rather man who models an ideal Spirit on the basis of his concrete existence; nor need man grovel before this, his own creation. Transposed to cultural theory, the claim now reads: it is not the conscious ideas men hold, their "imagination," which order their real-productive activity; what they are conscious of is only an appearance or expression of this activity. This conception of history, wrote Marx and Engels, "has not, like the idealistic view of history, in every period to look for a category, but remains constantly on the real *ground* of history; it does not explain practice from the idea but explains the formation of ideas from material practice" (1965, p. 50). Thus, as opposed to a fundamental appreciation on Marx's part that men transform nature, produce, according to a construct (see also below pp. 130–33), all conception now tends to be banished from the infrastructure to reappear as the construct of its material transformations. The anthropological objection would be that Marx arrives in this way at a truncated view of the symbolic process. He apprehends it only in its secondary character of symbolization—Boas's "secondary formation"—the model of a given system in consciousness, while ignoring that the system so symbolized is *itself symbolic.* There is again the fault, shared by Marx with certain functionalist-dualists, of limiting symbol to "ideology," thus allowing action to slip into the kingdom of the pragmatic. Dealing with meaning only in its capacity as the expression of human relations, Marx lets escape through the theoretical mesh the meaningful constitution of these relations.

This semiotic helps to situate the role of language in the developed theory of historical materialism.

The Genealogy of Conceptual Thought

We have seen that Marx makes a distinction between two types of discourse, a "language of real life" and the words in which men conceive their social existence; and that the second is held to be contingent upon the first. The emphasis on the role of praxis in history thus privileges the real forces experienced in production over the way men figure them. The material conditions of production become decisive insofar as men, if they are to effectively satisfy their needs, must "come to terms" (in the double sense of the phrase) with these conditions as they are. Both subject and object may be active poles in the Marxian theory of knowledge (Livergood 1967), *but it is not the object that needs the subject*. It is man who is the "limited" and "suffering" being. Hence the reciprocity implied in the idea of dialectic is in reality subsumed by a more powerful linear logic of objective need-satisfaction. The pragmatic logic of work forms a grid of material constraint to which all relations and conceptions are functionally submitted. That this praxis takes place in a world already symbolized, a social construction of reality, may be acknowledged, but it cannot stand up to the true nature of things any more than production could proceed effectively unless grounded in material reason. In the event, the symbolic determination of needs—which is to say the relative cultural system of objects—is theoretically dissolved within the absolute objective action of their satisfaction. The historical intention is mystified as the practical-natural premise—namely, that needs must be satisfied. Thus is culture eliminated from the act of its own reproduction.

More particularly, speech and thought shine with a borrowed light. For all *theoretical* purposes, which follow from all practical ones, language is not in play at the moment of concrete experience but must conform reflexively and pragmatically to that experience. Experience is first of all, and always primarily, the production of necessities: "life involves *before* everything else eating and drinking, a habituation, clothing and many other things. The *first historical act* is thus the production of means to satisfy these needs, the production of material life itself" (Marx and Engels 1965, p. 39; emphasis mine). It is specifically not germane to the argument that men can be distinguished from other animals by consciousness or the like; what is important is that men begin to distinguish themselves from animals when they begin to produce their means of subsistence (ibid., p. 31). Consciousness takes shape as a sequitur to this production, and language as the "practical consciousness" arising from the necessity of relations between men in the course of it (ibid., p. 42). Hence, only after having considered the "primary historical relationships"—production of subsistence, of new needs, of the family and modes of cooperation—only then "do we find that man also possesses consciousness" (ibid.; cf. Schaff 1970, p. 75). Engels, who participated in the formulation of the argument, took it quite literally and produced an account of the transition from ape to man on this basis:

The mastery over nature which begins with the development of the hand, with labour, widened man's horizon at every turn. . . . On the other hand, the development of labour necessarily helped to bring the members of society closer together by multiplying cases of mutual support, joint activity, and by making clear the advantage of this joint activity to each individual [note the utilitarian logic]. In short, men in the making arrived at the point where *they had something to say* to one another. . . . First comes labour, after it, and then side by side with it, articulate speech. [Engels 1940, p. 283–84]

The pseudohistory merely dramatizes a fundamental systemic point: that language is instrumental, very much as Malinowski considered it. Born in the attempt to master the world, its classifications are translations of the utilitarian distinctions set up by praxis, signs whose determinate value is a utility function.[9]

So in a late commentary (1881) on A. Wagner's textbook of political economy, Marx adduces just such a theory of the *pensée sauvage*—a theory of interest to anthropology not only because it addresses the "primitive" directly, but because it addresses it in a way that is indeed pure Malinowski. The passage in question has recently been widely cited as an illustration of Marx's basic theory of knowledge. Its phrasing as a myth of origin is again interesting. Schmidt calls it "a kind of genealogy of conceptual thought"—and it surely bears no more relation to the actual past than what Evans-Pritchard discovered in the genealogies of Nuer lineages. But more important for the moment, in displaying the original identity of speech and "the language of real life," Marx here gives us his idea of their essential connection: that the word is always cognate to the terms of the

9. Venable observed that for Marx and Engels the various features by which men might be distinguished from animals, including language, were "merely derivative, not ultimate," presumably by comparison with the consciousness developed in production. The difficulties in this position—namely, In what does such consciousness consist?—are only exacerbated by Engels's assertion that human and animal mentation, the latter as exemplified by Dido, Engels's dog, differ only in degree. " 'All activity of the understanding we have in common with animals: *induction, deduction,* and hence also *abstraction* (Dido's generic concepts: quadrupeds and bipeds), *analysis* of unknown objects (even the cracking of a nut is a beginning of analysis), *synthesis* (in animal tricks), and, as the union of both, *experiment* (in the case of new obstacles and unfamiliar situations). In their nature all these modes of procedure—hence all means of scientific investigation that ordinary logic recognizes—are absolutely the same in men and the higher animals. They differ only in degree (of development of the method in each case)' " (Engels, in Venable 1966 [1945], p. 66).

deed, for the two have a common root and sense in material utility. Continuity and discontinuity in the concept are introduced by the differentiations in the external world which experience has taught to be of practical value. Marx will now allow the idealist professor—here Wagner, but the criticism repeats that of Feuerbach, not to mention Malinowski's criticism of E. B. Tylor—that men begin by standing in a theoretical relation to objects of the world; they begin by acting, eating, appropriating these objects. We arrive thus at the anthropological crux: what is missed by Marx is that men begin *as men,* in distinction to other animals, precisely when they experience the world as a concept (symbolically). It is not essentially a question of priority but of the unique quality of human experience as meaningful experience. Nor is it an issue of the reality of the world; it concerns which worldly dimension becomes pertinent, and in what way, to a given human group by virtue of a meaningful constitution of the objectivity of objects. Marx, however, was a presymbolic social theorist. Language for him was a process of naming, the concordance of a social and a material text. The first classification men make is the distinction between things that are pleasurable and painful, edible and inedible. In language, it is nature itself that speaks, in the beginning without metaphor. The human power of bestowing a value on natural differences is reduced to an echo of practical-intrinsic significance. Marx's "genealogy of conceptual thought" is Malinowski's totemism:

Genealogy of Conceptual Thought

Totemism

For the doctrinaire professor, man's relation to nature is from the beginning not practical, i.e. based on action, but theoretical. . . . Man stands in a relation with the objects of the external world as the means to satisfy his needs. But men do not begin by standing "in this theoretical relation with objects of the external world." Like all animals they begin by eating, drinking, etc., i.e. they do not stand in any relation, but are engaged in activity, appropriate certain objects of the external

Tylor's theory of animism made early man contemplative and rational; field work shows the savage *interested* in fishing and gardening. . . . In totemism we see therefore not the result of early man's speculations about mysterious phenomena, but a blend of utilitarian anxiety about the necessary objects of his surroundings, with some preoccupation in those which strike his imagination and his attention, such as beautiful birds, reptiles world by means of their actions, and in this way satisfy their needs (i.e. they begin with production). As a result of the repetition of this process it is imprinted in their minds that objects are capable of "satisfying" the "needs" of man. Men and animals also learn to distinguish "theoretically" the external objects which serve to satisfy their needs from all other objects. At a certain level of later development, with the growth and multiplication of men's needs and the types of action required to satisfy these needs, they gave names to whole classes of these objects, already distinguished from other objects on the basis of experience.

That was a necessary process, since in the process of production, i.e., the process of the appropriation of objects, men are in a continuous working relationship with each other and with individual objects, and also immediately become involved in conflict with other men over these objects. Yet this denomination is only the conceptual expression of something which repeated action has converted into experience, namely the fact that for men, who already live in certain social bonds (this assumption follows necessarily from the existence of language), certain external objects serve to satisfy their needs.

and dangerous animals. . . . [Totemism] expresses primitive man's interest in his surroundings, the desire to claim an affinity and to control the most important objects. . . .

The road from the wilderness to the savage's belly and consequently to his mind is very short, and for him the world is an indiscriminate background against which there stand out the useful, primarily the edible, species of plants and animals.

Thus we find our questions answered; man's selective interest in a limited number of animals and plants and the way this interest is ritually expressed and socially conditioned appear as the natural result of primitive existence, of the savage's spontaneous attitudes towards natural objects and of his prevalent occupations. From the survival point of view, it is vital that man's interest in the practically indispensable species should never abate, that his belief in his capacity to control them should give him strength and endurance in his pursuits and stimulate his observation and knowledge of the habits and natures of animals and plants.

Totemism appears thus as a blessing bestowed by religion

[Marx cited in Schmidt 1971,   on primitive man's efforts in
pp. 110–11][10]   dealing with his useful surround-
                                  ings, upon his "struggle
                                  for existence." [Malinowski
                                  1954, pp. 20, 44, 46–47]

I should like to emphasize—while reserving full discussion for later—
that this theory of knowledge was inherent in Marx's point of departure—
that it was a continuous underpinning of the project from its "humanist"
through its "scientific" phases. Here one might invoke the testimony of
Kolakowski. Unaware, it seems, of the text on Wagner, Kolakowski found
"in embryo" in Marx's early writings, notably the *Paris Manuscripts,* an
idea of cognition that leads directly to the "genealogy of conceptual
thought." For on this basis Kolakowski himself practically reproduces the
genealogy, in a passage that bears close resemblance at once to Marx and
Malinowski:

> Human consciousness, the practical mind, although it does not pro-
> duce existence, produces existence as composed of individuals divided
> into species and genera. From the moment man in his onto- and
> phylogenesis begins to dominate the world of things intellectually—
> from the moment he invents instruments that can organize it and then
> expresses this organization in words—he finds the world already con-

10. Schmidt goes on to explicate this passage in a way that is both anthropologically painful,
and even in its salvaging final sentence, no real distinction from Malinowski. For if the
classifications of primitive man are not naively realistic but historically mediated relations
to the objects, this merely explains the "religious" guise of the naturalistic interest.
Schmidt writes: "Production comes into existence as a result of sensuous needs. All those
human functions that go beyond the immediacy of the given develop with production.
Nature appears at first to be an undifferentiated, chaotic mass of external materials. From
repeated intercourse with nature, which is common to men and animals alike, there
emerges an initial crude classification of natural objects according to the yardstick of the
pleasure or pain produced by them. The elementary theoretical achievement of this level
of development is the establishing of distinctions, the isolation of the objects with
pleasurable associations from the others. The nominalist classification of natural objects,
with the intention of exerting genuine control over them, corresponds to the economically
more advanced and hence more organized human groups and the contradictions emerging
in it. The particular is subsumed in the abstract-general. In the view of Marx (as of
Nietzsche), man's 'will to power' over things and his fellows underlies his intellectual
activity. The Spirit is originally empty. The concepts formed by it are the product of
accumulated practical experience. Its value is limited to the instrumental. Despite the
materialism of this view, we must insist that Marx did not see in concepts naively realistic
impressions of the objects themselves, but rather reflections of the historically mediated
relations of man to those objects" (1971, p. 111).

structed and differentiated, not according to some alleged natural classification but according to a classification imposed by the practical need for orientation in one's environment. The categories into which this world has been divided are not the result of a convention or a conscious social agreement; instead they are created by a spontaneous endeavour to conquer the opposition of things. It is this effort to subdue the chaos of reality that defines not only the history of mankind, but also the history of nature as an object of human needs—and we are capable of comprehending it only in this form. The cleavages of the world into species, and into individuals endowed with particular traits capable of being perceived separately, are the product of the practical mind, which makes the idea of opposition or even any kind of difference between it and the theoretical mind ridiculous. [Kolakowski 1969, p. 46]

In the words of a modern Marxist linguist: *"Les hommes parlent comme le leur suggère la vie, la pratique"* (Schaff 1967 [1964], p. 172). Not that Schaff and other sophisticated linguists working in a Marxist framework believe—any more than did Marx himself—that words or grammatical categories simply copy the sensuous properties of the world. On the contrary, for the members of a given speech community their language harbors classifications of the world which organize their experience of it. Vološinov writes: "It is not experience that organizes expression, but the other way around—*expression organizes experience*. Expression is what first gives experience its form and specificity of direction" (1973 [1930], p. 85). The issue then becomes, Whence the categories of expression? The answer to this is, In the social practice as generated from the distinctions set up in the action of the economic base—in other words, from the logic of concrete experience. Vološinov writes:

This is the order that the actual generative process of language follows: *social intercourse is generated (stemming from the basis* [economic infrastructure]); *in it verbal communication and interaction are generated; and in the latter, forms of speech performance are generated; finally, this generative process is reflected in the change of language forms.* [1973 (1930), p. 96][11]

11. Schaff writes similarly that grammatical structure, like vocabulary, will influence perception. But it does so because this grammatical structure itself, "has been socially fashioned on the basis of determinate social *practice;* it is the reflection of a concrete situation and constitutes the response to practical questions derived from that situation" (1967 [1964], p. 184).

Two words on the historicization of materialism exemplified by such determinations as "the first historical act . . ." or the so-called genealogy of conceptual thought. On one hand, "history" here consists of the speculative transformation of a structural relation between base and superstructure into a temporal priority. The procedure actually involves several logical phases, beginning essentially in a functional a priori. Marx first transposes the human necessity of gaining a livelihood into the structural dominance of production, then posits the primacy of production as an actual precedence in time. Marx would thus draw from the functional imperative that "man must be able to live in order to make history" the conclusion that "life involves before everything else eating and drinking," and thereupon project this temporal sequence into a real historical event— "the first historical act is thus the production of means to satisfy these needs." In brief, Marx turns a theoretical space into a hypothetical time. History, or at least a theory of history, is deduced from a valuation of functions; that is, from the premise that the satisfaction of human physical-biological needs is the most continuous and compelling of all man's activities, hence the *prerequisite* to all others. Parenthetically, it is just as habitual for certain structuralists to oppose this procedure on its first premise—and thereby to violate their own. Objection is taken on the grounds that there are other "needs" as compelling as eating—and not merely sex but, for instance, the necessity for classification, if only to stipulate those continuities and discontinuities between groups of men that make possible a society. But such rebuttal is never definitive, because it accepts the functionalist framework of the adversary. It submits the symbolic classification, which is the defining and indicative condition of culture, to the discourse of functional practicality. Who then can decide between "needs" that are equally indispensable? How can one assign priorities among functions the absence of any one of which would render humanity impossible? Structuralism would err in descending to the arguments of functionalism. It can only turn an advantage into a stalemate. There was already a better idea in hand: the indisputable conception, which can also be affirmed from the texts of Marx, that not even the infrastructure responds directly to biological "needs." The symbolic system is a sine qua non even of praxis, insofar as the term applies to any historical society.

There is, on the other hand, another kind of theoretical imperative involved in the determination of a "first historical act" or the intention of a speculative prehistory of conception. Clearly, the drive toward origins is built into the formulation of history as scientific theory: "Assume a particular state of development in the productive forces of man and you will get. . . ." The positivist formula is a license to conceive any historical condition as in fact tabula rasa; to project this method into a "first time" is only the essential form of the same consciousness. But more important, the rights allowed by a scientific theory of history here join the demands of an equally empirical theory of knowledge to make of *every time* an origin. To situate the concept as a secondary formation of experience, Marx has to make the same kind of arbitrary entrance into meaningful action, do the same kind of analytic surgery, as is involved in the scientist invocation of a "given state of the productive forces." That is, the deed which in actuality proceeds in the terms of a particular word—a particular-historical scheme of the productive forces—is taken in isolation, abstracted, and made to precede the word. The symbolic specifications of reality that are historically in effect are suspended in order to give play to eternal and general material realities. Fictive origins of mankind to one side, even the dialectics of actual history will know such a moment of practical creation—that is, when the entire cultural order is restructured along the lines of a revealed material reason. There comes a decisive analytic moment when the previous society is destroyed, in order to take action de novo, and as such to derive meaning from its necessities. For even if—as Marx describes the process in *Pre-Capitalist Economic Formations*—its own reproduction is the finality of any society, in the course of so reproducing itself by action in nature society is apt to change that nature and thereby its own. It reorders itself on a new material basis. The transformative quality of the dialectic is thus not a metaphysic force for Marx, as some have argued, but responds to a more fundamental power: the force of an objective rationality which must seize conditions "as they really are" on pain of social destruction by material contradiction. The "language of real life" triumphs over any received construction put upon the world, and "new conceptions, new modes of intercourse, new needs, and new speech" then follow in the wake of society's historical passage. The "historical" mind thus effects a rupture in the symbolic totality, to discover origins in a universal practical discourse of things that society had already conceived in its own terms.[12]

12. "Once the *City of Rome* had been built and its surrounding land cultivated by its citizens, the conditions of the community were different from what they had been before. The object of all these communities is preservation, i.e. *the production of the individuals which constitute them as proprietors, i.e. in the same objective mode of existence which also forms the relationship of the members to each other, and therefore forms the community itself. But this reproduction is necessarily new production and the destruction*

Naturalization of the Materialist Conception of History

Society may orchestrate a discourse of things, but as historical materialism subordinates the meanings by which a given society deals with objectivity to the material coordinates of the work situation, it does not develop a general concept of either one: either the significant properties of goods or the actual rationality of labor. The first problem, how to account for the kinds of goods a society will produce, their precise form and content, is a question without answer in Marx's theory. "These questions about the *system of needs* and *system of labours*—at what point is this to be dealt with?" (Marx 1973 [1857–58], p. 528). How indeed to account for what a particular human group is pleased to consider "satisfaction"? Nothing is as variable, naturalistically arbitrary, or analytically fundamental as the "system of needs." But what would be an anthropological theory of production, in particular or in the comparative? Historical materialism has failed to answer to the nature of use-values, or more precisely, to the cultural code of persons and objects which orders the "needs" of such use-values (cf. Baudrillard 1968; 1972). The generation of productive finalities, hence of the "system of labours," is left unexplained, a theoretical void: attributed to an unexamined historical variability, or else reduced, even with relations of production, to the natural necessities of eating and drinking. The absence of cultural logic in the theory of production thus becomes a standing invitation to all sorts of naturalism.

Yet it must be stressed that we owe to Marx the appreciation of what is missing. As emphatically as he insisted that man must eat before all else, and accordingly that all analysis of men must be "empirical," that is, that it start "in the right place—with man's material needs" (McLellan 1970, p. 180)—for all this, it was Marx who taught that the contents of human need are not exhausted by any such reference to physical necessity. "Need" in human society is an historical product, by comparison with which the biological imperative is unspecified, abstract. However, Marx only presented the concept of the need to eat; he did not develop the

---

of the old form. . . . Thus the preservation of the ancient community implies the destruction of the conditions upon which it rests, and turns it into its opposite . . . . The act of reproduction itself changes not only the objective conditions—e.g., transforming village into town, the wilderness into agricultural clearings, etc.—but the producers change with it, by the emergence of new qualities, by transforming and developing themselves in production, forming new powers and new conceptions, new modes of intercourse, new needs, and new speech" (Marx 1964, pp. 92–93).

concept of its historical properties. In fact, he compressed the latter within the former, insofar as he considered use-value as corresponding transparently to human needs. Nevertheless, it was Marx who observed that man produces universally, in contrast to animals, who appropriate only "what is strictly necessary." An animal, he wrote,

> produces only under the dominion of immediate physical needs, whilst man produces even when he is free from physical need and only truly produces in freedom thereof. An animal produces only itself, whilst man reproduces the whole of nature. An animal's product belongs immediately to its physical body, whilst man freely confronts his product. An animal forms things in accordance with the standard and need of the species to which it belongs, whilst man knows how to produce in accordance with the standard of any species, and knows how to apply everywhere the inherent standard to the object. Man therefore also forms things in accordance with the laws of beauty. [Marx 1961 (1844), pp. 75–76][13]

It is not to beauty that I appeal, but to the determination of a production that is undertaken within a symbolic order, within culture. Marx spends much time in *Capital* explaining why a certain quantity of wheat is equivalent in value to X hundredweight of iron. While the answer to the rate of equivalence in terms of average necessary social labor is surely brilliant, it does not tell us why wheat and why iron: why certain commodities are produced and exchanged and not others. Throughout *Capital* these questions remain unanswered, in the assurance that the answers are self-evident. In the determination of workers' means of subsistence, Marx writes, "there enters a historical and moral element"; nevertheless, "in a given country at a given period, the average *quantity*[!] of the means of subsistence necessary for the labourer is practically known" (1967 [1867], 1:171; emphasis mine).[14] If the commodity, as Marx says, is a mysterious thing, "abounding in metaphysical subtleties and theoretical niceties," this mystery does not extend to its external properties. As a use-value, the commodity is perfectly intelligible: it satisfies human needs. Insofar as an object

---

13. Cf. Lukács on the determination of handicrafts when their production is an art, as opposed to the evolution of commodities when they are allowed to advance "purely economically" (1971, p. 236).

14. Besides, the long-run tendency of capitalism will reduce the workers subsistence to the biological minimum, thus making a juncture with the theoretical transparency of "needs."

is a value in use, there is nothing mysterious about it, whether we consider it from the point of view that by its properties it is capable of satisfying human wants, or from the point of view that those properties are the product of labour. *It is as clear as noon-day,* that man, by his industry, changes the forms of materials furnished by Nature, in such a way as to make them useful to him. [Ibid., p. 71; emphasis mine]

But notice that to achieve this transparency of signification by comparison with commodity-fetishism, Marx was forced to trade away the social determination of use-values for the biological fact that they satisfy "human wants." This in contrast to his own best understanding that production is not simply the reproduction of human life, but of a definite way of life.

From such (cultural) understanding it would follow that all utilities are symbolic. Insofar as "utility" is the concept of "need" appropriate to a certain cultural order, it must include a representation, by way of concrete properties of the object, of the differential relations between persons—as contrasts of color, line, or fabric between women's clothes and men's signify the cultural valuation of the sexes. The "system of needs" must always be relative, not accountable as such by physical necessity, hence symbolic by definition. But for Marx, only in the abstract commodity-form do relations between persons appear as relations between things, and such "fetishism" he distinguishes from use-value exactly as the socially significant is different from the perceptually self-evident, the symbolic from the "natural." "So far no chemist has ever discovered exchange-value in a pearl or a diamond" (Marx 1967 [1867], 1:83). The "mysterious" quality of the commodity form alone merits a definition equivalent to the Saussurean notion of sign—"social things whose qualities are at the same time perceptible and imperceptible to the senses" (ibid., p. 72)—even as the attribution of meaning to a thing in the form of exchange-value is alone comparable to the formation of language (ibid., p. 74).

For Marx, then, the commodity had a double nature: its value as opposed to itself, or its exchange-value as opposed to its utility: the first an assigned function of society and not given in the object as such, the second responding to human needs and intrinsic to the object qua object. These distinctions are repeatedly made in the *Grundrisse.* The (exchange-) value of a commodity, Marx there writes, necessarily has an existence different from the commodity itself,

and in actual exchange this separability must become a real separation, because the natural distinctness of commodities must come into contradiction with their economic equivalence, and because both can exist

together only if the commodity achieves a double existence, not only
natural but also a purely economic existence, in which latter it is a
mere symbol, a cipher for a relation of production, a mere symbol of
its own value. . . . As a value, the measure of [the commodity's] ex-
changeability is determined by itself; exchange value expresses precisely the relation in which it replaces other commodities; in real exchange it is exchangeable only in quantities which are linked with its
natural properties and which correspond to the needs of the participants in exchange. [Marx 1973 (1857–58) pp. 141–42]

The extent to which the economy has been naturalized by this problematic is only partially grasped in the implication of the foregoing to the effect
that the social (meaningful) dimension of commodity production rests on
an underlying system of natural needs and of the objective properties of
goods to satisfy them (cf. ibid., p. 147). Marx also draws the logical
conclusion that this system in use-value, precisely because it is universal
and natural, falls properly outside the domain of political economy. Hence
that which distinguishes one historical economy and society from another,
its particular "system of needs" and "system of laborers," finds no place
in the theory of historical materialism. *For want of an adequate theory of
meaning, the material side of the process is absent from Marx's study of
economy:*

> The commodity itself appears as unity of two aspects. It is *use value,*
> i.e., object of the satisfaction of any system whatever of human needs.
> This is its material side, which the most disparate epochs of produc-
> tion may have in common, and whose examination therefore lies
> beyond political economy. [Ibid., p. 881][15]

Marx at one point of the *Grundrisse* did explain a certain luxury production, that is, production of silk. Here he resolved all contradiction between
the production of luxuries and the production of necessities, as well as

15. But see pp. 267–68 of the same *Grundrisse,* where Marx has clear misgivings about this
position and again poses the question, never answered, of the system of needs: "Use
value [is] presupposed even in simple exchange or barter. But here, where exchange takes
place only for the reciprocal use of the commodity, the use value, i.e. the content, the
natural particularity of the commodity has as such no standing as an economic form. Its
form, rather, is exchange value. The content apart from this form is irrelevant; it is not a
content of the relation as a social relation. But does this content as such not develop into a
system of needs and production? Does not use value as such enter into the form itself, as a
determinant of the form itself, e.g. . . . . the different forms of labour?—agriculture, industry—etc. . . . Above all it will and must become clear . . . to what extent use value exists
not only as presupposed matter, outside economics and its forms, but to what extent it
enters into it."

between the production of needs by production and the naturalness of needs, by deriving the production of silk from the produced need for guano:

> The crafts themselves do not appear *necessary* ALONGSIDE self-sustaining agriculture, where spinning, weaving etc. are done as a secondary domestic occupation. But e.g. if agriculture itself rests on scientific activities—if it requires machinery, chemical fertilizer acquired through exchange, seeds from distant countries etc. . . . then the machine-making factory, external trade, crafts etc. appear as *needs* for agriculture. Perhaps guano can be procured for it only through the export of silk goods. Then the manufacture of silk no longer appears as a luxury industry, but as a necessary industry for agriculture. It is therefore chiefly and essentially because, in this case, agriculture no longer finds the natural conditions of its own production within itself . . . that what previously appeared as a luxury is now a necessity, and that so-called luxury needs appear e.g. as a necessity for the most naturally necessary and down-to-earth industry of all. [Ibid., pp. 527–28; we are not told why the guano exporters need the silk]

Avineri has clearly seen the problem in the analysis of the economic base. The ''wants'' invoked by Marx are not sufficient to account for their object, which is always particular and historical. Marx thus fails to spell out the process by which ''wants'' are formulated. According to Avineri, Marx was ''aware'' of the ''philosophical dilemma'':

> If human wants are mediated through human consciousness and activity, men's minds must have an intentional capacity for the satisfaction of these needs which is not by itself a product of these needs. Sometimes Marx has been criticized for failing to attend to the need for such an autonomous intentional capacity. This problem is a serious problem, but in *Das Kapital* Marx, aware of it, attributes to human mind the capacity to evolve a model of the final product prior to the physical existence of the product itself. The way in which Marx treats this problem strongly suggests that he did not lose sight of the philosophical dilemma involved, though he did not spell out the process through which the ideal model is created in man's mind prior to material production. [Avineri 1971, p. 81]

Indeed, Avineri shows that Marx's awareness of ''the process through which the ideal model is created in man's mind prior to material production'' was more acute than could be judged by readers of the English edition of *Capital*. First published in the Soviet Union, this translation excises from the famous comparison of animal and human labor its key concluding phrase. Avineri (ibid.) restores that phrase in a footnote (here added to the original text in brackets):

> We pre-suppose labour in a form that stamps it as exclusively human. A spider conducts operations that resemble those of a weaver, and a bee puts to shame many an architect in the construction of her cells. But what distinguishes the worst architect from the best of bees is this, that the architect raises his structure in imagination before he erects it in reality. At the end of the labour-process, we get a result that already existed in the imagination of the labourer at its commencement [i.e., had already pre-existed ideally]. [*Capital* 1:178]

But the work by which Marx transforms the preexistent image of production into its objective consequence cannot be laid to the nervousness of the Russian intelligentsia alone. It is detailed by Marx in the critical introductory section of the *Grundrisse,* where he takes up the relations between production, distribution, exchange, and consumption.

The intention of this discussion is to establish the organic unity of these several elements of production, elements which appear to the participating individual as separate acts and to the economist as independently motivated. Marx shows that they are complementary aspects of the one material process, necessarily interdependent, in a state of reciprocal interaction. From the analysis of their relationships, however, Marx concludes that production in the narrow sense of the labor-process is the "actual starting point" and the "predominating factor" in the production-form as a whole. The other elements, notably consumption, take the theoretical position of factors of this factor. Althusser was in one sense correct in congratulating Marx for here effecting the "disappearance" of anthropology—more correct perhaps than was intended, as the reference was to the naive anthropology (*Homo economicus*) of the classical economists (Althusser and Balibar 1970, pp. 167–68).

The part of the text explaining the interaction of production and consumption is of most interest to a still-existing anthropology. In addition to the consumption of materials that occurs in production (consumptive-production), and the production of persons, for example, that occurs in consumption (productive-consumption), Marx explicates in all its complexity the relation between the two moments. Consumption completes production by supplying the subject, whose use of a product makes it a product. A garment becomes a real garment only by wear: "a product, as distinguished from a mere natural object, proves to be such, first *becomes* a product, in consumption" (Marx, in McLellan 1971a, p. 25). Moreover, consumption stands to production as its necessity, "i.e., by providing the ideal, inward, impelling cause which constitutes the prerequisite of production" (ibid.). There follows a passage very much like the one Avineri adduced from the later *Capital:*

> Consumption furnishes the impulse for production, as well as its object, which plays in production the part of its guiding aim. It is clear that while production furnishes the material object of consumption, consumption provides the *ideal object* of production, as its *image,* its want, its impulse and its purpose. [Ibid., emphases mine]

The key words, as we shall see, are "impulse" and "want," for as opposed to the specificity of "image" or "ideal object," the former imply an indeterminacy of form and content which allows Marx to find the true definition of the object, and the real beginning of the process, in production rather than consumption. In providing consumption with its object, production not only in turn completes consumption, but determines its actual form—that is, a definite good which defines the manner and content of consumption. Otherwise, consumption has only the shapelessness of a biological want. It is production that creates the specific desire through the mediation of an object-form—something in the way that modern economists understand the "demonstration effect" or the generation of demand by supply:

> it is not only the object that production provides for consumption. It gives consumption its definite outline, its character, its finish. . . . For the object is not simply an object in general, but a definite object, which is consumed in a certain definite manner prescribed in its turn by production. Hunger is hunger; but the hunger that is satisfied with cooked meat eaten with fork and knife is a different kind of hunger from the one that devours raw meat with the aid of hands, nails and teeth. Not only the object of consumption, but also the manner of consumption is produced by production; that is to say, consumption is created by production not only objectively but also subjectively. Production thus creates the consumers. . . .
>
> Production not only supplies the want with a material, but supplies the material with a want when consumption emerges from its first state of natural crudeness and directness—and its continuation in that state would in itself be the result of a production still remaining in a state of natural crudeness—it is itself, as a desire, mediated by its object. The *want for it which consumption experiences is created by its perception of the product.* . . . Production thus produces not only an object for the subject, but also a subject for the object. [Ibid., pp. 25–26; emphasis mine]

The passage is famously difficult; let us try to see clearly what is happening. Essentially what is happening is a transposition of the relationship between production and consumption from reciprocity to hierarchy. Consumption, which started out in mutual interdependence with production, is in the end subordinated to production: a change of status to which corresponds a change of time, from the "pre-existing image" to the objective consequence. This redefinition of the relationship depends on assigning consumption all the vagueness of an "impulse," while allowing to production all the definiteness of the object. Here then is a condensed symbol of the anthropological deception in Marx's program: the relapse from "imagination" to "perception," and so from culture to nature. As "want" or "impulse," consumption is at this moment situated in the realm of the natural; while as the source of the object-form, production alone is historical. The need-without-shape, moreover, is realized as content by perception of the object; thus all consumption, including its influence upon production, depends on the historical movement of production. I stress the "perception." The seeing eye here is not the organ of tradition but the instrument of desire. The mind, therefore, does not organize experience but follows it. Production is "the actual starting point":

> The important point to be emphasized here is that whether production and consumption are considered as activities of one individual or of separate individuals, they appear at any rate as aspects of one process in which production forms *the actual starting point and is, therefore, the predominating factor.* Consumption, as a natural necessity, *as a want,* constitutes an internal factor of productive activity, *but the latter is the starting point of realization and, therefore, its predominating factor, the act* in which the entire process recapitulates itself. The individual produces a certain article and turns it again into himself by consuming it; but he returns as a productive and self-reproducing individual. Consumption thus appears as a factor of production. [Ibid., p. 27; emphases mine]

This section of the *Grundrisse* on the organic unity of the production-elements has been the subject of much attention in recent Marxology. Habermas sees in it Marx's philosophical inclination—as opposed to his substantive practice—to reduce the relations of production to the labor-process itself, ignoring the cultural dimensions of economic organization (1971). For Althusser, as already noted, the same passages illustrate Marx's skillful avoidance of an anthropology such as was current among economists of the day: the founding of the economic process in a human subject and an autonomous domain of "need" rather than in production itself. The two commentaries make a link with each other, and also a transition to a different anthropology of the economy.

Althusser explains Marx's escape from the older anthropology this way: First, the structure of production determines what proportion goes to individual consumption (as opposed to productive-consumption). As for the structure of people's consumption, it of course varies historically. Beyond that, it depends on one hand on "effective demand," that is, purchasing power. Purchasing power in turn depends on the distribution of income, which is the return to property, while property itself is the legal expression of relations of production. Yet clearly, the relations of production will not thus account for the nature of what is produced, only for the differential demand by class. Therefore, a second generative factor of need enters Althusser's exposition, namely, "the *nature* of the products available, which are, at a given moment, the result of the technical capacities of production" (Althusser and Balibar 1970 [1968], p. 166). From this Althusser concludes there was no need in the problematic for a subject with a need, inasmuch as the "nature as well as the quantity" of the product can be grounded in production itself. But of course, nothing has really been specified about the character of production besides the reference to unexplicated historical differences—unless the nature of the product is to be understood to correspond specifically and mechanically to the "technical capacities" of the productive forces. In the latter event, we are in a full praxis anthropology, which is in fact what Habermas claims Marx achieves in the *Grundrisse* by collapsing the relations of production into the labor process itself, and thus the cultural logic into the instrumental.[16]

What Habermas is saying is that Marx's elimination of culture is effected by ignoring the historical determination of the relations of production, that Marx instead would derive the relations from the techno-logic of the work situation. In part, Habermas argues, this collapse of social relations to practicalities is a "terminological equivocation" in the relevant passages of the *Grundrisse:* a concept of production so broad as to give Marx "the opportunity of insisting that production also produces the institutional framework in which production takes place" (Habermas 1971,

---

16. E.g., "Is there anywhere where our theory that the organisation of labor is determined by the means of production is more brilliantly confirmed than in the human slaughter industry [i.e., the army]?" (Marx to Engels, 7 July 1866, in Marx and Engels 1936, p. 209; emphasis mine; cf. Marx 1933 [1845], p. 28).

p. 238). But there is a particular type of reasoning concealed in the "equivocation," and the interesting thing to us is that it recapitulates exactly the argument we have just discerned in the collapse of consumption into production. The relations of production are likewise reduced to dependence on the productive forces by rendering the former natural and the later historical. And everything depends again on pseudohistorical phrasing of this theoretical priority. The relations of production appear in an original, natural, and inchoate form, out of which they are taken and fashioned in new form by the productive forces. The relations are posited theoretically as pre-economic; their specific formulation is the work of the labor process:

> Should it be maintained that, at least to the extent that production depends on a certain distribution of the instruments of production, distribution in that sense precedes production and constitutes its pre-requisite, it may be replied that production has in fact its prerequisite conditions, which form factors of it. These may appear at first to have a natural, spontaneous origin [Habermas says, "Here Marx is probably thinking of natural qualities of social interaction such as sex, age, and kinship relations"]. By the very *process of production* they are changed from natural to historical, and if they appear in one period as a natural prerequisite of production, they *formed* at other periods its historical result. Within the sphere of production itself they undergo a constant change. For example *the application of machinery* produces a change in the distribution of the instruments of production as well as in that of the products, and modern land ownership on a large scale is as much the result of modern trade and modern industry as that of the application of the latter to agriculture. [Marx, in McLellan 1971a, pp. 30–31, emphases mine]

Marx's theoretical technique here consists of rendering the cultural relations of production natural in order to posit the natural logic of production as the primary cultural (historical) fact. Judging from a similar process in naturalistic theories of anthropology, this seems to be the main secret of praxis interpretation in all its varieties. In any event, the "rational kernel" of historical materialism is work.[17] The labor process mediating human

---

17. "The concrete expression of this human activity [i.e., the life-process of definite individuals, out of which the social structure is continually evolving] is work, the creation of tools of human activity that leaves its impact on the world. Since he calls work man's specific attribute, Marx conceives history as the continuum of modes of work over generations. The preeminence in Marx's discussion of economic activity does not derive from the preeminence of material economic values, but from Marx's view of man as *homo faber*" (Avineri 1971, p. 77).

subjectivity ("needs") and the objective world brings into play an inescapable facticity of nature and technical means, a concrete foundation on which the rest of the cultural architecture is erected. Habermas's objection is that by such arguments as that of the Introduction to the *Grundrisse,* Marx makes culture as a whole a sequitur to the nature of things. The method generates the human world out of interest in technical control of natural processes, the immanent social and practical necessities of such control, and the transformations of the objective world effected in the course of it.[18] Whatever the "aims," "ideal images," or the like which may be presupposed, the labor process nevertheless engages a reason stronger than imagination and independent of will. So long as human material needs are primary, the intrinsic logic of productivity is fundamental and constituting, the social structure evolving out of the life process of individuals "as they really are." In the final analysis, therefore, as it appears in many of Marx's most explicit statements of theoretical principle, the historical logic is frankly techno-logic. The hand-operated mill gives one kind of society, the steam mill another:

> Social relations are intimately linked to the productive forces. In acquiring new productive forces men change their mode of production, and in changing their mode of production, the manner of gaining their livelihood, men change their social relations. The hand-mill will give society with a suzerain; the steam mill, society with industrial capitalism. The same men who establish social relations in conformity with their material productivity, also produce principles, ideas and categories conforming to their social relations. Thus ideas, categories are as little eternal as the relations they express. They are *historical* and *transitory* products. [Marx 1968 (1847), p. 119]

Or again:

> Darwin has interested us in the history of Nature's Technology, i.e., in the formation of the organs of plants and animals, which organs serve as instruments of production for sustaining life. Does not the history of the productive organs of man, of organs that are the material

18. So then Sartre's criticism of Marx's epistemology: "Yet the theory of knowledge continues to be the weak point in Marxism. When Marx writes: 'The materialist conception of the world signifies simply the conception of nature as it is without any foreign addition,' he makes himself into an *objective observation* and claims to contemplate nature as it is absolutely. Having stripped away all subjectivity and having assimilated himself into pure objective truth, he walks in a world of objects inhabited by object-men" (1963, p. 32n).

basis of all social organization, deserve equal attention? And would not such a history be easier to compile, since, as Vico says, human history differs from natural history in this, that we have made the former, but not the latter? Technology discloses man's mode of dealing with nature, the process of production by which he sustains his life, and thereby also lays bare the mode of formation of his social relations, and of the mental conceptions that flow from them. [1967 (1867) 1:372n]

Then, again, another passage of the *German Ideology* that is worth considerable reflection:

The way in which men produce their means of subsistence depends first of all on the nature of the actual means of subsistence they find in existence and have to reproduce. This mode of production must not be considered simply as being the reproduction of the physical existence of the individuals. Rather, it is a definite form of activity of these individuals, a definite form of expressing their life, a definite *mode of life* on their part. As individuals express their life, so they are. What they are, therefore, coincides with their production, both with *what* they produce and *how* they produce. The nature of individuals thus depends on the material conditions determining their production.

This production only makes its appearance with the increase of population. In its turn this presupposes the intercourse of individuals with one another. The form of this intercourse is again determined by production (Marx and Engels 1965, pp. 31–32). [19]

This passage of *The German Ideology* is another key text in which the "two moments" of historical materialism are again conjoined. I have already evoked this text—and in the next chapter I will return to it again—for its clear statement that men's production, as historical production, is

19. Engels's version, in a famous letter to H. Starkenburg (25 January 1894), is much less nuanced: "What we understand by the economic conditions which we regard as the determining basis of the history of society are the methods by which human beings in a given society produce their means of subsistence and exchange the products among themselves (in so far as division of labor exists). Thus the *entire technique* of production and transport is here included. According to our conception this technique also determines the method of exchange and, further, the division of products, and with it, after the dissolution of tribal society, the division into classes and hence the relations of lordship and servitude and with them the state, politics, law, etc. Under economic conditions are further included the geographical basis on which they operate and those remnants of earlier stages of economic development which have actually been transmitted and have survived—often only through tradition or the force of inertia, also of course the external milieu which surrounds this form of society" (in Marx and Engels 1936, pp. 516–17).

not referable simply to physical (biological) necessities. That being the case, it follows that *what* men produce and *how* they produce it depends on the cultural scheme of men and things. The content and manner of production do not follow from what men and things "really are," that is, as apart from this cultural attribution. The last sentences of the text could well be taken as a logical rupture with the first. For where Marx had first determined the cultural coordinates of production, the organization of production as a "mode of life," in the end he determines the mode of life, including the organization of production, by the material coordinates. The "form of intercourse," which includes the relations of production, is again the sui generis outcome of the production process. We thus return to Habermas's criticism.

Habermas's criticism is based on the observation that Marx's philosophical formulation is inconsistent with his historical investigations. In the latter—in *Capital,* for example—the relations of production enjoy a theoretical status distinct from and at least as powerful as that of the productive forces. But Marx's abstract reflection is with a mind singular to the forces. In *principle* he reduces "the self-generative act of the human species to labor." The effect is a "positivist atrophy of epistemology." Instrumental reason is enfranchised at the expense of the "symbolic interaction" ordering the relations of production, and through them acting cognitively within the labor process itself (Habermas 1971, p. 42). Habermas's objection is that culture is left out of the philosophy:

> For the [substantive] analysis of the development of economic formations of society [Marx] adopts a concept of the system of social labor that contains more elements than are admitted to in the idea of a species that reproduces itself through social labor. Self-constitution through social labor is conceived *at the categorical level* as a process of production, and instrumental action, labor in the sense of material activity, or work designates the dimension in which natural history moves. *At the level of his material investigations,* on the other hand, Marx always takes account of social practice that encompasses both work and interaction. The processes of natural hisotry are mediated by the productive activity of individuals and the organization of their interrelations. These relations are subject to norms that decide, with the force of institutions, how responsibilities and rewards, obligations and charges to the social budget are distributed among members. The medium in which these relations of subjects and groups are norma-

tively regulated is cultural tradition. It forms the linguistic communication structure on the basis of which subjects interpret both nature and themselves in their environment. [Habermas 1971, pp. 52–53]

Historical Materialism and Utilitarianism

One could ask if Marx ever abandoned—as some have claimed—his understanding of man as a "species being" compelled to evidence himself through the appropriation of the sensuous world. Or was this view of human nature not essential to the naturalism of the developed theory of materialism? In the *Paris Manuscripts,* Marx had indeed defined his position—by opposition at once to idealism and materialism—as a "naturalism" or "humanism." It is worthwhile to investigate briefly the idea of man thus set out. For it could be another continuity, the most subtle, existing as an almost ghostly presence within the later historical materialism—yet acting there, as in Western society generally, as a powerful "phantom in the brains of men." The continuity would consist specifically in the rationality of utilitarianism, established first as a frame of discourse on human nature, then penetrating the analysis of history—at once in the objective guise of resource maximization at the point of society's interaction with nature and in the subjective form of materialistic motivation, revealed as the truth of the social ideology. The continuity is bourgeois economizing.

I am making a very large claim: that the species to which Marx's "species-being" belongs is *Homo economicus.* It was, however, a special variety. Marx's vision of the human condition in the *Paris Manuscripts* seems rather a spiritualized "market mentality," combining human needs (of self-realization), natural scarcities (of objective means), and man's progressive liberation from this dismal condition by purposive action—his progressive enrichment through increasingly effective exercise of his appropriative powers and interchange with other men. Even the "alienation" of the early phases of this career involves that dualist opposition of man and society characteristic of a bourgeois functionalism. Marx often insisted that the individual is *the social being,* and yet his concept of alienation depended broadly on "the antithesis between man and his social being" (McLellan 1971*b*, p. 106). Alienation seems like the reverse (proletarian) side of the idea of an enterprising man, in relation to whose subjective project of satsifaction society stands as an external condition. In any event, communism is the outcome of this struggle, a transcendence of alienation that, in Marx's terms (1961 [1844], p. 109), "produces the *rich* man profoundly endowed with all his senses"; that is, the man who is able to perceive truly and thus realize his own essence by the appropriation of the essential nature of things.[20] Conversely, man in the original state is a limited, "suffering being," a creature of need and impulse passionately bent on the objects of his existence:

> *Man* is directly a *natural being*. As a natural being and as a living natural being he is on the one hand furnished with *natural powers of life*—he is an *active* natural being. These forces exist in him as tendencies and abilities—as *impulses*. On the other hand, as a natural, corporeal, sensuous, objective being he is a *suffering*, conditioned and limited creature, like animals and plants. That is to say, the objects of his impulses exist outside him as objects independent of him; yet these objects are *objects* of hs need—essential *objects*, indispensable to the manifestation and confirmation of his essential powers . . . .
>
> An unobjective being is a *nullity*—an *un-being* . . . .
>
> Man as an objective, sensuous being is therefore a *sufferng* being—and because he feels what he suffers, a *passionate* being. Passion is the essential force of man energetically bent on its object. [Ibid., pp. 156–58]

It is important to the credibility of my argument to note that this reading of Marx's concept of human nature as a metaphor of capitalist rationality is neither unusual nor idiosyncratic. If the concept has not always been situated just this way, still the identification of such a needs-means-ends paradigm is a common finding of recent commentary. Several passages of Ollman's excellent book *Alienation* (1971) might serve to exemplify this:

> Marx sums up his account of man as a natural and sensuous creature, by referring to him as "suffering, limited, and conditioned." Man suffers because of what he undergoes. To be sensuous, according to Marx, is necessarily to suffer. Man cannot obtain everything he needs to realize his natural powers, since, in one way or another, it is the whole world which is required. There will always be a woman (or

---

20. Note then that the direction of culture is in one sense an escape from the symbolic, toward the senses, hence the ultimate unity of human and natural science. Symbolism here, as in the later works, is treated with mistrust, as the distortion and mystification of reality (e.g., in religion). Inasmuch as the symbolic is a mistaken idea, to suppose that culture is contingent on the idea would be a mistake.

man), food etc., which is unavailable, if only for a moment, and whatever is denied him causes suffering . . . . Because he feels what he undergoes, because to undergo is to suffer, man is said to be a passionate being. Passion is the quality which animates the individual's effort to obtain his objects. Viewed from the vantage point of the feeling subject, it is this effort itself.

Finally, man is said to be a limited being because of the restrictions which surround his desires and activities on all sides. . . . The availability of objects in nature and their particular qualities control man in all his attempts to do; they regulate when and how his powers can be used. [Ibid., p. 82]

Marx attributes to man certain powers, which he divides into natural and species, and maintains that each of these powers is reflected in one's consciousness by a corresponding need; the individual feels needs for whatever is necessary to realize his powers. The objects of nature, including other men, provide the matter through which these powers are realized and, consequently, for which needs are felt. Realization occurs through the appropriation of objects which accord in kind and level of development with these powers themselves. "Appropriation" is Marx's most general expression for the fact that man incorporates the nature he comes into contact with into himself. Activity enters this account as the chief means by which man appropriates objects and becomes, therefore, the effective medium between the individual and the outer world. Marx sees such activity in three special relationships to man's powers: first, it is the foremost example of their combined operation; second, it establishes new possibilities for their fulfillment by transforming nature and, hence, all nature imposed limitations; and third it is the main means by which their own potential, as powers, is developed. [ibid., pp. 137–38; see Kolakowski 1969, pp. 38–60, for a very similar explication of the *Paris Manuscripts*.]

Marx never abandoned this concept of "needs," nor a concept of production, therefore, as purposive action toward their satisfaction. On the contrary, the later historical materialism depends on the same naturalistic determination of labor as a need-satisfying process—the more so, we have seen, as use-value had to be distinguished from exchange-value by its direct correspondence to human wants. Similarly for "class interest." C. Wright Mills remarked that "Marx's view of class consciousness . . . is as utilitarian and rationalist as anything out of Jeremy Bentham" (1962, p. 115). But if Marx did not exorcise the utilitarian framework, neither did he ever feel compelled to define it, to precisely state the nature of the material advantage characteristic of human action in the world—so far as I am aware.[21]

The nature of economic rationality appears in Marx's historical analyses as self-evident, as somehow following directly from the natural necessity of production. If the content of production was a question without an answer in Marx's economics, here was an answer without a question. Yet everything depends on the rationality of production, the instrumental efficiency of the labor process. For such must constitute the material conditions beyond men's will on the practical experience of which they construct their social and intellectual existence. Perhaps if the question had been specifically posed, rather than assumed with the received idea that production is the satisfaction of human needs, the entire theoretical edifice built on material activity would have been redesigned. Is there indeed *a* logic of work? One would be forced to reply by one of two naturalistic models, neither themselves satisfactory in theory or history (cf. Sahlins 1969). Either it is a bourgeois strategy of maximization, such as Marx seems to presuppose, although no one has better argued its social relativity. Or it is an ecological model of "survival," which, since it speaks only to a minimum necessary functioning, leaves the precise intensity of resource use unspecified, anything over the minimum being "adaptive." And if there is not then *a* logic of work, can there be a constituting *material* logic of work? The point is that material effectiveness, practicality, does not exist in any absolute sense, but only in the measure and form projected by a cultural order. Selecting its material means and ends from among all possible ones, as well as the relations under which they are combined, it is society which sets the productive intentions and intensities, in a manner and measure appropriate to the entire structural system. There remains, as

---

21. Ollman also felt this lack, and was obliged to break his "fundamental rule of remaining within Marx's categories" in order to explain. His explanation was precisely to the present point; the behavior implied in Marx's notion of work, of "activity," was acquisitive rationality: "Marx views work as 'rational' in the sense that man grasps the nature of what he wants to transform and is able to direct his movements accordingly. . . . In ordinary language, 'to act rationally' means to understand the 'why' and 'wherefore' of what one is doing and *to proceed in the most efficient way* when doing it. . . . The act of choosing itself shows will to be another building block in reason. However, it is in Marx's portrayal of man's life activity as purposive that its rationality is most evident. . . .

The mental process that goes on when the individual feels particular needs and tries to *satisfy them in the most efficient manner* he knows may justly be labelled 'reasoning.' Such reasoning, of course, is carried on within carefully prescribed boundaries determined by the state of his powers and of nature" (Ollman 1971, pp. 114–15; emphasis mine; see again Kolakowski 1969, p. 44).

logic, only the meaningful system of culture. Historical materialism installs one such cultural logic as the definition of everyone's material necessity.

With this criticism we return to anthropology, or particularly to that anthropology which has conceived culture as an intervention in nature. Moreover, we are now in a better position to restore our own society to the world. For to say historical materialism is relative to that society, if it seems to set the West apart from the Rest, must also suggest that our own system is no less meaningfully founded than the others. The next chapter begins by exploring some semiotic dimensions of our economy, with a view toward a more general synthesis, both theoretical and human.

4

La Pensée Bourgeoise

Western Society as Culture

The field of political economy, constructed exclusively on the two values of exchange and use, falls to pieces and must be entirely reanalyzed in the form of a GENERALIZED POLITICAL ECONOMY, which will imply the production of symbolic exchange value [*valeur d'echange/signe*] as the same thing and in the same movement as the production of material goods and of economic exchange value. The analysis of the production of symbols and culture is not thus posed as external, ulterior, or "superstructural" in relation to material production; it is posed as a *revolution of political economy itself,* generalized by the theoretical and practical intervention of symbolic exchange value.

Baudrillard
1972, p. 130
translation, M.S.

Historical materialism is truly a self-awareness of bourgeois society—yet an awareness, it would seem, within the terms of that society. In treating production as a natural-pragmatic process of need satisfaction, it risks an alliance with bourgeois economics in the work of raising the alienation of persons and things to a higher cognitive power. The two would join in concealing the meaningful system in the praxis by the practical explanation of the system. If that concealment is allowed, or smuggled in as premise, everything would happen in a Marxist anthropology as it does in the orthodox economics, as if the analyst were duped by the same commodity fetishism that fascinates the participants in the process. Conceiving the creation and movement of goods solely from their pecuniary quantities (exchange-value), one ignores the cultural code of concrete properties governing "utility" and so remains unable to account for what is in fact produced. The explanation is satisfied to recreate the self-deception of the society to which it is addressed, where the logical system of objects and social relations proceeds along an unconscious plane, manifested only through market decisions based on price, leaving the impression that

166

production is merely the precipitate of an enlightened rationality. The structure of the economy appears as the objectivized consequence of practical behavior, rather than a social organization of things, by the institutional means of the market, but according to a cultural design of persons and goods.

Utilitarianism, however, is the way the Western economy, indeed the entire society, is experienced: the way it is lived by the participating subject, thought by the economist. From all vantages, the process seems one of material maximization: the famous allocation of scarce means among alternative ends to obtain the greatest possible satisfaction—or, as Veblen put it, getting something for nothing at the cost of whom it may concern. On the productive side, material advantage takes the form of added pecuniary value. For the consumer, it is more vaguely understood as the return in "utility" to monetary disbursements; but even here the appeal of the product consists in its purported functional superiority to all available alternatives (cf. Baudrillard 1968). The latest model automobile—or refrigerator, style of clothing, or brand of toothpaste—is by some novel feature or other more convenient, better adapted to "modern living," more comfortable, more healthful, sexier, longer-lasting, or better-tasting than any competing product.[1] In the native conception, the economy is an arena of pragmatic action. And society is the formal outcome. The main relations of class and politics, as well as the conceptions men entertain of nature and of themselves, are generated by this rational pursuit of material happiness. As it were, cultural order is sedimented out of the interplay of men and groups severally acting on the objective logic of their material situations:

> Till jarring interests of themselves create
> The according music of a well-mixed state. . . .
> Thus God and Nature linked the general frame,
> And bade Self-love and Social be the same.
> [Alexander Pope, *Essay on Man*]

Such is the mode of appearance of our bourgeois society, and its common average social science wisdom. On the other hand, it is also common

---

1. Of course we know at some level that these claims are fraudulent, but this knowledge is only further evidence of the same principle, namely, the ordering power of gain. Having penetrated the secrets of advertising, taken away all substance and sense, what else is left but the gainful motive underneath all social form? Now, by the very abstractness and nakedness in which we discover it, its power is confirmed—even more so by the illusion that we have been able to determine it behind the mask of false claims.

anthropological knowledge that the "rational" and "objective" scheme of any given human group is never the only one possible. Even in very similar material conditions, cultural orders and finalities may be quite dissimilar. For the material conditions, if always indispensable, are potentially "objective" and "necessary" in many different ways—according to the cultural selection by which they become effective "forces." Of course in one sense nature is forever supreme. No society can live on miracles, thinking to exist by playing her false. None can fail to provide for the biological continuity of the population in determining it culturally—can neglect to provide shelter in producing houses, or nourishment in distinguishing the edible from the inedible. Yet men do not merely "survive." They survive in a definite way. They reproduce themselves as certain kinds of men and women, social classes and groups, not as biological organisms or aggregates of organisms ("populations"). True that in so producing a cultural existence, society must remain within the limits of physical-natural necessity. But this has been considered axiomatic at least since Boas, and not even the most biological of cultural ecologies can claim any more: "limits of viability" are the mode of the practical intervention of nature in culture (cf. Rapapport 1967). Within these limits, any group has the possibility of great range of "rational" economic intentions, not even to mention the options of production strategy that can be conceived from the diversity of existing techniques, the example of neighboring societies, or the negation of either.

Practical reason is an indeterminate explanation of cultural form; to do any better, it would have to assume what it purports to explain—the cultural form. But allow me a justifiable "nervousness." Insofar as this applies to historical materialism, it is Marx who here criticizes Marx, if through the medium of a later anthropology. The point of these objections had already been anticipated in Marx's understanding of production as devoted not simply to the reproduction of the producers, but also to the social relations under which it is carried out. The principle is, moreover, interior to Marx's work in an even more general form. I repeat a seminal passage of *The German Ideology:* "This mode of production must not be considered simply as being the reproduction of physical existence of individuals. Rather it is a definite form of activity of these individuals, a definite form of expressing their life, a definite *mode of life* on their part" (Marx and Engels 1965, p. 32). Thus it was Marx who taught that men never produce absolutely, that is, as biological beings in a universe of physical necessity. Men produce objects for given *social* subjects, in the course of reproducing subjects by *social* objects.

Not even capitalism, despite its ostensible organization by and for pragmatic advantage, can escape this cultural constitution of an apparently
objective praxis. For as Marx also taught, all production, even where it is
governed by the commodity-form, by exchange-value, remains the production of use-values. Without consumption, the object does not complete
itself as a product: a house left unoccupied is no house. Yet use-value
cannot be specifically understood on the natural level of "needs" and
"wants,"—precisely because men do not merely produce "housing" or
shelter": they produce dwellings of definite sorts, as a peasant's hut, or a
nobleman's castle. This determination of use-values, of a particular type of
house as a particular type of home, represents a continuous process of
social life in which men reciprocally define objects in terms of themselves
and themselves in terms of objects.

Production, therefore, is something more and other than a practical logic
of material effectiveness. It is a cultural intention. The material process of
physical existence is organized as a meaningful process of social being—
which is for men, since they are always culturally defined in determinate
ways, the only mode of their existence. If it was Saussure who foresaw the
development of a general semiology devoted to "the role played by signs
in social life," it was Marx who provided the *mise-en-scène*. Situating
society in history, and production in society, Marx framed the problematic
of an anthropological science yet unborn. For the question he proposed to
it contains its own answer, inasmuch as the question is the definition
of symbol itself: How can we account for an existence of persons and
things that cannot be recognized in the physical nature of either?

We have seen that Marx nevertheless reserved the symbolic quality to
the object in its commodity-form (fetishism). Assuming that use-values
transparently serve human needs, that is, by virtue of their evident properties, he gave away the meaningful relations between men and objects
essential to the comprehension of production in any historical form. He left
the question without an answer: "About the *system of needs* and the *system
of labours*—at what point is this to be dealt with?"

In order to frame an answer, to give a cultural account of production, it
is critical to note that the social meaning of an object that makes it useful to
a certain category of persons is no more apparent from its physical properties than is the value it may be assigned in exchange. Use-value is not less
symbolic or less arbitrary than commodity-value. For "utility" is not a
quality of the object but a significance of the objective qualities. The
reason Americans deem dogs inedible and cattle "food" is no more perceptible to the senses than is the price of meat. Likewise, what stamps trous-

ers as masculine and skirts as feminine has no necessary connection with their physical properties or the relations arising therefrom. It is by their correlations in a symbolic system that pants are produced for men and skirts for women, rather than by the nature of the object per se or its capacity to satisfy a material need—just as it is by the cultural values of men and women that the former normally undertake this production and the latter do not. No object, no thing, has being or movement in human society except by the significance men can give it.[2]

Production is a functional moment of a cultural structure. This understood, the rationality of the market and of bourgeois society is put in another light. The famous logic of maximization is only the manifest appearance of another Reason, for the most part unnoticed and of an entirely different kind. We too have our forebears. It is not as if we had no culture: no symbolic code of objects—in relation to which the mechanism of supply-demand-price, ostensibly in command, is in reality the servant.

Consider, for example, just what Americans do produce in satisfying basic "needs" for food and clothing.[3]

Food Preference and Tabu in American Domestic Animals

The aim of these remarks on American uses of common domestic animals will be modest: merely to suggest the presence of a cultural reason in our

2. In one respect, that of being less bound to a specific situation, use-value is more arbitrary than exchange-value, although in stricter association with concrete properties of the object. Marx was surely correct in understanding the commodity-value as a differential meaning established in the discourse of things, i.e., standing as the concept (*le signifié*) of a given object only by relations developed in the commercial discourse and not by reference to concrete properties. In the latter respect, commodity-value is the more abstract. In order to enter into these determining relations, however, the object must be a use-value, i.e., have a conventional meaning assigned to its objective properties, such as to give it "utility" to certain persons. Since this meaning is a differential *valuation* of the properties, it cannot be grasped by the senses; but it is always connected to the sensible—hence use-value is the more concrete value. On the other hand, the utility-meaning can be invoked outside any specific action, being taken as the meaning of the object as such. But exchange-value is determinable only from the economic interaction of commodities, and differently in each such situation. It is bound to and stipulated within the discourse of commodities; outside the context of exchange, the object resumes the status of a use-value. Viewed thus, use-value is the more arbitrary; exchange-value is a pragmatic "shifter."

3. The discussion which follows is but a marginal gloss on the larger analysis of notions of edibility and relations to domestic animals launched by Douglas (1966, 1971); Leach (1964), and Lévi-Strauss (1966). See also Barthes (1961), R. Valeri (1971), and, on certain correspondences between social and zoological categories, Bulmer (1967) and Tambiah (1969). The intent here is not so much to contribute to the semiotic analysis as to stress the economic implications.

food habits, some of the meaningful connections in the categorical distinctions of edibility among horses, dogs, pigs, and cattle. Yet the point is not only of consuming interest; the productive relation of American society to its own and the world environment is organized by specific valuations of edibility and inedibility, themselves qualitative and in no way justifiable by biological, ecological, or economic advantage. The functional consequences extend from agricultural "adaptation" to international trade and world political relations. The exploitation of the American environment, the mode of relation to the landscape, depends on the model of a meal that includes a central meat element with the peripheral support of carbohydrates and vegetables—while the centrality of the meat, which is also a notion of its "strength," evokes the masculine pole of a sexual code of food which must go back to the Indo-European identification of cattle or increasable wealth with virility.[4] The indispensabilitty of meat as "strength," and of steak as the epitome of virile meats, remains a basic condition of American diet (note the training table of athletic teams, in football especially). Hence also a corresponding structure of agricultural production of feed grains, and in turn a specific articulation to world markets—all of which would change overnight if we ate dogs. By comparison with this meaningful calculus of food preferences, supply, demand, and price offer the interest of institutional means of a system that does not include production costs in its own principles of hierarchy. The "opportunity costs" of our economic rationality are a secondary formation, an expression of relationships already given by another kind of thought, figured a posteriori within the constraints of a logic of meaningful order. The tabu on horses and dogs thus renders unthinkable the consumption of a set of animals whose production is practically feasible and which are nutritionally not to be despised. Surely it must be practicable to raise *some* horses and dogs for food in combination with pigs and cattle. There is even an enormous industry for raising horses as food for dogs. But then, America is the land of the sacred dog.

A traditional Plains Indian or a Hawaiian (not to mention a Hindu), might be staggered to see how we permit dogs to flourish under the strictest interdictions on their consumption. They roam the streets of major

---

4. Cf. Benveniste (1969, vol. 1) on Indo-European *pasu vīra;* for example: "it is as an element of mobile wealth that one must take the avestic *vīra* or *pasu vīra.* One designates by that term the ensemble of movable private property, men as well as animals" (p. 49). Or see the extensive discussion of the Latin *pecu, pecunia,* and *peculium* (pp. 55 ff.).

American cities at will, taking their masters about on leashes and depositing their excrements at pleasure on curbs and sidewalks. A whole system of sanitation procedures had to be employed to get rid of the mess—which in the native thought, and despite the respect owed the dogs themselves, is considered "pollution." (Nevertheless, a pedestrian excursion on the streets of New York makes the hazards of a midwestern cow pasture seem like an idyllic walk in the country.) Within the houses and apartments, dogs climb upon chairs designed for humans, sleep in people's beds, and sit at table after their own fashion awaiting their share of the family meal. All this in the calm assurance that they themselves will never be sacrificed to necessity or deity, nor eaten even in the case of accidental death. As for horses, Americans have some reason to suspect they are edible. It is rumored that Frenchmen eat them. But the mention of it is usually enough to evoke the totemic sentiment that the French are to Americans as "frogs" are to people.

In a crisis, the contradictions of the system reveal themselves. During the meteoric inflation of food prices in the spring of 1973, American capitalism did not fall apart—quite the contrary; but the cleavages in the food system did surface. Responsible government officials suggested that the people might be well-advised to buy the cheaper cuts of meat such as kidneys, heart, or entrails—after all, they are just as nutritious as hamburger. To Americans, this particular suggestion made Marie Antoinette seem like a model of compassion (see fig. 10). The reason for the disgust seems to go to the same logic as greeted certain unsavory attempts to substitute horsemeat for beef during the same period. The following item is reprinted in its entirety from the *Honolulu Advertiser* of 15 April 1973:

PROTEST BY HORSE LOVERS

WESTBROOK, Conn. (UPI)—About 25 persons on horseback and on foot paraded outside Carlson's Mart yesterday to protest the store's selling horsemeat as a cheap substitute for beef.

"I think the slaughter of horses for human consumption in this country is disgraceful," said protest organizer Richard Gallagher. "We are not at a stage yet in the United States where we are forced to kill horses for meat."

"Horses are to be loved and ridden," Gallagher said. "In other words, horses are shown affection, where cattle that are raised for beef . . . they've never had someone pet them or brush them, or anything like that. To buy someone's horse up and slaughter it, that, I just don't see it."

—Mrs. Virginia Knauer, the President's advisor on consumer affairs.

'No matter how you slice it...'

Figure 10   From the *Honolulu Advertiser,* 2 March 1973

    The market began selling horsemeat—as "equine round," "horse-meat porterhouse" and "horseburger"—on Tuesday, and owner Kenneth Carlson said about 20,000 pounds were sold in the first week.

    Most butchers who sell horsemeat have purchased "real old, useless horses" which would otherwise be sold "for dogfood and stuff like that," Gallagher said. But "now they're picking up the young horses. We can't buy these horses now, because the killers are outbidding us."

The principal reason postulated in the American meat system is the relation of the species to human society. "Horses are shown affection, where cattle that are raised for beef... they've never had someone pet them or brush them, or anything like that."[5] Let us take up in more detail

---

5. "Supposing an individual accustomed to eating dogs should enquire among us for the reason why we do not eat dogs, we could only reply that it is not customary; and he would

the domesticated series cattle-pigs-horses-dogs. All of these are in some measure integrated in American society, but clearly in different statuses, which correspond to degrees of edibility. The series is divisible, first, into the two classes of edible (cattle-pigs) and inedible (horses-dogs), but then again, within each class, into higher and less preferable categories of food (beef vs. pork) and more and less rigorous categories of tabu (dogs vs. horses). The entire set appears to be differentiated by participation as subject or object in the company of men. Moreover, the same logic attends the differentiations of the edible animal into ''meat'' and the internal ''organs'' or ''innards.'' To adopt the conventional incantations of structuralism, ''everything happens as if'' the food system is inflected throughout by a principle of metonymy, such that taken as a whole it composes a sustained metaphor on cannibalism.

Dogs and horses participate in American society in the capacity of subjects. They have proper personal names, and indeed we are in the habit of conversing with them as we do not talk to pigs and cattle.[6] Dogs and horses are thus deemed inedible, for, as the Red Queen said, ''It isn't etiquette to cut anybody you've been introduced to.'' But as domestic cohabitants, dogs are closer to men than are horses, and their consumption is more unthinkable: they are ''one of the family.'' Traditionally horses stand in a more menial, working relationship to people; if dogs are as kinsmen, horses are as servants and nonkin. Hence the consumption of horses is at least conceivable, if not general, whereas the notion of eating

---

be justified in saying that dogs are tabooed among us, just as much as we are justified in speaking of taboos among primitive people. If we were hard pressed for reasons, we should probably base our aversion to eating dogs or horses on the seeming impropriety of eating animals that live with us as our friends'' (Boas 1965 [1938], p. 207).

6. French and American naming practices appear to differ here. Lévi-Strauss's observations on the names the French give animals (1966, pp. 204 ff.) apply only fractionally to American custom. A brief ethnographic inquiry is enough to show that the latter is quite complex in this regard. The general rule, however, is that named/unnamed: inedible/edible. The names of both dogs and horses (excluding racehorses) are sometimes ''like stage names, forming a series parallel to the names people bear in ordinary life, or, in other words, metaphorical names'' (ibid., p. 205)—e.g., Duke, King, Scout, Trigger. More often, however, the names used in English are descriptive terms, likewise metamorphical, but taken from the chain of discourse, Smokey, Paint, Blue, Snoopy, Spot, etc. The French reserve such names for cattle. Our cattle are generally unnamed, except for milk cows, which often have two-syllable human names (Bessie, Ruby, Patty, Rena—these were collected from informants). Work horses—as distinguished from riding horses—also had human names. Differences between related societies in these regards, as Lévi-Strauss (1973) points out, represent different cultural *découpages* or superpositions of the animal on the human series.

dogs understandably evokes some of the revulsion of the incest tabu.[7] On the other hand, the edible animals such as pigs and cattle generally have the status of objects to human subjects, living their own lives apart, neither the direct complement nor the working instrument of human activities. Usually, then, they are anonymous, or if they do have names, as some milk cows do, these are mainly terms of reference in the conversations of men. Yet as barnyard animals and scavengers of human food, pigs are contiguous with human society, more so than cattle (cf. Leach 1964, pp. 50–51). Correspondingly, cut for cut, pork is a less prestigious meat than beef. Beef is the viand of higher social standing and greater social occasion. A roast of pork does not have the solemnity of prime rib of beef, nor does any part of the pig match the standing of steak.

Edibility is inversely related to humanity. The same holds in the preferences and common designations applied to edible portions of the animal. Americans frame a categorical distinction between the "inner" and "outer" parts which represents to them the same principle of relation to humanity, metaphorically extended. The organic nature of the flesh (muscle and fat) is at once disguised and its preferability indicated by the general term "meat," and again by particular conventions such as "roast," "steak," "chops," or "chuck"; whereas the internal organs are frankly known as such (or as "innards"), and more specifically as "heart," "tongue," "kidney," and so on—except as they are euphemistically transformed by the process of preparation into such products as "sweetbreads."[8] The internal and external parts, in other words, are respectively assimilated to and distinguished from parts of the human body—on the same model as we conceive our "innermost selves" as our

7. Leach develops this point in his important paper on English animal categories as fitting into a systematic set of correspondences between relations to people and relations to animals according to degrees of distance from self (1964, pp. 42–47 and appendix). Leach claims the scheme has wide validity, although not universality; of course, it would require some permutation for peoples who (for example) eat domestic dogs. The Hawaiians treat dogs destined for eating with great compassion, "and not infrequently, condescend to treat them with Poi [pounded taro] from their mouths" (Dampier 1971, p. 50). Dogs destined for eating, however, are never allowed to touch meat (Corney 1896 [1821], p. 117). It is not clear whether they are eaten by the family who raised them, or like Melanesian pigs, similarly coddled in the household, reserved for prestations to others.

8. The meat taxonomy is of course much more complex than these common appellations. Steak, for instance, has a whole vocabulary of its own, in which some organic reference occurs, although usually not the terms applied to the human body (sirloin, T-bone, etc.). Calves' liver is an exception to this entire discussion, the reasons for which I do not know.

"true selves"—and the two categories are accordingly ranked as more or less fit for human consumption. The distinction between "inner" and "outer" thus duplicates within the animal the differentiation drawn between edible and tabu species, the whole making up a single logic on two planes with the consistent implication of a prohibition on cannibalism.

It is this symbolic logic which organizes demand. The social value of steak or roast, as compared with tripe or tongue, is what underlies the difference in economic value. From the nutritional point of view, such a notion of "better" and "inferior" cuts would be difficult to defend. Moreover, steak remains the most expensive meat even though its absolute supply is much greater than that of tongue; there is much more steak to the cow than there is tongue. But more, the symbolic scheme of edibility joins with that organizing the relations of production to precipitate, through income distribution and demand, an entire totemic order, uniting in a parallel series of differences the status of persons and what they eat. The poorer people buy the cheaper cuts, cheaper because they are socially inferior meats. But poverty is in the first place ethnically and racially encoded. Blacks and whites enter differentially into the American labor market, their participation ordered by an invidious distinction of relative "civilization." Black is in American society as the savage among us, objective nature in culture itself. Yet then, by virtue of the ensuing distribution of income, the "inferiority" of blacks is realized also as a culinary defilement. "Soul food" may be made a virtue. But only as the negation of a general logic in which cultural degradation is confirmed by dietary preferences akin to cannibalism, even as this metaphorical attribute of the food is confirmed by the status of those who prefer it.

I would not invoke "the so-called totemism" merely in casual analogy to the *pensée sauvage*. True that Lévi-Strauss writes as if totemism had retreated in our society to a few marginal resorts or occasional practices (1963*a;* 1966). And fair enough—in the sense that the "totemic operator," articulating differences in the cultural series to differences in natural species, is no longer a main architecture of the cultural system. But one must wonder whether it has not been replaced by species and varieties of manufactured objects, which like totemic categories have the power of making even the demarcation of their individual owners a procedure of social classification. (My colleague Milton Singer suggests that what Freud said of national differentiation might well be generalized to capitalism, that it is narcissism in respect of minor differences.) And yet more fundamen-

tal, do not the totemic and product-operators share a common basis in the
cultural code of natural features, the significance assigned to contrasts in
shape, line, color and other object properties presented by nature? The
"development" that is effected by the *pensée bourgeoise* may consist
mainly in the capacity to duplicate and combine such variations at will, and
within society itself. But in that event, capitalist production stands as an
exponential expansion of the same kind of thought, with exchange and
consumption as means of its communication.

For, as Baudrillard writes in this connection, consumption itself is an
exchange (of meanings), a discourse—to which practical virtues,
"utilities" are attached only post facto:

> As it is true of the communication of speech, so it is likewise true of
> goods and products: consumption is exchange. A consumer is never
> isolated, any more than a speaker. It is in this sense that we must have
> a total revolution in the analysis of consumption. In the same way as
> there is no language simply because of an individual need to speak,
> but first of all language—not as an absolute, autonomous system but
> as a contemporary structure of the exchange of meaning, to which is
> articulated the individual interaction of speech—in the same sense
> neither is there consumption because of an objective need to consume,
> a final intention of the subject toward the object. There is a social
> production, in a system of exchange, of differentiated materials, of a
> code of meanings and constituted values. The functionality of goods
> comes afterward, adjusting itself to, rationalizing and at the same time
> repressing these fundamental structural mechanisms. [Baudrillard
> 1972, pp. 76–77][9]

The modern totemism is not contradicted by a market rationality. On the
contrary, it is promoted precisely to the extent that exchange-value and
consumption depend on decisions of "utility." For such decisions turn
upon the social significance of concrete contrasts among products. It is by

9. Moreover, there is to this notion of communication a fundamental base, set down by
Rousseau in his running debate with Hobbes: "But when it should prove true that this
unlimited and indomitable covetousness shall have developed in all men to the point
supposed by our sophist, still it would not produce that universal war of each against all of
which Hobbes ventures to trace the odious *tableau*. This unchecked desire to appropriate
all things is incompatible with that of destroying all fellow beings; and having killed
everyone the victor would have only the misfortune of being alone in the world, and could
enjoy nothing even as he had everything. Wealth in itself: What good does it do if it cannot
be communicated; and what would it serve a man to possess the entire universe, if he were
its only inhabitant?" (Rousseau 1964, 3:601).

their meaningful differences from other goods that objects are rendered exchangeable: they thus become use-values to certain persons, who are correspondingly differentiated from other subjects. At the same time, as a modular construction of concrete elements combined by human invention, manufactured goods uniquely lend themselves to this type of discourse. Fashioning the product, man does not merely alienate his labor, congealed thus in objective form, but by the physical modifications he effects he sediments a thought. The object stands as a human concept outside itself, as man speaking to man through the medium of things. And the systematic variation in objective features is capable of serving, even better than the differences between natural species, as the medium of a vast and dynamic scheme of thought: because in manufactured objects many differences can be varied at once, and by a godlike manipulation—and the greater the technical control, the more precise and diversified this manipulation—and because each difference thus developed by human intervention with a view toward "utility" must have a significance and not just those features, existing within nature for their own reasons, which lend themselves to cultural notice. The bourgeois totemism, in other words, is potentially more elaborate than any "wild" (*sauvage*) variety, not that it has been liberated from a natural-material basis, but precisely because nature has been domesticated. "Animals produce only themselves," as Marx taught, "while men reproduce the whole of nature."[10]

Yet if it is not mere existence which men produce but a "definite *mode of life* on their part," it follows that this reproduction of the whole of nature constitutes an objectification of the whole of culture. By the systematic arrangement of meaningful differences assigned the concrete, the cultural order is realized also as an order of goods. The goods stand as an object code for the signification and valuation of persons and occasions, functions and situations. Operating on a specific logic of correspondence between material and social contrasts, production is thus the reproduction of the culture in a system of objects.

One is led naturally to exploit the double meanings in such terms as

10. "Les objets ne constituent ni une flore ni une faune. Pourtant ils donnent bien l'impression d'une végétation proliférante et d'une jungle, où le nouvel homme sauvage des temps modernes a du mal à retrouver les réflexes de la civilisation. Cette faune et cette flore, que l'homme a produit et qui reviennent l'encercler et l'investir . . . il faut tenter de les décrire . . . en n'oubliant jamais, dans leur faste et leur profusion, qu'elles sont le *produit d'une activité humaine,* et qu'elles sont dominées, non par des lois écologiques naturelles, mais par la loi de la valeur d'échange" (Baudrillard 1970, pp. 19–20).

"fashion" and "fabricate": I take the American clothing system as the principal example.

Notes on the American Clothing System

Considered as a whole, the system of American clothing amounts to a very complex scheme of cultural categories and the relations between them, a veritable map—it does not exaggerate to say—of the cultural universe.[11] The first task will be to suggest that the scheme operates on a kind of general syntax: a set of rules for declining and combining classes of the clothing-form so as to formulate the cultural categories. In a study of *mode* as advertised in several French magazines, Roland Barthes discriminated for women's dress alone some sixty foci of signification. Each site or dimension comprised a range of meaningful contrasts: some by mere presence or absence, as of gloves; some as diversified as the indefinite series of colors (Barthes 1967, pp. 114 ff.).[12] It is evident that with a proper syntax, rules of combination, a formidable series of propositions could be developed, constituting so many statements of the relations between persons and situations in the cultural system. It is equally evident that I could not hope to do more than suggest the presence of this grammar, without pretense at having analyzed it.

There are in costume several levels of semantic production. The outfit as a whole makes a statement, developed out of the particular arrangement of garment parts and by contrast to other total outfits. Again there is a logic of the parts, whose meanings are developed differentially by comparison at this level, in a Saussurean way: as, for example,

11. Fashion in clothing is of course frequently commented upon by social scientists and is occasionally given empirical investigation (Barthes 1967; Richardson and Kroeber 1940; Simmel 1904; Stone 1959). But there is a much richer literature upon which one may draw for ethnographic purposes: the direct reflections of participants in the process. Our discussion makes use of the writings of such as admen, market researchers, designers, buyers, fashion editors and critics, and textbooks by teachers of home economics, design, and aesthetics. Moreover, the discussion does not deny itself the advantage of observation and self-reflection in the one situation where the ethnographer finally realizes the privileged position of the participant-observer, namely, in his own village. I do not claim to have exhausted any of these resources—very far from it.

For a treatment of costume analogous to that attempted here—which, however, came to my attention after this chapter had gone to press—see Bogatyrev 1971.

12. Although Barthes was exclusively concerned with the rhetoric of fashion as written (*le vêtement écrit*) rather than with the symbolic system of the clothing object as such, much of his discussion is pertinent to the present effort, and I have drawn heavily upon it.

the value of women's slacks is simultaneously determined by opposition to other garments of that locus, such as skirts or men's pants,
as well as by contrast to other examples of the same class (slacks) that
differ in color, pattern, or whatever. My concern in discussing this syntax
will be more with what is conveyed than with an account of the entire set of
rules. It will be enough to indicate that it provides a systematic basis for the
cultural discourse "fashioned" upon it:

> "Most people wear some sign, and don't know what it's saying.
> Choose your sign according to your audience," Malloy said . . . "a
> good dark suit, white shirt and conservative tie are a young man's best
> wardrobe friends, if he's applying for a white collar job in a big range
> of business and professional categories. They're authority symbols.
> It's that simple," he said. ["Fashion Column," *Chicago Daily News*,
> 11 Jan. 1974]

But there is another problem, somewhat more difficult. I should like to
move down a level to the constituent units composing the discourse: to
demonstrate here how particular social meanings are related to elementary
physical contrasts in the clothing object. It will be a movement also of
rapprochement with totemic thought. For the principle is very much the
same: a series of concrete differences among objects of the same class to
which correspond distinctions along some dimension of social order—as the
difference between blue collar and white is one between manual labor and
bureaucratic; the relative saturation or brightness of hue discriminates fall
from spring; or, "A sweet disorder in the dress / Kindles in clothes a
wantoness." (Herrick). By such means the set of manufactured objects is
able to comprehend the entire cultural order of a society it would at once
dress and address. (Two words whose derivation from a common root—as
Tylor said of "kindred" and "kindness"—expresses in the happiest way
one of the most fundamental principles of social life.)

The overall objective in all this, I should stress, is some contribution
toward a cultural account of production. It is to this end that I explore the
code of object properties and their meaningful combinations. The emphasis
on the code implies also that we shall not be concerned at present with how
individuals dress. This is not simply a decision for *langue* over *parole*.
How people dress is a far more complicated semiotic problem than can be
attempted here, including as it does the particular consciousness or self-
conceptions of the subject in a specific meaningful "context of the situation." Again, I touch too briefly on the related question of the manipulation of the fashion code within the clothing industry. However, if all such

limitations, which have a common reference to the system in action, render this account regrettably incomplete, they do have the advantage of focusing upon the position it is necessary to establish in advance, and without which all further analysis of action risks relapse into a vulgar pragmatics: that production is the realization of a symbolic scheme.

For notice what is produced in the clothing system. By various objective features an item of apparel becomes appropriate for men or women, for night or for day, for "around the house" or "in public," for adult or adolescent. What is produced is, first, classes of time and place which index situations or activities; and, second, classes of status to which all persons are ascribed. These might be called "notional coordinates" of clothing, in the sense that they mark basic notions of time, place, and person as constituted in the cultural order. Hence what is reproduced in clothing is this classificatory scheme. Yet not simply that. Not simply the boundaries, the divisions, and subdivisions of, say, age-grades or social classes; by a specific symbolism of clothing differences, what is produced are the meaningful differences between these categories. In manufacturing apparel of distinct cut, outline, or color for women as opposed to men, we reproduce the distinction between femininity and masculinity as *known* to this society. That is what is going on in the pragmatic-material process of production.

More specifically, what is going on is a differentiation of the cultural space as between town and country, and within the town between downtown and neighborhood—and then again, a contrast between all of these, as collectively making up a public sphere, and the domestic-familial domain. When a woman goes shopping, she normally "dresses *up*" a domestic costume, at least by the addition of peripheral display of elements such as jewelry; and the more so if she is shopping downtown rather than "in the neighborhood." Conversely, when a man returns home from "a hard day at the office," he dresses down a public style in a way consistent with the "familiarity" of the domestic sphere.[13]

13. Cf. Crawley's "principle of adaptation to state": "Dress expresses every social movement, as well as every social grade. It also expresses family, municipal, provincial, regional, tribal, and national character. At the same time it gives full play to the individual. A complete psychology of the subject would analyze all such cases with reference to the principle of adaptation" (Crawley 1931, p. 172). Some of the objective changes that accompany the fundamental proportion of public/private : impersonal/familial are conjured up by the stereotypic image of the good bourgeois returning home from "a hard day at the office": a banal scene in which the social passage is signified by the man successively removing his hat, kissing his wife, taking off his jacket, stripping away his tie (exaggerated gesture), opening his shirt collar (deep breath), sinking into his favorite

At the other extreme are the higher distinctions of national space: for example, the West Coast and East Coast, of which the marked subclasses are California and the Northeast (cf. Rosencranz 1972, pp. 263–64).

We also substantialize in clothing the basic cultural valuations of time—diurnal, hebdomodal, and seasonal. We have evening clothes and daytime clothes, "little afternoon dresses" and nighttime dress (pajamas). Each references the nature of the activities ordered by those times, in the way that weekday apparel is to Sunday "best" as the secular is to the sacred. The marked seasonal variations are spring and fall, the colors of these seasons usually conceived to parallel the vegetation cycle. (Outdoor color per se, however, seems to be inverted for summer and winter dress: spectral green and red mark the winter solstice [Christmas], whereas white is traditionally appropriate between Memorial Day [May 30] and Labor Day.)

A similar treatment could be made of the class, the sex, and the age-grade of clothing. All these social categories have determinate markers, characteristic variations on the object level. In the common ideology of producers and consumers, this consubstantiality of subject and object is predicated on an identity of essences, such that the silk is "womanly" as women are "silky." "Fine as silk," "soft as silk," the cloth opposes itself on one side to the masculinity of wool and on the other to the inferiority of cotton (cf. Dichter 1959, pp. 104 ff.).[14] But this Veblenesque

---

armchair, donning the slippers fetched by a well-trained child, spouse, or dog—and breathing a sigh of relief. A whole set of statements about the contrast between kinship and the "larger world" is going on. In Stone's sociological study of clothing in Vansburg, Michigan, it was observed that about 70 percent of manual and white-collar workers arrive at work in what they consider their work clothes, and about 60 percent change when they go home. More than 90 percent of their wives changed clothing before going shopping, and about 75 percent did so again upon returning home (Stone 1959, pp. 109–10). Lynes some time ago noticed that on weekends, since the (suburban) home has become an arena of do-it-yourself, the white-collar class has affected "workclothes" (e.g., blue jeans) in the domestic sphere—except for the "backyard barbeque," which is distinguished by bright and dashing holiday wear, "symbols of revolt against the conformity imposed on men by the daily routine of business" (1957, p. 69).

14. Varieties of cotton are again differentiated by sex according to heaviness and stiffness; so the common four-class paradigm in materials:

	male	female	
class	wool	silk	fine
mass	denim	"cotton"	

heavy ←——————→ light   coarse

In a book on advertising technique, Stephen Baker (1961, unpaginated) presents pictures of the same woman draped in four different fabrics. He comments: "Fabrics have sexual correlation of the height of luxury with the height of femininity is likely transposed by race, as for American blacks the male seems to be the marked sex whereas whites decorate the female.[15] Yet in turn, the correlation between black male and white female elegance along such dimensions as texture will be differentially inflected by class, insofar as race and class overlap, and it is a commonplace of the homegrown sociology that muted color and minor contrast are upper-class Establishment whereas brilliant color and major contrast are "mass" (Birren 1956). On the other hand, the silken sobriety of the upper-class white woman is exchanged in her daughter's clothes for the textures of youth: which brings us back full circle to wool by the common discrimination of youth and male from the adult female on the attributes of activity/passivity (ceremonial.)[16]

---

connotations. Wool is the least feminine of the four materials . . . . It makes a women appear businesslike, urban, sophisticated. Linen has a mixed image. If it is white, the fabric strongly suggests purity. It is more feminine than wool but has little seductive power. Linen is associated with clean, wholesome fun. The delicacy (and lightness) of lace makes it very much a woman's fabric. Rich in pattern, lace exudes an air of elegance, aloofness, yet soft femininity. Silk is the most sensuous of all materials. It shines and reflects the play of light. It is very soft and clings to a woman's body. This characteristic makes silk (or satin) bring out the seductive qualities of the wearer."

15. Cf. Schwartz (1958) on clothing among American blacks. One observation of this empirical study that seems quite generalizable is that "the least significant motive underlying the selection and wearing of certain items of clothing is protection from the elements" (p. 27).

16. An empirical study of favored costumes of upper-class college and middle-aged women developed contrasts of the following type (N. Taylor, cited in Rosencranz 1972, pp. 214–15):

	Young College Women	Middle-aged Women
Garment	Dark gray wool dress and coat; scarf of gray, black, and red paisley	Black silk ottoman suit
Shoes	Black brogans	Black silk pumps with bow
Hose	"Hint" of gray	Black sheer
Handbag	Black calf	Black silk
Bracelet	Silver with pearls	Gold
Pin	-------	Diamond sunburst
Ring	Pearl	Pearl and diamond

From the above information and preceding discussion one could probably make a few guesses about production: for example, that (other things being equal, and they are

Gender and age-grade serve to illustrate another property of the grammar: certain mechanisms of opening the set to make it more complex without, however, a revision in principle. Even in expansion, the system seems to adhere to Sapir's dictum that fashion is custom in the guise of a departure from custom. New species and subspecies are permuted, for example, by a combinatory synthesis of existing oppositions. In designer's categories, the received distinction between infants and schoolchildren has latterly been segmented into "infants," "toddlers," "preschoolers," and "schoolchildren"; adolescents are likewise not what they used to be, but "preteens," "subteens," and "teens" (Rosencranz 1972, p. 203). In the same way, various categories of homosexuality can be evolved by particular combinations of male and female apparel, to the extent that we now have six more or less clearly distinguishable sartorial sexes. But at the line between adolescent and adult, a second type of permutation is currently in evidence: the adaptation of an existing distinction from elsewhere in the system, a kind of metaphorical transfer, to signify a change of content in a traditional opposition. The received idea of an "adolescent revolution" doubtless predisposed the change, but since the Vietnam War the conflict with the constituted (i.e., adult) authorities has been specifically idiomized politically, and so in apparel by the contrast, adolescent/adult: worker/ capitalist, with youth appropriating the blue jeans and work shirts of *society's* underclass. Perhaps nothing could better prove the absence of practical utility in clothing, since work is one of the last things youth has in mind. But the example serves as well to reveal the singular quality of capitalist society: not that it fails to work on a symbolic code, but that the code works as an open set, responsive to events which it both orchestrates and assimilates to produce expanded versions of itself.

Parenthetically: this view of production as the substantialization of a cultural logic should prohibit us from speaking naively of the generation of demand by supply, as though the social product were the conspiracy of a few "decision-makers," able to impose an ideology of fashion through the deceits of advertising. In Marx's phrase, "The educator himself needs educating." It is not as if the producers' *parole* becomes our *langue*. Nor

---

many), the amount of black silk produced is correlated with the number of middle-aged, upper-class white females in the population—which is itself a product of the total organization of society (notably including production). The proposition is at once banal and totally unself-evident. It is hardly in the nature of things that silk has some affinity with white middle-aged women, although it is in *the culture of the things*.

need one indulge in the converse mystification of capitalist production as a response to consumers' wants: "We always try to adapt," says the head of public relations for the company that has profited most from the recent expansion of blue jeans sales.[17] But who then is dominant, the producer or the consumer? It should be possible to transcend all such subjective representations for an institutional description of capitalist production as a cultural process. Clearly this production is organized to exploit all possible social differentiation by a motivated differentiation of goods. It proceeds according to a meaningful logic of the concrete, of the significance of objective differences, thus developing appropriate signs of emergent social distinctions. Such might well describe the specialization of age differences in clothing, or the metaphoric transfer of blue jeans—especially if it is noted that the iconic integration of social and object distinctions is a dialectic process. The product that reaches its destined market constitutes an objectification of a social category, and so helps to constitute the latter in society; as in turn, the differentiation of the category develops further social declensions of the goods system. Capitalism is no sheer rationality. It is a definite form of cultural order; or a cultural order acting in a particular form. End of parenthesis.

I turn to another type of variation in costume, this corresponding to the division of labor broadly considered, to suggest the presence of systematic rules for social categorization of the clothing form. First, however, we must establish the classification on the social level. In his discussion of the *monde* in the *mode,* Barthes distinguishes two alternate ways in which the social significance of costume is conceived (1967, pp. 249 ff.). These are, in effect, two modalities of social discourse, the active and the passive: doing and being, *faire* and *être,* activity and identity. Adapting the distinction to present purposes, one might say that the first has to do with functions; it indexes costume according to the type of activity, such as sport or manual labor. The second relates to occupational status—the characteristic habit of the industrial worker, the farmer, the waitress, the doctor, the soldier. Again, in the following very general and oversimplified table of

---

17. Not to deny that such may be the genuine mode of appearance to the participants in the process: " 'I don't think I ever figured it would come to this,' " says Haas, who along with his brother Peter, the (Levi-Strauss) company president, was responsible for molding Levi's into its present structure. " 'Basically, what we've tried to do is to serve society's needs.' "

" 'The consumer still determines what he wants,' " says Bud Johns, the company's public relations director. " 'We always try to adapt' " (Blue jeans: Uniform for a casual world," *Chicago Tribune,* 5 May 1975).

functions (fig. 11), I abbreviate a considerable argument, and more than one assumption:

The main assumption is the validity of Veblen's distinction of ceremony and workmanship in American categories of activity and clothing. The key to the entire table is this principle. In each opposition, the marked or ceremonial function is placed to the left, the unmarked and workmanlike to the right, the whole then a set of differentiations of the master distinction between work and leisure (cf. Veblen 1934 [1899]). If this assumption is allowed as more or less ethnographically correct, and the consequences likewise worked out through the classes and subclasses in a faithful way, two remarkable regularities in the system of clothing are presented to view. The first might be called the *rule of ceremonial correspondence*. It refers to the analogous differentiation of costume in any two functional classes similarly ordered on the opposition of ceremony and workmanship. Consider, for example, the "dress clothes" affected by men on "special occasions" (*fête*), culminating perhaps in formal tuxedo for very ritualized affairs (e.g., marriages, gala) or, slightly less formally, the highly styled dark suit. Notice then that these outfits specifically resemble the "conservative" suits worn by business executives, in a way corresponding to their respective differences from sportive wear in the area of amusement and white-collar dress in the domain of work. The latter two—by their relative "informality," permissible color schemes, and so forth—again resemble each other; indeed, to the extent that a younger office worker may be discriminated from the higher corporate executives precisely by his "sports jacket." Yet exactly the same differences characterize, in a general way, the opposition between the more formal costumes of amusement and the relative undress permitted when "doing nothing; just sitting around the house" (*sans projet*). Or again, it is the difference between the blue jeans or overalls of an industrial worker and the more stylized uniforms of waitresses, deliverymen, and other service workers. This particular opposition also reappears on the leisure side in the sporting outfits of hunting or skiing, which are like uniforms even as they are differentiated from the "casual clothes" of the spectator.[18] It is thus a rule of analogy in the oppositions of ceremony/workmanship, at whatever level they may appear in the system. The terms of any opposition correspond to the terms of any other, such that the marked (ceremonial) costumes of any two classes

---

18. Or consider the following example of stylization in relation to ceremonial hierarchy noted by Jacinski in one factory: " 'Suntan trousers and shirts but no ties for inspectors; slacks and sport shirts for lead men; slacks, white shirts, and ties for assistant foremen; and the same, plus a jacket, for the foreman' " (Quoted by Ryan 1966, p. 66).

Figure 11   Schema of functions signified in American clothing

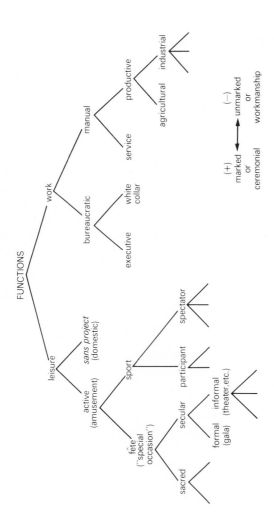

resemble each other by an analogous differentiation from the unmarked (workmanlike) costumes of their respective classes. Or more formally:

(1) $M_x/\overline{M}_x \cong M_y/\overline{M}_y$—which says that the opposition (/) of marked (M) and unmarked ($\overline{M}$) in any given class ($_x$) corresponds ($\cong$) to $M/\overline{M}$ in any other class ($_y$).

Besides the similarities in the differences, there are also differences in the similarities—a tuxedo is still more "stylized" than a business suit, as domestic clothes (especially for night) are more "undressed' and "casual" than work clothes—which leads to a second rule: *rule of ceremonial exaggeration*. The rule is that, on one hand, the marked costume in a more ceremonial opposition is itself more ceremonial than its counterpart in some workmanlike opposition: as the uniforms of active sport are more colorful and cut with more flair than the uniform of the waitress or the milkman. On the other hand, the unmarked costume of the ceremonial opposition is even less workmanlike than its counterpart on the more workmanlike side: as the spectator's outfit is more "casual" than the industrial worker's. The same might be said of the opposition of *fête* and sport within the category "amusement," as compared with executive and clerical in the category of managerial work, even as the last pair is at once more ceremonial (the executive suit) and less workmanlike (white collar) than, again, the service versus industrial worker. The rule, therefore, is that the opposition stipulated within a workmanlike class is exaggerated by the corresponding opposition in a more ceremonial class. The exaggeration occurs in both directions: the ceremonial outfit is more ceremonial at its marked pole, less workmanlike at its unmarked pole. Formally:

(2) $M_x^1 > M_y^2 :: M_x^1 < M_y^2$, where the superscripts (1, 2, 3 ... n) represent a factor of workmanlike function and $>$ and $<$ represent relative formality.

Or, by diagram (fig. 12):

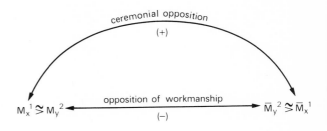

Figure 12   Rule of ceremonial exaggeration

I spare the reader a corresponding discussion of the modality of "being," which, as it responds to a proliferating specialization of occupation, is even more protean than the system of functions.[19] But it seems legitimate to pause at this juncture to explain what claims are being made for exercises of the sort just indulged in. The overall aim is to respond to a question initially posed by Marx, but so far as I know without answer in his or any other Economics: What kind of theoretical account can be given for production as a *mode of life*? I propose here an example of the beginning of such a cultural account: example, because it is concerned only with the system of clothing in modern America; beginning, because it has been concerned so far mostly with the general syntax, social classes of the clothing object, and certain rules of its social declension. But it is necessary to be still more cautious. The claim made for the rules of ceremonial correspondence is only that they suggest such a syntax. To have any higher pretensions, the discussion would have to stipulate the kinds of clothing features to which the rules apply—features of color, color contrast, line and outline, type and congruence of garment pieces, kinds of accessories, qualities of texture—and the modes of their combination. The full scope of the project is very large; this is only an example of the suggestion of a beginning.

In the same spirit I would discuss the symbolic process on the lowest level of constituent elements and their specific meanings. What I have in mind is the determination of minimal distinctive contrasts in object features, as in line, color, or texture, that signify differences in social meaning. Not to claim here, either, any novelty in the attempt, or any superiority by virtue of an apparent systematics to the observations many others have made:

> So far as I know, overalls are a garment native to this country . . . the standard or classical garment at the very least . . . of the southern rural American working man: they are his uniform, the badge and proclamation of his peasantry . . . the basis, what they are, can best be seen

19. On occupational differentiation of clothing, see, for example, Ryan 1966, p. 62; Horn 1968. One of Stone's Vansburg informants commented as follows on the changes wrought by recent agricultural specialization: " 'A few years ago you could tell any farmer. They used to wear denim overalls all the time. Now they have diversified farming, so the clothes have changed, too. Well, some still wear denims. Those in the dairy business have uniforms. Those in the poultry business have white uniforms. Those in beef wear women's skirts and corduroy pants—out in the field, they have to wear something heavier. It's altogether different than it was thirty years ago' " (Stone 1959, pp. 120–21).

when they are still new; before they have lost shape and color and texture; and before the white seams of their structure have lost their brilliance. . . . In the strapping across the kidneys they again resemble work harness, and in their crossed straps and tin buttons.

And in the functional pocketing of their bib, a harness modified to the convenience of a used animal of such high intelligence that he has use for tools. . . . A new suit of overalls has among its beauties those of a blue print: and they are a map of a working man.

The shirts too; squarely cut and strongly seamed; with big square pockets and with metal buttons: the cloth stiff, the sweat cold when it is new, the collar large in newness and standing out in angles under the ear. [James Agee, *Let Us Now Praise Famous Men* (1941, pp. 265–67)]

It is these elementary meaningful units—the squareness of the pockets, the stiffness of the cloth, the crossed straps—that the present discussion intends. There is at a higher level a lexicon of the producible units: types of cloth such as silk or wool, kinds of upper garment such as shirts and blouses: products as such, entering integrally into the total outfit and usually contributing several conceptions to the whole. But these are already complex constructions whose meaningful import is predicated on constituent details of the form. In a work which ridicules the conceit that our clothes are in any sense "modern" or "civilized," Rudolfsky writes:

Any piece of fabric can be charged with sexuality by simply working it into a precise shape. The resulting form might determine the actual sex. . . .

The overlap of a blouse, a jacket or a coat determines the sex of the article. By buttoning a garment on the right side, it becomes suitable for men only and definitely unsuitable for women. Whatever the quaint explanations of folklore are, the right side of the body has always been male, the left side female; this orientation survived despite its irrationality. [Rudolfsky 1947, pp. 126–27]

One might easily adduce a number of similar elementary features that differentiate the gender of clothes. Men's sleeves, for instance, are characteristically more tailored than women's and extend the full length of the arm by comparison with three-quarter (or less) lengths which expose the lower extremity—contrasts exactly repeated on the lower limbs in trousers and skirts.[20] The masculine fabric is relatively coarse and stiff, usually heavier, the feminine soft and fine; apart from the neutral white, masculine

20. As has often been remarked, there is an asymmetry in the gender of almost all objects, including clothing: it is feminine things that are marked and exclusive; male objects,

colors are darker, feminine light or pastel. The line in men's clothing is square, with angles and corners; women's dress emphasizes the curved, the rounded, the flowing, and the fluffy. Such elements of line, texture, and the like are the minimal constituents, the objective contrasts which convey social meaning.

I refrain from calling them "vestemes," but if necessary they might be deemed ECUs—for "elementary constituent units" and as a pun on McLuhan's dictum that "conformity to a fashion literally gives currency to a style." I propose to consider just three classes of elementary units: texture, line, and color.

Texture first, mainly to illustrate that significance is developed from binary contrasts of signifiers. Texture operates semantically on a number of objective oppositions—heavy/light, rough/smooth, hard/soft,—several of them simultaneously pertinent to any given cloth. Marilyn Horn, in a text subtitled "An Interdisciplinary Study of Clothing" (1968, p. 245), compiles a fair list of textural dyads, supposing each pair the two poles of a graded continuum of variation. I myself would be pressed to discriminate between several of the pairs, but one must incline to Horn as expert and informant. In any event, the cloth may be:

dull	-----	shiny
rough	-----	smooth
uneven	-----	flat
grainy	-----	slippery
coarse	-----	fine
bulky	-----	gossamer
heavy	-----	light
compact	-----	porous
bristly	-----	downy
crisp	-----	limp
stiff	-----	pliable
hard	-----	soft
rigid	-----	spongy
inelastic	-----	stretchy
warm	-----	cool
scroopy	-----	waxy

even such things as razors or electric shavers, are often used by women or appear in feminine versions. On the gender of objects, see Levy 1968; Baker 1961.

The presumption is that such objective differences are at once observable and socially significant (see note, p. 182 above). Any piece of cloth is a particular combination, then, of several textural qualities. Insofar as each quality bears some meaning, in contradistinction to its objective opposite, the texture communicates a parataxic set of propositions concerning age, sex, activity, class, time, place, and the other dimensions of cultural order.

The structural lines figuring in the cut or patterns of costume make up an analogous class of meaningful contrasts. Significance seems to be correlated with at least three characteristics of line: direction, form, and rhythm. *Direction* refers to orientation in relation to a ground: thus, vertical and horizontal and the mediating oblique, the last again divisible into left (downward left to right) and right (upward left to right) (fig. 13).

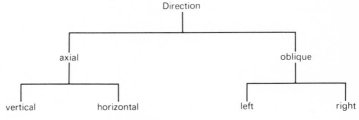

Figure 13   Direction in line

Notice that it is already a small paradigm of the cultural constitution of meaning that an oblique line proceeding downward from right to left is considered by Europeans to slant "up," whereas a line downward from the left slants "down." The distinction "up"/"down" is perfectly arbitrary, if sometimes implicitly accepted experimentally (e.g., Poffenberger and Barrows 1924). Supposing the lines are "read" from left to right, the distinction renders them the potential objectification of any ranked social relation similarly conceived in terms of "up" and "down," "higher" and "lower."[21] The second dimension of line, *form,* refers to its properties as straight or curved, with a mediate angular or zigzag. *Rhythm* is the periodicity of the curve or angle: an indefinite series usually idiomized as movement or velocity from the "slow" or "undulating" to the "rapidly oscillating" but which may also include a significant variation in amplitude.

21. This cultural construction of a line as "going upward to the right," which a Japanese would conceive just the reverse way, is a small but interesting indication that action, including language, proceeds in a world already symbolized and interacting nondiscursively with the conventional code of action.

With the aid of some vintage psychology and aesthetic commentary on the meaning of line, it is possible to present cultural valuations for certain contrasts of line. The experimental psychology can only be suggestive: typically designed to elicit the expressive or affective value of lines, the procedure tests the relation to the individual subject rather than that between objective and social representations as such. Nevertheless, the responses of mood at least indirectly imply cultural interpretations. For further reflection I append therefore an early example of experiment on "the feeling-value of line," the Poffenberger and Barrows study just cited, reporting percentage responses of five hundred educated subjects to a set of eighteen different lines (1924). The lines differed in form as curved or angular; no straight lines were included. For rhythm, both periodicity and amplitude were simultaneously operating, while direction comprised only the horizontal and the two obliques. There was no vertical orientation. The subjects were asked to assign values to the lines presented from a list of thirteen adjectives, such as "sad," "quiet," "lazy." The principal results are summarized in table 1 (p. 194).

Results of this kind are enhanced by another type of information, such as is provided by trained aestheticians, whose descriptions of the significance of the concrete often achieve specifically cultural dimensions. In a fascinating text, *The Art of Color and Design,* Maitland Graves (1951), for example, provides several comments of the following sort on line: "The slightly curved or undulating line is loose and flexible. Because of harmonic transition in the change of direction, it has flowing continuity." The "slow, lazy movement," Graves goes on to say, is "passive," "gentle," "soft," "voluptuous," and "feminine" (p. 202). The straight line, in contrast: "suggests rigidity and precision. It is positive, direct, tense, stiff, uncompromising, harsh, hard, unyielding." One might then add— perhaps without taking undue advantage of the prerogative of informant— that the straight line is, by comparison, masculine. Graves makes an analogous comparison of the vertical and the horizontal, with such additional connotations as strength and authority. Here everything depends on the relation to a ground, and as Graves describes it, most naively, to *the ground.* The horizontal line: "is in harmony with the pull of gravity, that is, at rest. It is quiet, passive, calm, it suggests repose. . . . The vertical is suggestive of poise, balance, and of strong, firm support. Vertical lines . . . are severe and austere; they symbolize uprightness, honesty or integrity, dignity, aspiration and exaltation" (ibid., p. 210).

Now, how does one get from the object feature of the ECU (e.g., straight/curved) to its cultural significance (masculine/feminine)? One

Table 1   Feelings and Their Appropriate Lines

	Form		Rhythm			Direction			
	Curve	Angle	Slow	Medium	Fast	Horizontal	Up	Down	
1. Sad	86.3	14.3	86.8	6.9	6.9	12.1	4.2	84.3	Slow descending curve
2. Quiet	97.2	3.0	81.5	7.2	8.5	90.2	5.8	4.2	Slow horizontal curve
3. Lazy	74.0	26.1	72.3	19.9	7.9	38.7	9.9	51.5	Slow descending curve
4. Merry	79.7	20.4	11.5	54.4	34.2	16.4	79.5	4.2	Medium rising curve
5. Agitating	17.4	82.8	4.5	39.1	56.6	23.1	68.8	8.3	Rapid rising angle
6. Furious	10.7	89.2	9.7	44.0	46.2	16.4	62.8	20.7	Rapid or medium rising angle
7. Dead	53.0	46.2	70.3	6.3	22.6	46.6	2.2	50.4	Slow horizontal or descending curve or angle
8. Playful	76.0	23.7	9.8	51.8	38.1	28.2	65.0	6.5	Medium rising curve
9. Weak	69.2	30.6	53.6	14.0	32.2	31.6	8.0	60.2	Slow descending curve
10. Gentle	89.6	10.3	51.7	22.2	26.0	73.7	15.5	10.7	Slow horizontal curve
11. Harsh	7.1	92.9	11.8	62.5	25.7	40.1	30.6	29.3	Medium horizontal curve
12. Serious	35.5	64.2	50.5	28.2	21.0	64.4	19.1	16.2	Slow horizontal angle
13. Powerful	15.3	85.4	27.8	52.7	19.9	37.9	55.5	7.0	Medium rising angle

Source: Poffengerger and Barrows 1924.

must beware of the simple naturalistic trap. The meaning is not a self-evident icon, immanent in the sign; the mental process is something more than an association of resemblances present to the senses. It is hardly enough to remark that men are on average straighter than women—even if the fact that plenty of men are rounder than plenty of women could some-how be disregarded. The problem is infinitely more interesting and subtle and, when one reflects upon it, altogether incorrectly posed in the initial question. *So far as production is concerned,* it is unnecessary to "get to" the cultural gender from the geometric form, as to the signified from the signifier, because from the beginning, as it were, each of these is alter-nately the meaning of the other. In the society as constituted, "rounded" and "soft" are as much the definition of women as "feminine" is the definition of the line. Gender and line: each is the signification of the other and each stands to the other as the physical sign whose meaning is being determined. From this point of view, the difference between men and women is also "objective," a distinction of the concrete-perceptual type, in relation to which such object notions as "straight" and "curved," "hard" and "soft," "rigid" and "yielding" play the role of the concept. As we understand the difference in line to be a distinction of sex, so we understand the distinction of sex in terms of line.

But more, a second moment of reflection on the language suggests that as much can be said for a great number of social distinctions: they are characteristically idiomized in geometric terms. Our social world is pre-sented as an enormous object world—and vice versa. Death is a "decline" to the "end" of immobility and prostration; hence in the Poffenberger experiment, the line of "slow" horizontal or "descending" curve is "dead." But likewise, status is a "standing" among men, understood in the terms of "higher" and "lower," as a command is something before which we "incline" or "yield." Some people are "upright"; others are "crooked" or at least "devious." Some are even "deviants." Some are "strong," others are "weak." Certain are "forceful"; "force" also is an attribute of constituted authority. We speak "directly" or "indirectly." We act "rigidly" or "flexibly." We have "near" kinsmen and "distant" kinsmen, on some of whom we may "lean" while others we "support." It would be easy to go on indefinitely, but I shall cut the discussion "short" to make the "point." The point is that the social world is commonly figured by the so-called objective, which precisely as it is figurative here functions as the idea. Consequently, when it comes to the manufacture of a product, of a clothing set which objectifies the proportion straight/

curved: masculine/feminine, no greater privlege has to be given to the attribution of gender to shape than of shape to gender. The correspondence already exists in full before and outside that moment when ''any piece of fabric can be charged with sexuality by simply working it into a precise shape'' (Rudolfsky). Only a particular realization of that correspondence, the cloth is a total social fact, at once material and conceptual, which seamlessly interweaves the spatial meaning of sex with the sexual meaning of space.

Production, then, is the practice of a much more pervasive logic of the concrete, which logic is itself produced as a symbolic appropriation of nature. It is not merely species which are ''good to think.'' Lévi-Strauss's famous dictum is applicable to all kinds of naturally occurring things and relations. The whole of nature is the potential object of the symbolic praxis, whose cunning, rather like Hegel's Reason, consists in this: that it puts to the service of its own intentions those relations among things existing by their own properties. The difference between vertical and horizontal line may carry with it a commonly experienced ''resistance'' and ''submission'' to a well-known ''force.'' Hence the suitability of a contrast provided by nature to a distinction present in culture—for instance, between authority and subordination. Nor need we be deceived by the apparent objectivity of the sign, which is only the result of a dialectic process in which the natural fact was first seized culturally in order to be reapplied naturally. Nature rigidly separated from man, as Marx said, does not exist for man. The notions of ''force,'' ''resistance,'' and the like are already valuations, relative cultural representations of the natural process. Contrary to our received perspectives, this sort of metaphor does not really proceed from the concrete to the abstract, from nature to culture. Such would suppose that language's power of classification mysteriously fails at the moment of ''real'' experience, that it can merely then give forth a new name, which is to say degenerate into a signal. We can be sure that ''force'' was a spiritual relation before it became an objective fact. And, correspondingly, the material appropriation of nature we call ''production'' is a sequitur to its symbolic appropriation.

Saussurean principle, therefore, is not violated, whatever the apparent resemblances between object-sign and cultural referent. More than a reflection, the sign is a conception of objective differences. Arbitrariness thus retains a double historical guarantee. Which features of nature are harnessed by culture to its own intentions remains a relative determination: that particular contrast of line to represent gender is not the only one possible. Conversely, the specific content of any particular contrast on the object level is not given with the difference: whether the upright line is to represent honesty, masculinity, or authority, and if authority, what kind, none of this can be said apart from a determinate cultural system. Yet at the same time, the historical appropriation of concrete contrasts must carry into the order of culture at least two *conditions of nature* if it is to function as social discourse. First, the selection of a given material opposition—as straight/curved:masculine/feminine—must be *true*: the penalty of a contradiction between the perceptible object contrasts and the relationships signified is meaninglessness and, ultimately, silence. In use the sign is relatively motivated, if according to a certain cultural scheme. And second, then, the condition of perceptible resemblance, itself relative and indeterminate (as merely a condition of noncontradiction), argues the encompassment within the symbolic system of specific natural structures: those of perception itself. This is an activity of appropriation and exploitation, the employment of sensible contrasts and relations as a semiotic code. In the event, when color, for example, is harnessed to the symbolic work—granted that neither the extent nor the specific content of color symbolism is naturally determined—the relationships that subsist among cultural meanings will correspond formally to relationships among hues laid down in perception.

At this point we are no longer concerned to demonstrate that color contrasts function as elementary constituents of significance in production. There is abundant evidence to this effect, not only for clothing but for household furnishings, automobiles, and all sorts of goods. The class of color operators is again complex, making use of distinctions of hue (including neutrals), saturation, value (brightness), and the several ways these are combined in multicolor patterns.[22] The problem of present interest is to discover whether there is any structure common to the relations between color-meanings and the perception of color differences. Such a structure would itself be without specific meaning, merely a formal *combinatoire* of oppositions and compatibilities. Its presence would, for some, testify to the limitations placed on the symbolic system by the nature of perception (or of the mind). But said more positively and perhaps more fruitfully, the *combinatoire* would testify to the employment of structures already present to the mind in the social project of symbolic production.[23]

22. Cf. Arnheim 1974; Birren 1956; Wexner 1954; Kintner 1940; Murray and
    Deabler 1957; Graves 1951; Sargent 1923; Baker 1961; among others, and the texts on
    clothing previously cited by Ryan, Rosencranz, and Horn.
23. See below on the cultural employment of mental structures. This kind of phrasing
    has certain advantages over the usual appeal to innate structures, which tends to be

Let us take up in this connection the oft-cited example of the traffic signal: an opposition of red and green mediated by yellow. For Leach (1970, p. 16–21), this segmentation of the spectrum operated by the mind is in a fundamental part iconic, experientially motivated by an association of red with blood, ''which certainly goes back to very early paleolithic times'' (p. 19). Out of this ''natural fact'' comes the significance of red as danger. In another part, however, the traffic signal seems arbitrary, since the selection of green for contrast is a learned convention—other colors (blue, black, white yellow) could also be selected for contrast with red. Finally, the analysis depends too on a physicalist notion of color as presented on a spectrum of wavelength, by virtue of which it is said that yellow is intermediate between red and green. Thus, brought together on inconsistent principles, each of these postulates is also inadequate in itself, and the total effect rather obscures the natural structure of the symbol system and the relation between that structure and the assignment of meaning.

Very briefly: the first argument, on the naturalness of red as danger, attempts to reduce the symbolic process to a nomenclature of meanings immanent in experience. It is not only that the explanation thus violates Saussurean canons of value as a relation of differentiation in a system of signs; by the same token, it neglects that the ''blood'' signified by red would not be blood as such but the (cultural) meaning of blood. Hence the motivated iconic relation that Leach supposes—*as is true of all signs proper* (American usage)—is a moment within and dependent upon preexistent symbolic values (V. Valeri 1970).[24] The second of Leach's arguments concerning the arbitrary selection of green for contrast with red

---

reductionist even as it is static and a negative determination by natural constraints. The implication of the alternative phrasing is to retain the primacy of the cultural over the mental, while suggesting some notion of mediation between the two. It supposes some functional connection—the pervasiveness of the mental structure rendering it suitable for symbolic communication—and certain dynamic possibilities, at least in the sense that the symbolic project is at liberty to develop various potentialities of mental structure and to do so to a variable extent. One might sum up the position by giving a slight displacement to the classic Durkheimian dictum, arguing that representations are general insofar as they are collective (social), not collective merely insofar as they are general (mental).

24. The generality of this point, that human sign behavior (motivated) is always a secondary formation of symboling (unmotivated), may be argued on grounds that the very *découpage* of object signifiers presupposes the process of valuation, thus the position and content of the object-sign in a meaningful order, on which basis motivation proceeds. It also follows that the concepts of both the object-sign and its signified, here redness and blood-danger, will likely ''outrun'' (Barthes) the formal motivation connecting them, so

ignores the salient relations of attraction and opposition between red and
green as complementary colors, on the level of both perception and
conception—a point to which we will return in a moment. The last of
Leach's postulates supposes that the common experience of color takes the
form of a refracted spectrum, but this is very rare in nature by comparison
with object colors, where blue's claim to mediacy between red and green
would be as good as yellow's. The moral: the analysis should aim singu-
larly at the correspondences between the structure of symbolic meanings
and the structure of perception, avoiding en route the parallel ideological
pitfalls of physicalism and associationalism. For the first is not the way the
world is presented to the mind, nor the second the way it is represented.
And again, the elicitation of correct correspondences between the perceptual and meaningful would show not the delimination of culture by nature,
but the appropriation of nature by culture.

The following is merely a suggestion of such an analysis, taking departure from the observation that the color relations of the traffic signal seem
to be duplicated in other symbolic domains of Western culture. This logically ensues provided the principle of the signal is generalized as follows:
red is opposed in meaning to green, while yellow is mediate in the sense
that it is like red in opposition to green but also like green in opposition to
red. Yellow, for a simple example, shares with red the significance of
danger in the flag of quarantine, which also unites it with "sickly green" in
contradiction to the vigor and energy of red.[25] Or, to take the correlated
domains of age and sexuality: as compared to the charged sexuality and
virility of red, green and yellow are forms of relative impotency, although

---

that the attempt to furnish an explanation by iconic resemblance will never be empirically satisfactory. Thus red in Western society is not always negative or indicative of
danger, as Leach has it. Red also has implications of health, strength, virility or
marked sexuality, and *fête* ("red-letter day"). The several meanings do have a common
marked or "advancing" value, by comparison especially with the senses of white and
green, which is corollary to differences in the perception of the distance of objects
reflecting longer wave lengths. By the combination of relative nearness (chromatic aber-
ration effect) and the high levels of saturation achieved by reds over a variety of wave-
lengths and brightness values, this hue is the most "penetrating" of colors. Red, indeed, is the most color (cf. Graves 1951; Gregory 1966; Bidwell 1899; Southall 1937).
It is this contrastive feature of red that makes it especially valuable in coding.

25. By testimony of the *Oxford English Dictionary*, green used in reference to human com-
plexion implies a "pale, sickly or bilious hue, indicative of fear, jealousy, ill-humour or
sickness"; whereas red, when said of lips or cheeks, indicates "a natural, healthy
color." In the discussion which follows, I make use of various authorities on color
meanings cited on p. 197, note, as well as dictionaries of slang and usage, principally
Mathews 1951; Partridge 1967; and Wentworth and Flexner 1967. See also Spengler
1956, 1:242 ff.

at the opposite poles of immaturity and maturity, fresh, inexperienced youth and a ripe old age whose course has been run—"my way of life / Is fall'n into the sere, the yellow leaf." Yet in the passions, yellow and green become tangent again in meanings of jealousy and envy. However as a "warm" color, yellow—cheerful yellow—joins red and orange as "positive and aggressive, restless or stimulating" (Graves 1951, p. 401), as against the cooler greens and blues, which are "transcendent," "spiritual," and "non-sensuous" (Spengler 1956, p. 246). Red is courage and war; green (with blue) passive, quiescent, peaceable; yellow as cowardice is the pretext of the one but the reality of the other. And notice how the system expands to include blue in a particular way. Just as green is to red, whatever yellow is, blue is the contrary: depressed ("the blues") where yellow is cheerful; loyal and genuine ("true blue") where yellow is deceitful and cowardly. Blue has a meaning comparable to yellow's about once in a blue moon. As we have seen, however, blue entertains similarities with green in opposition to the warm reds and yellows; on the other hand, blue's constancy distinguishes it from the recklessness of new and young green;[26] and indeed where green is the nascent, blue is the eternal and immortal. In the same way, blue is both like and distinguished from red: noble (blue-blood) and king in an age of monarchy, blue and red in another time become the party of order and the revolution. Red is the color of saints and martyrs in Christianity and blue, correlatively, of faith and piety; but red is also the mark of sinners—yet then, "the blues" once referred more specifically to the "blue devils." In sum, one may draw up a set of relationships of the following sort between red, green, yellow, and blue (fig. 14):

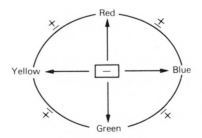

Figure 14   Relations of color meaning

26. The *OED* quotes Chaucer: "To newe things your lust is ever kene / in stede of blue, thus may ye were al grene."

The point I will make is that the diagram serves exactly as well for perception, if the relations of semantic intermediacy ($\pm$) between adjacent colors are taken for compatibility or simultaneous presence in object-colors and the semantic oppositions ($-$) are taken for complementarity. This structure can be built up on the perceptual level from a few elementary propositions, well known to color science and aesthetics. First, the four hues in question (along with the neutrals black and white) are peculiarly suited to the semantic function because they alone are perceptually unique, not decomposable into other hues. I speak specifically of vision, which is a totally different matter from the mixing of pigments. As a matter of perception, no other hues can be seen in the values usually named as "blue," "red," "yellow," and "green" (Hurvich and Jameson 1957; Hering 1964 [1920]; Linksz 1964; Pokorny and Smith 1972).[27] Yet where these four are perceptually unique, all other hues are seen as some mixture of two of them; as orange is perceived to be compounded of red and yellow, purple of blue and red, and so forth. Accordingly, red, green, yellow, and blue are deemed the "primary" or "primal" hues of perception in the scientific literature—and in the aesthetic literature, sometimes the "primitive" colors. The last makes a nice connection with Berlin and Kay's (1969) conclusion that, after black and white, these four are the first "basic color terms" to emerge in natural languages, and that their spectral position (on a chart of maximum saturation) is similar cross-culturally.[28] A second pertinent observation is that each of the four "primitives" will mix visually with only two of the other three, but never with the third. Blue may

27. Also note that only four hues in the spectrum—a blue of about 475 nm, a green of ca. 505 nm, a yellow of ca. 578 nm, and a red of the complement 495 nm—remain constant in color appearance despite changes in intensity.

28. There is some paradox in the conclusion that the "basic" color terms should have similar spectral referents in widely different cultures. The paradox is that, after all, these are not the "basic" color terms of any language, but abstract concepts of color, disengaged from any particular object. At a more "basic" level everywhere are the myriad of color terms recognized in their object form (as lemon-yellow, sea green, etc., cf. Conklin 1955). Why then should a concept that is clearly a secondary formation nevertheless have specific and apparently universal "basis"? The present discussion suggests an answer: that these hues, precisely as they have the perceptual qualities of distinctiveness, complementarity, etc., at certain loci—which lend them to meaningful contrast—are the most suitable for semantic employment in rituals, production exchange-value discrimination, and the like. Colors are in practice semiotic codes. Precisely as they subserve this significance, only certain color precepts are appropriately singled out as "basic," namely, those that by their distinctive features and relations can function as signifiers in informational systems. See Sahlins, in press.

appear in combination with red or green (to make, e.g., purple or cyan), as also may yellow; but one never sees a yellowish blue or a bluish yellow. Likewise red and green are each compatible in perception with blue and yellow, yet not with each other: there are no reddish greens or greenish reds. (See the several sources on color perception previously cited, as well as Hering 1964[1920]; Hurvich 1960; Hurvich and Jameson 1957). Third observation: there is good perceptual as well as physiological sense to conceiving these color relationships as "compatibilities" and "oppositions." Where the members of each complementary dyad, blue-yellow and red-green, will separately synthesize with the members of the other, the complementary hues themselves not only oppose but evoke each other in a classic pattern of negation and correlation.[29] Green is banished from the sensation of red, only to reappear as the afterimage of red or the effect given by red to a neutral background—a relation perfectly reciprocal and also true of blue and yellow. Each pair of complements, moreover, is linked in perception by contrast to the other dyad. Under increasing intensity, blue and yellow increase in brightness more rapidly than green and red; the latter retain their values longer under decreasing intensity (Bezold-Brücke effect). Or, as the stimulus size is reduced, the ability to discriminate blue and yellow deteriorates progressively by comparison with green and red. The linkage is again confirmed pathologically by the existence of distinctive red-green and yellow-blue syndromes of color blindness. All these perceptual facts, finally, have a ground in the physiology of color vision, specifically the "opponent-process" mechanism of transmission from eye to brain—an understanding first developed for man but recently supported by electrophysiological data from monkeys and fish. The evidence is that the transmission of color sensation (as distinct from retinal photoreception) is organized as a triadic set of binary processes: red-green, blue-yellow, and black-white. Each of these processes fires impulses to the brain in a privative manner through cells which respond to one of the complementary pair but exclude the other; for example, the red-green process is activated either as $+R-G$ or $-R+G$ (see Pokorny and Smith 1972; Hurvich and Jameson 1957).

---

29. Linksz writes: "Red and green are a dyad of opposing colors and so are yellow and blue. Either member of one dyad cancels the other, antagonizes the other or—as Stilling (1880) described it—destroys the other" (1964, p. 2). But this antagonism has also an aspect of reciprocal reinforcement, as Goethe long ago remarked: "Red and green (or yellow and blue), as he expressed it, demand each other at the same time; they promote each other, further each other" (ibid.).

In sum, the perceptual system of primitive hues can be described as follows: It is composed of two dyads of opposed colors, red-green and yellow-blue, and four dyads of compatible colors, red-yellow, red-blue, green-blue, and green-yellow. This is exactly the same system as is figured in the preceding diagram of semantic relationships (fig. 14). The claim is that such correspondence between symbolic and perceptual structures represents a mobilization of the latter in the project of the former.

In its economic dimension, this project consists of the reproduction of society in a system of objects not merely useful but meaningful; whose utility indeed consists of a significance. The clothing system in particular replicates for Western society the functions of the so-called totemism. A sumptuary materialization of the principal coordinates of person and occasion, it becomes a vast scheme of communication—such as to serve as a language of everyday life among those who may well have no prior intercourse of acquaintance.[30] "Mere appearance" must be one of the most important forms of symbolic statement in Western civilization. For it is by appearances that civilization turns the basic contradiction of its construction into a miracle of existence: a cohesive society of perfect strangers. But in the event, its cohesion depends on a *coherence* of specific kind: on the possibility of apprehending others, their social condition, and thereby their relation to oneself "on first glance." This dependence on seeing helps to explain, on one hand, why the symbolic dimensions have nevertheless not been obvious. The code works on an unconscious level, the conception built into perception itself. It is precisely the type of thought generally known as "savage"—thought that "does not distinguish the moment of observation and that of interpretation any more than, on observing them one first registers the interlocutor's signs and then tries to understand them; when he speaks, the signs expressed carry with them their meanings" (Lévi-Strauss 1966, p. 223). On the other hand, this dependence on the glance suggests the presence in the economic and social life of a logic completely foreign to the conventional "rationality." For rationality is time elapsed, a comparison: at least another glance beyond, and a weighing

---

30. "With briefest visual perception, a complex mental process is aroused, resulting within a very short time, 30 seconds perhaps [*sic*], in judgment of the sex, age, size, nationality, profession and social caste of the stranger together with some estimate of his temperament, his ascendence, friendliness, neatness; and even his trustworthiness" (G. Allport, cited in Horn 1968, p. 109; cf. Linton 1936, p. 416).

of the alternatives. The relation between logics is that the first, the symbolic, defines and ranks the alternatives by the ''choice'' among which rationality, oblivious of its own cultural basis, is pleased to consider itself as constituting.

5   Conclusion   Utility and the Cultural Order

In this chapter, I develop a few of the implications of the last, the excursion into capitalist economy as a cultural system, by placing it in the context of the preceding theoretical discussions. The summary successively addresses the general problem of symbolic and pragmatic interpretations of culture and the question, tabled at the beginning of the inquiry and unresolved to this point, of the distinctiveness of Western culture. The several programmatic suggestions and propositions developed here amount to the evident and first conclusions of the essay as a whole.

One evident matter—for bourgeois society as much as the so-called primitive—is that material aspects are not usefully separated from the social, as if the first were referable to the satisfaction of needs by the exploitation of nature, the second to problems of the relations between men. Having made such a fateful differentiation of cultural components— having dissociated the cultural order into subsystems of different purpose—we are forced to live forever with the intellectual consequences. That is, each "subsystem" is subjected initially to a different kind of analysis, in the terms of material and social properties, respectively, and then referred to a different teleo-logic: the articulation to nature in the service of a practical interest on one hand, the maintenance of order between persons and groups on the other. We would then be left with one type of problem, which has in fact haunted anthropology from the beginning; namely, how to account for the functional relations between aspects that had at first been conceived as distinct. Much of anthropology can be considered a sustained effort at synthesizing an original segmentation of its object, an analytic distinction of cultural domains it had made without due reflection, if clearly on the model presented by our own society. But the project was doomed from the beginning, because the very first act had consisted in ignoring the unity and distinctiveness of culture as a symbolic structure, hence the reason imposed from within on the relations to an external nature. The error was to surrender this reason to various practicalities and then be forced to decide how one set of requirements is reflected in the relations devoted to another—the economic to the social, the social to the ideational, the ideational to the economic. But it follows that a retotalization is not effected merely by considering material goods, for example, in the context of social relations. The unity of the cultural order is constituted by a third and common term, meaning. And it is this meaningful system that defines all functionality; that is, according to the particular structure and finalities of the cultural order. It follows that no functional explanation is ever sufficient by itself; for functional value is always relative to the given cultural scheme.

As a specific corollary: no cultural form can ever be read from a set of "material forces," as if the cultural were the dependent variable of an inescapable practical logic. The positivist explanation of given cultural practices as necessary effects of some material circumstance—such as a particular technique of production, a degree of productivity or productive diversity, an insufficiency of protein or a scarcity of manure—all such scientist propositions are false. This does not imply that we are forced to adopt an idealist alternative, conceiving culture as walking about on the thin air of symbols. It is not that the material forces and constraints are left out of account, or that they have no real effects on cultural order. It is that the nature of the effects cannot be read from the nature of the forces, for the material effects depend on their cultural encompassment. The very form of social existence of material force is determined by its integration in the cultural system. The force may then be significant—but significance, precisely, is a symbolic quality. At the same time, this symbolic scheme is not itself the mode of expression of an instrumental logic, for in fact there is no other logic in the sense of a meaningful order save that imposed by culture on the instrumental process.

The problem of historical materialism—a problem it shares with all naturalistic theories of culture—is that it accepts the practical interest as an intrinsic and self-explanatory condition, inherent in production and therefore inescapable in culture. For Marx, as we have seen, at the moment of production two logics are in play. The interaction of labor, techniques, and resources proceeds at once by the laws of nature and the intentions of culture: by the objective quantities and qualities and by the quantitative and qualitative objectives. But in the problematic of praxis, the symbolic logic is subordinated to the instrumental, within production and therefore throughout society. As the reason in production is a practical interest, the satisfaction of men's needs, it is of a piece with the natural process it sets in motion. Culture is organized in the final analysis by the material nature of things and cannot in its own conceptual or sociological differentiations transcend the reality structure manifested in production.

At first glance the confrontation of the cultural and material logics does seem unequal. The material process is factual and ''independent of man's will''; the symbolic, invented and therefore flexible. The one is fixed by nature, the other is arbitrary by definition. Thought can only kneel before the absolute sovereignty of the physical world. But the error consists in this: that there is no material logic apart from the practical interest, and the practical interest of men in production is symbolically constituted. The finalities as well as the modalities of production come from the cultural side: the material means of the cultural organization as well as the organization of the material means. We have seen that nothing in the way of their capacity to satisfy a material (biological) requirement can explain why pants are produced for men and skirts for women, or why dogs are inedible but the hindquarters of the steer are supremely satisfying of the need to eat. No more are the relations of production—the division of labor by culturally defined categories and capacities—deducible from materially determined categories and capacities of the population. It is imprecise to speak of a confrontation of *two* logics in production; logic is the property of conception alone, which has before it an inchoate force wanting in meaning or social content. The situation in culture in general is like that which Rousseau argued against Grotius and Hobbes—as well as Caligula—in respect of political institutions. Force is a physical attribute to which men must yield if they cannot do otherwise; but the question is, What makes submission a duty? To say that Might makes Right, Rousseau observed, is to mistake the cause for the effect. In the same way, the material forces in production contain no cultural order, but merely a set of physical possibilities and constraints selectively organized by the cultural system and integrated as to their effects by the same logic that gave them cause.

The material forces taken by themselves are lifeless. Their specific motions and determinate consequences can be stipulated only by progressively compounding them with the coordinates of the cultural order. Decompose the productive forces to their material specifications alone; suppose an industrial technology, a population of men, and an environment. Nothing is thereby said about the specific properties of the goods that will be produced, or about the rate of production or the relations under which the process shall proceed. An industrial technology in itself does not dictate whether it will be run by men or by women, in the day or at night, by wage laborers or by collective owners, on Tuesday or on Sunday, for a profit or for a livelihood; in the service of national security or private gluttony; to produce hand-fed dogs or stall-fed cattle, blue collars or white dresses; to pollute the rivers and infect the atmosphere or to itself slowly rust away like the Singer sewing machine posed majestically in front of the house of an African chief. If one further assumes a certain rate of production, as is given by the total relations of production, something more can be said about the required labor period, the character of cooperation, and the division of labor, including a hierarchical distinction between managerial and manual tasks. Still, if cooperation is required, it is not indicated that it shall exclude women; if a period of labor, not that it shall be on weekdays rather than weekends; if manager and worker, not that the former has the qualities of an entrepreneur or his agent and the latter those of a wage laborer. Add in private property and production for exchange-value; now the hierarchy becomes bourgeois and proletariat. Make the cultural distinctions of sex, ethnicity, and race, and the bourgeois in charge is likely to be a WASP male, the worker—also male—a black or a Pole. And so on. The material forces become so under the aegis of culture.

Do we neglect the play of purely natural forces, the biological necessities and the action of natural selection? Ecology, as we have noticed and everyone seems to agree, is brought into cultural play as a set of limit conditions, a range of tolerance in the exploitation of the environment or the satisfaction of biological requirements beyond which the system as constituted can no longer function—is "selected against." Yet it is insufficiently stressed in ecological studies that before there can be natural selection there is a cultural selection: of the relevant natural facts. Selection is not a simple natural process; it originates in a cultural structure, which by its own properties and finalities defines the environmental context specific to itself; decides, that is to say, the effective form and intensity of the selective forces. Even in biological studies, as Monod observes, this determination by the adapting organism is too often misrepresented as a purely environmental fact:

> Other difficulties about accepting the selective theory are to be traced to its having been too often understood or represented as placing the sole responsibility for selection upon conditions of the external environment. This is a completely mistaken conception. For the selective

pressures exerted by outside conditions upon organisms are in no case unconnected with the teleonomic [i.e., internal regulatory] performances characteristic of the species. Different organisms inhabiting the same ecological niche interact in very different and specific ways with outside conditions (among which one must include other organisms). The specific interactions, which the organism itself "elects," at least in part, determine the nature and orientation of the selective pressure the organism sustains. [Monod 1972 (1970), pp. 125–26]

At the same time, insofar as the environment is given effect by a cultural order, it is important to be precise about the character of the determinism attributable to selective conditions. "Adaptation" is invoked to explain the properties, persistence, or, most weakly, the mode of functioning of a cultural form. But selective advantage is a stipulation of minimum positive functioning: anything within the natural limits, anything that does not subject the people or the system to material destruction, is advantageous from the point of view of adaptation, just as a minimum significant advantage between species or societies decides any competitive struggle for resources. Beyond that, whether the positive functioning is optimal, minimal, or somewhere in between is a matter of indifference to nature. She rules only on the question of existence, not on specific form. Or to look at it the other way around, selection as a "limit of viability" is a negative determination, stipulating only what cannot be done, but licensing indiscriminately (selecting for) anything that is possible. So far as the definite properties of the cultural order are conceived, the laws of nature are indeterminate. For all their facticity and objectivity, the laws of nature stand to the order of culture as the abstract to the concrete: as the realm of possibility stands to the realm of necessity, as the given potentialities to the one realization, as survival is to actual being.

That is because nature is to culture as the constituted is to the constituting. Culture is not merely nature expressed in another form. Rather the reverse: the action of nature unfolds in the terms of culture; that is, in a form no longer its own but embodied as meaning. Nor is this a mere translation. The natural fact assumes a new mode of existence as a symbolized fact, its cultural deployment and consequence now governed by the relation between its meaningful dimension and other such meanings, rather than the relation between its natural dimension and other such facts. All of this of course within the material limits. But if nature "rigidly separated from man does not exist for man" (Marx), then the nature which does exist has surrendered its own reason in the combination. From the moment of cultural synthesis, the action of nature is mediated by a conceptual scheme "by the operation of which matter and form, neither with any independent existence, are realized as structures, that is as entities which are both empirical and intelligible" (Lévi-Strauss). Such being the fate of nature culturalized, nature as it exists in itself is only the raw material provided by the hand of God, waiting to be given meaningful shape and content by the mind of man. It is as the block of marble to the finished statue; and of course the genius of the sculptor—in the same way as the technical development of culture—consists in exploiting the lines of diffraction within the material to his own ends. That marble is refractory; there are certain things one cannot do with it—such are the facts of nature and the action of selection. But it is the sculptor who decides whether the statue is to be an equestrian knight contemplating his victories (and how many legs the horse has off the ground) or a seated Moses contemplating the sins of his people. And if it be objected that it is the composition of the marble which compels the form of the statue, it should not be forgotten that this block of marble was chosen from among all possible ones because the sculptor saw within it the latent image of his own project.

Too often, also, it is assumed that if "primitive" societies are not organized by a strict material rationality, at least we are. So far as concerns Western society, at least we are safe in the utilitarian postulates of practical interest first elaborated by economic science and applied thence to all domains of our social action. I have offered a brief analysis of food and clothing in America by way of a challenge to this conventional wisdom. The objects and persons of capitalist production are united in a system of symbolic valuations. But if our own economy does not elude the human condition, if capitalism too is a symbolic process, wherein lies the uniqueness of Western "civilizations"?

Perhaps in nothing so much as the illusion that it is otherwise—that the economy and society are pragmatically constructed. Yet the situation is not so simple, for even the illusion has a material basis. One could not have failed to notice from our brief sketch of the American clothing system that many of the main symbolic distinctions in the clothing object follow upon the organization of production. If weekend clothes differ from weekday, night from day, downtown from uptown, men's clothes from women's, not to mention the various forms of business and work clothes, the difference is made in every case along the lines of economic relations. One might say that if production reflects the general scheme of society, it is looking at itself in a mirror. But it is saying the same thing, and in a way that does not neglect the understanding of our own system already achieved while opening a comparison with others, to observe that in Western culture the economy is the main site of symbolic production. For us the production of goods is at the same time the privileged mode of symbolic production and transmission. The uniqueness of bourgeois society consists not in the fact that the economic system escapes symbolic determination, but that the economic symbolism is structurally determining.

What I am suggesting is another way of thinking about the cultural design, instead of the received division into component purposive systems, economy, society, and ideology, or infrastructure and superstructure, each composed of distinct kinds of relations and objectives, and the whole hierarchically arranged according to analytic presuppositions of functional dominance and functional necessity. Instead, we ought to have a perspective that reflects the long-standing anthropological appreciation of the diversity of cultural emphases, if made more precise by the understanding, also long-standing, that these represent differing institutional integrations of the symbolic scheme. Here the economy appears dominant, all other activities reflecting in their own categories the modalities of production relations; there everything seems "bathed in a celestial light" of religious conceptions. In other words, the cultural scheme is variously inflected by a dominant site of symbolic production, which supplies the major idiom of other relations and activities. One can thus speak of a privileged institutional locus of the symbolic process, whence emanates a classificatory grid imposed upon the total culture. And speaking still at this high level of abstraction, the peculiarity of Western culture is the institutionalization of the process in and as the production of goods, by comparison with a "primitive" world where the locus of symbolic differentiation remains social relations, principally kinship relations, and other spheres of activity are ordered by the operative distinctions of kinship. We have to do not so much with functional dominance as with structural—with different structures of symbolic integration. And to this gross difference in design correspond differences in symbolic performance: between an open, expanding code, responsive by continuous permutation to events it has itself staged, and an apparently static one that seems to know not events, but only its own preconceptions. The gross distinction is between "hot" societies and "cold," development and underdevelopment, societies "with" and "without" history—and so between large societies and small, expanding and self-contained, colonizing and colonized.

I stress that the comparison is a crude one, the singling out of a polar contrast, without any intention of proposing a typology of the cultures of the world. Even at the level of gross comparison, one neglects the large category of "lukewarm" archaic civilizations (cf. de Heusch 1971), with a dominant symbolic focus in the state-religious sector, which penetrates decisively into the economy and the agricultural-peasant hinterlands. Nor is any implication here intended or denied with respect to contemporary socialist societies. Permit me merely the broad contrast of Western and "tribal"; it could prove useful to the objectives of finer classification, and above all to the self-awareness of capitalist society.

What I am trying to get at is a difference between bourgeois and primitive society in the nature and productivity of the symbolic process, which is the counterpart of a variance in institutional design. With respect to the last, one rehearses the well-known, for the distinctive quality of Western civilization at the level of institutional structure has been remarked at least since Marx, and of primitive society at least since anthropology. The former is characterized by the structural separation of functional spheres—economic, social-political, and ideological—severally organized as special-purpose systems by particular kinds of social relations (market, state, church, etc.). Since the objectives and relations of each subsystem are distinct, each has a certain internal logic and a relative autonomy. But since all are subordinated to the requirements of the economy, this gives credibility to the kind of reflectionist theory which perceives in the superstructure the differentiations (notably of class) established in production and exchange. In primitive society, economic, political, and ritual action are organized by the one generalized kinship structure. Anthropologists, therefore, especially the British social anthropologists, have tended to posit a different kind of structural dominance for this type of society: one which would see in politics, ritual, or the economy the reflection of relations between persons and groups and the exigencies of maintaining these relations. My point is not that these observations have been incorrect. On the contrary, they are essential, and no structuralist or symbolist analysis is entitled to ignore the differences in institutional design. For they correspond to different modes of symbolic production, contrasting both in objective medium and in dynamic capacity.

The two cultural orders elevate certain institutional relations to a position of dominance, as the site from which the symbolic grid is precipitated and the code objectified. In bourgeois society, material production is the dominant locus of symbolic production; in primitive society it is the set of social (kinship) relations. In the Western plan, the relations of production constitute a classification reiterated throughout the entire cultural scheme, inasmuch as the distinctions of persons, time, space, and occasion developed in production are communicated throughout, to kinship, politics, and the rest, despite the discontinuities in institutional quality. At the same time, as the accumulation of exchange-value proceeds by way of use-value, capitalist production develops a symbolic code, figured as the meaningful differences between products, which serves as a general scheme of social classification. And this economic integration of the whole, the transmission of both grid and code, social differentiation and objective contrast, is assured by the market mechanism—for everyone must buy and sell to live, but they can do so only to the extent that they are empowered by their relations to production.

Let us begin an explication of the cultural differences by consideration of the type of code, as this follows from and sums up the earlier discussions. We commence then with a fundamental similarity: that capitalist production is as much as any other economic system a cultural specification and not merely a natural-material activity; for as it is the means of a total mode of life it is necessarily the production of symbolic significance. Nevertheless, because it appears to the producer as a quest for pecuniary gain, and to the consumer as an acquisition of "useful" goods, the basic symbolic character of the process goes on entirely behind the backs of the participants—and usually of economists as well, insofar as the meaningful structure of demand is an exogenous "given" of their analyses. The differentiation of symbolic value is mystified as the appropriation of exchange-value. But it is not enough to demystify: the anthropological point is that in the bourgeois system there is indeed no difference between the two, because the logic of production is a differential logic of cultural meanings.

The reasoning is simple and violates no conventional understanding of the capitalist process. The accumulation of exchange-value is always the creation of use-value. The goods must sell, which is to say that they must have a preferred "utility," real or imagined—but always imaginable—for someone. In an article entitled "Symbols by Which We Buy," S. J. Levy writes: "Buridan's ass starved to death equidistant between two piles of attractive hay; he wouldn't have had the problem if one pile had been a bit more asinine" (1968, p. 56).[1] Production for gain is the production of a

---

1. Compare the economist's "utility" with C. S. Peirce's general notion of the sign as "something which stands to somebody for something in some respect or capacity" (1932, chap. 2, p. 228).

symbolically significant difference; in the case of the consumer market, it is the production of an appropriate social distinction by way of concrete contrast in the object. The point is implicit in the apparent ambiguity of the term "value," which may refer to the price of something or the meaning of something (as the differential concept of a word), or in general to that which people hold "dear," either morally or monetarily. Anthropologists, incidentally, are quite familiar with this ambiguity, if not always entirely conscious of it, since many adopt it to illustrate the universality of rational economic behavior—even where market exchange is specifically absent. The people are nevertheless economizing their resources; it's just that they are interested in "values" other than the material—brotherhood for example.

But the same connection is made more effectively by Saussure, in a passage which deserves the place in the study of Western economy that is accorded in the anthropological economics to the famous text of the Maori sage Tamati Ranapiri on the *hau* of the gift (Mauss 1966 [1923–24]).[2] Just as Ranapiri's remarks revealed that for the Maori a ritual construction has its counterpart in a material exchange, so Saussure's text, by its use of exchange-value to illustrate the conceptual value of the sign, must suggest to an unsuspecting Western world that its ostensible quest for the material is mediated by the symbolic:

all values are apparently governed by the same paradoxical principle. They are always composed:
(1) of a *dissimilar* thing that can be exchanged for the thing of which the value is to be determined; and
(2) of *similar* things that can be *compared* with the thing of which the value is to be determined.
Both factors are necessary for the existence of a value. To determine what a five-franc piece is worth one must therefore know: (1) that it can be exchanged for a fixed quantity of a different thing, e.g., bread; and (2) that it can be compared with a similar value of the same system, e.g., a one-franc piece, or with coins of another system (a dollar, etc.). In the same way a word can be exchanged for something dissimilar, an idea; besides, it can be compared with something of the same nature, another word. Its value is therefore not fixed so long as

2. See the interpretation in Sahlins 1972. I take the opportunity to repeat here a point made to me independently by Gayle Rubin and Lawrence Adelson that the common referent of the constraint of the *hau* in ritual and material exchange is the one gift that is both fertile and must be reciprocated: women. Moreover, the structure of the transaction is one of "generalized exchange," which is a background structure in many Polynesian societies.

one simply states that it can be "exchanged" for a given concept, i.e., that it has this or that signification: one must compare it with similar values, with other words that stand in opposition to it. Its content is really fixed only by the concurrence of everything that exists outside it. . . . Instead of pre-existing ideas then, we find in all the foregoing examples *values* emanating from the system. When they are said to correspond to concepts, it is understood that the concepts are purely differential and defined not by their positive content but negatively by their relations with other terms in the system. Their most precise characteristic is in being what the others are not. [Saussure 1966 (1915), pp. 115, 117]

Just so, exchange-value is acquired by producing objects that are not the same as other products: objects that have a differential meaning in the society as organized—Cadillacs as opposed to Chevrolets, suits as opposed to overalls, steak as opposed to entrails. Rational production for gain is in one and the same motion the production of symbols. And its acceleration, as in opening up new consumer markets, is exactly the same as opening up the symbolic set by a permutation of its logic; because, (1) in order to be exchanged for something else (money), the goods produced must (2) contrast in one or another original property with all other goods of the same general kind. The peculiarity of this bourgeois totemism perhaps lies merely in its *sauvagerie*. For by the development of market-industrial production, that is, the institutional dominance given to the economy, the traditional functional relation between the cultural series and the natural series is today reversed: rather than serving the differentiation of society by a differentiation of objects, every conceivable distinction of society is put to the service of another declension of objects. Fetishism and totemism: the most refined creations of the civilized mind.

The second indicative characteristic of economic dominance: the relations of production compose the main classificatory grid for Western society. Mauss wrote of the *hau* as if the exchange of things were by Maori conceptions the exchange of persons, even as Marx observed rather the opposite of our own thinking: the bond of persons is a relation between things (cf. White 1959*b*, pp. 242–45). If, as is frequently noticed of "primitive" exchange, every transaction has a social coefficient, a relationship between the participants of one kind or another that regulates the material terms of their interaction, of ourselves it seems true that every transaction has a material term that supplies important dimensions of the social relationship. Even apart from business dealing, in what is sometimes called "life" as opposed to "work"—in the association of neighbors, the membership of a church, a country club, or a Friday-night poker game—there enters a decisive economic element: a reflection, direct or indirect but always essential, of the relations of production. And note that it is not just the condition of income which comes into play, but a determination of time which likewise develops from the structure of production, and a similarly generated specification of space. Moreover, no institution, however ordered by other principles or oriented to other purposes, is immune from such structuration by the economic forces. The domestic realm is as much determined by negation of the workaday world as by intrinsic kinship conceptions. Its internal organization, as is well known, varies by economic class, and the relations between husband and wife are generally saturated by the economic distinction between "breadwinner" and "dependent." In the tribal design the several functional moments, including production, are decisively ordered by kinship standing, such that the classification germane to any particular activity represents some transposition of the scheme operative in kinship. But money is to the West what kinship is to the Rest. It is the nexus that assimilates every other relation to standing in production. "Money greed, or mania for wealth," Marx wrote, "necessarily brings with it the decline and fall of the ancient communities. Hence it is the antithesis to them. It is itself the community [*Gemeinwesen*], and can tolerate none other standing above it" (1973 [1857–58], p. 223).

Thus does the economy, as the dominant institutional locus, produce not only objects for appropriate subjects, but subjects for appropriate objects. It throws a classification across the entire cultural superstructure, ordering the distinctions of other sectors by the oppositions of its own—precisely as it uses these distinctions for purposes of its own (gain). It effects what might be called "symbolic synapses."[3] conjunctions of oppositions from distinct cultural planes which thus take the form of homologous differentiations—such as work/leisure:weekday/weekend; or downtown/uptown:impersonality/familiarity. Certain of these proportions are clearly constructed by analogy, as the clothing combination adolescent/adult:worker/capitalist. But if they embody logical processes and are used to think (therefore to be in) the cultural world, still they cannot be considered unmotivated, the product of a pure speculative interest. They

---

3. Such synapses are the logical product of what James Boon has designated "action values" in a paper (1972) which attempts to isolate the actual moment—the "Traviata moment" it might be called from his excellent example—of the unison of meanings from formally distinct codes.

suppose—perhaps only in an unconscious way—connections that are already present in the social life. They already exist in the social praxis.

This last point is important in two ways. The first we had already remarked in the context of tribal society, but it is worth reiterating of the "civilized" concrete thought: the interest taken in such conceptual correspondences as worker/capitalist:youth/adult is in no way an idealism. Their recognition by the anthropologist or economist, like their existence in the society, reflects a real experience of that society—if always the only kind of real social experience, namely, that mediated symbolically. The anthropologist did not put them there, any more than the people just made them up and thereupon decided to live by them. They are the true armature of the cultural order, and the anthropologist in arranging them in a way faithful to experience does no more than discover that order. In doing so—and this is the second implication—he acts in something of the same way as a market researcher, an advertising agent, or a fashion designer, unflattering as the comparison might be. For these hucksters of the symbol do not create de novo. In the nervous system of the American economy, theirs is the synaptic function. It is their role to be sensitive to the latent correspondences in the cultural order whose conjunction in a product-symbol may spell mercantile success (fig. 15).

Or perhaps more frequently, theirs is to respond to the ceaseless reformulation of symbolic relations within the national social life. Such change proceeds, on one side, from constant revision of the economic grid, changes in the structure of production which impose new coordinates on other social relationships. This revision of the grid of course reflects the power of an industrial productivity—given the distribution of income predicated on relations of production—to saturate a symbolic correspondence by an appropriate product, and the consequent movement of capital toward a new differentiation of symbolic value in pursuit of greater exchange-value. On the other hand, reformulation of the symbolic correspondences may be initiated from the opposite direction: from events unfolding in superstructural spheres—wars, a new radical movement, an increase in the divorce rate, a return to religion—such as alter the context of production. We think of these as a kind of cultural climate, just as we think of designers as plucking their ideas out of thin air. But the fashion expert does not make his collection out of whole cloth; like Lévi-Strauss's famous bricoleur, he uses bits and pieces with an embedded significance from a previous existence to create an object that works, which is to say that sells—which is also to say that objectively synthesizes a relation between cultural categories, for in that lies its salability.

Figure 15   The sexing of objects in advertising display. Advice to
advertisers from Stephen Baker, *Visual Persuasion*
(1961).

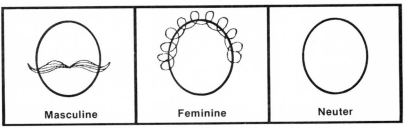

Masculine   **Feminine**   **Neuter**

Almost every object has a "sex" of its own. This fact is important to keep in mind when choosing
symbols or props for an illustration.

Potato   **Tomato**   **Apple**

The rough texture of a potato helps make it a masculine article. A tomato, soft and pretty, has become a symbol of femininity. An apple has no sex (it grows on "masculine" trees, but in the Bible it
served as a symbol of feminine beguilement).

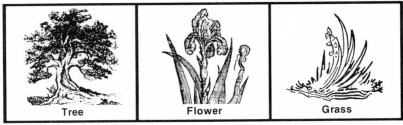

Tree   **Flower**   **Grass**

Trees (and wooden textures) reek of masculinity. Delicacy of flowers (and girls' liking for them)
assures their place in a woman's domain. Grass, on the other hand, has no claim to any particular
gender.

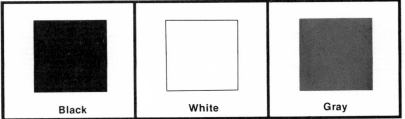

Black   **White**   **Gray**

Black has strength and opacity. These qualities make it appear more masculine than feminine. The
translucency of white (and its virginal quality) gives it a maidenly appearance. Gray is in between and
therefore neuter.

| Train | Ship | Automobile |

A train is a "he." It suggests power, adventure, energy. A ship, by virtue of its sleek, graceful appearance, has managed to become a "she." The car used to be more masculine than feminine, but in this modern world it is rapidly becoming bisexual.

| Wool | Silk | Cotton |

Wool (tweedy textures) is associated more with men's suits than ladies' dresses. Silk has a different connotation altogether; its softness and pliability make it more "feminine." Cotton can be either gender.

| Dog | Cat | Horse |

A dog is usually "he." A cat—characteristically a calculating animal—is "she." Both looks and personalities give these creatures a "sex" of their own. A horse can be "he" or "she," depending on the anatomy.

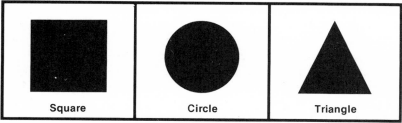

| Square | Circle | Triangle |

The harsh, angular edges of square objects (as shown on previous page) suggest masculine temper while the round shape of a circle implies the gentleness of a woman. A triangle stands undecided.

We arrive thus at a final distinguishing quality of Western civilization: that it responds transformationally to events, incorporates historical perturbations as structural permutations, according to a general code of significance. It is important to stress, however, that this is a quantitative difference within a qualitative identity. History is always structured by society; there are only more or less dynamic modes of effecting this. Nor do the principles of historical structuration differ so much in kind as in locus. The tribal peoples are capable of the very same transpositions and reformulations of the symbolic code, the generation of new oppositions out of old—only there it goes on mainly between societies and so appears as simple variation, whereas here it goes on within the one system and thus presents a compounded growth ("development"). History there takes place at the juncture of societies, such that an entire culture area may present a marvelous set of variations, in base as well as superstructure, of societies, "all of them similar, but none the same, whose chorus points the way to a hidden law." For us, by virtue of a different institutional mode of the symbolic process, history is enlisted, in basically the same ways, but in the complication of the one society.

In its reliance upon symbolic reason, however, our culture is not radically different from that elaborated by the "savage mind." We are just as logical, philosophical, and meaningful as they are. And however unaware of it, we give to the qualitative logic of the concrete as decisive a place. Still, we speak as if we had rid ourselves of constraining cultural conceptions, as if our culture were constructed out of the "real" activities and experiences of individuals rationally bent upon their practical interests. The final alienation is a kind of de-structuration. Marx wrote that primitive society could not exist unless it disguised to itself the real basis of that existence, as in the form of religious illusions. But the remark may be truer of bourgeois society. Everything in capitalism conspires to conceal the symbolic ordering of the system—especially those academic theories of praxis by which we conceive ourselves and the rest of the world. A praxis theory based on pragmatic interests and "objective" conditions is the secondary form of a cultural illusion, and its elaborate empirical and statistical offspring, the "etic" investigations of our social sciences, the intellectual titillation of an "emic" mystification.

What is finally distinctive of Western civilization is the mode of symbolic production, this very disguise in the form of a growing GNP of the process by which symbolic value is created. But such institutionalization of the symbolic process only makes it more elaborate, as well as less subject to control and more dangerous. More elaborate because it encourages all the human capacities of symbolic manipulation within a single social order, and thus generates an enormous cultural growth. More dangerous, then, because in the interest of this growth it does not hesitate to destroy any other form of humanity whose difference from us consists in having discovered not merely other codes of existence but ways of achieving an end that still eludes us: the mastery by society of society's mastery over nature.

References

Agee, James, and
Walker, Evans

1941. *Let us now praise famous men.* Boston: Houghton Mifflin.

Althusser, Louis

1969. *Montesquieu: La politique et l'histoire.* Paris: Presses Universitaires de France.

1970 [1965]. *For Marx.* New York: Random House, Vintage Books.

Althusser, Louis, and
Balibar, Etienne

1970 [1968]. *Reading Capital.* New York: Pantheon Books.

Arnheim, Rudolf

1974. *Art and visual perception* (new version). Berkeley: University of California Press.

Avineri, Shlomo

1971. *The social and political thought of Karl Marx.* Cambridge: Cambridge University Press.

Baker, Stephen

1961. *Visual persuasion.* New York: McGraw-Hill.

Barthes, Roland

1961. Pour une psycho-sociologie de l'alimentation contemporaine. *Annales,* pp. 977–86.

1967. *Système de la mode.* Paris: Seuil.

1970 [1964]. *Elements of semiology.* Printed as *Writing degree zero and elements of semiology.* Boston: Beacon Press.

Bateson, Gregory

1958. *Naven.* 2d ed. Stanford: Stanford University Press.

1972. *Steps to an ecology of mind.* New York: Ballantine.

Baudrillard, Jean

1968. *Le système des objets.* Paris: Denoël-Gonthier.

1970. *La société de consommation.* Paris: S.G.P.P.

1972. *Pour une critique de l'économie politique du signe.* Paris: Gallimard.

223

Bauman, Zygmunt   1973. *Culture as praxis.* London: Routledge and
                             Kegan Paul.

Benedict, Ruth   1961 [1934]. *Patterns of culture.* Boston:
                             Houghton Mifflin.

Benveniste, Emile   1969. *Le vocabulaire des institutions indo-
                             européenes. Vol. 1. Economie, parenté, societé.*
                             Paris: Editions de Minuit.

                             1971. *Problems in general linguistics.* Coral
                             Gables: University of Miami Press.

Berger, Peter L., and   1967. *The social construction of reality.* Garden
Luckman, Thomas   City: Doubleday, Anchor Books.

Berlin, Brent, and   1969. *Basic color terms.* Berkeley: University of
Kay, Paul   California Press.

Bernstein, Richard J.   1971. *Praxis and action.* Philadelphia: University
                             of Pennsylvania Press.

Bidwell, Shelford   1899. *Curiosities of light and sight.* London:
                             Swan Sonnenschein.

Biersack, Aletta   1974. Matrilineality in patrilineal systems: The
                             Tongan case. Paper submitted in candidacy for
                             the Ph.D. in anthropology, University of Michigan.

Birren, Faber   1956. *Selling color to people.* New York:
                             University Books.

                             1961. *Color psychology and color therapy.* New
                             York: University Books.

Boas, Franz   1965 [1938]. *The mind of primitive man.* New
                             York: Free Press.

                             1966a [1911]. *Introduction to handbook of
                             American Indian languages,* published with J. W.
                             Powell, *Indian linguistic families of America north
                             of Mexico,* ed. Preston Holder. Lincoln: University
                             of Nebraska Press.

                             1966b [1940]. *Race, language, and culture.*
                             New York: Free Press.

Bogatyrev, Peter   1971 [1937]. *The functions of folk costume in
                             Moravian Slovakia.* Mouton: The Hague.

Bohannan, Paul   1955. Some principles of exchange and invest-
                             ment among the Tiv. *American Anthropologist*
                             57:60–70.

Boon, James   1972. Further operations of "culture" in anthro-
                             pology: A synthesis of and for debate. *Social
                             Science Quarterly* 52:221–52.

Boon, James, A., and Schneider, David M.
1974. Kinship vis-à-vis myth: Contrasts in Lévi-Strauss' approaches to cross-cultural comparison. *American Anthropologist* 76:794–817.

Bott, Elizabeth
1972. Psychoanalysis and ceremony and a rejoinder to Edmund Leach, in *The interpretation of ritual,* ed. J. S. La Fontaine, pp. 205–37, 277–82. London: Tavistock.

Bourdieu, P.
1971. La maison Kabyle ou le monde renversé. In *Echanges et communications: Mélanges offerts à Lévi-Strauss,* ed. P. Maranda and J. Pouillon, pp. 739–58. Paris: Mouton.

Braidwood, Robert J.
1957. *Prehistoric man.* 3d ed. Chicago Natural History Museum Popular Series, Anthropology, no. 37.

Bulmer, R.
1967. Why is the cassowary not a bird? A problem of zoological taxonomy among the Karam of the New Guinea highlands. *Man,* n.s., 2:5–25.

Cassirer, Ernst
1933. Le langage et la construction du monde des objets. *Journal de Psychologie Normale et Pathologique* 30:18–44.

1951 [1932]. *The philosophy of the Enlightenment.* Princeton: Princeton University Press.

Charbonnier, G.
1969. *Conversations with Lévi-Strauss.* London: Jonathan Cape.

Collins, Paul W., and Vayda, Andrew P.
1969. Functional analysis and its aims. *Australian and New Zealand Journal of Sociology* 5:153–56.

Conklin, Harold C.
1955. Hanunóo color categories. *Southwestern Journal of Anthropology* 4:339–44.

Cook, Scott
1974. "Structural substantivism": A critical review of Marshall Sahlins' *Stone Age Economics. Comparative Studies in Society and History* 16: 355–79.

Corney, Peter
1896 [1821]. *Voyages in the Northern Pacific.* Honolulu: Thos. G. Thrum.

Cornforth, Maurice
1971 [1963]. *The theory of knowledge.* 3d ed. New York: International Publishers.

Crawley, Ernest
1931. *Dress, drinks, and drums.* London: Methuen.

Cunningham, Clark E.
1973. Order in the Atoni house. In *Right and Left,* ed. R. Needham, pp. 204–38. Chicago: University of Chicago Press.

Dampier, Robert

1971. *To the Sandwich Islands on the H.M.S. Blonde.* Honolulu: University of Hawaii Press.

Deane, Rev. W.

1921. *Fijian society.* London: Macmillan.

Dichter, Ernest

1959. *The strategy of desire.* Garden City, New York: Doubleday.

Dornstreich, Mark O., and Morren, George E. B.

1974. Does New Guinea cannibalism have nutritional value? *Human Ecology* 2(1):1–2.

Doroszewski, W.

1933. Quelques remarques sur les rapports de la sociologie et de la linguistique: Durkheim et F. de Saussure. *Journal de Psychologie* 30: 82–91.

Douglas, Mary

1966. *Purity and danger.* London: Routledge and Kegan Paul.

1971. Deciphering a meal. In *Myth, symbol, and culture,* ed. Clifford Geertz. New York: Norton.

1973*a*. Self-evidence. *Proceedings of the Royal Anthropological Institute of Great Britain and Ireland for 1972,* pp. 27–43.

1973*b*. *Rules and meanings.* Harmondsworth, Middlesex: Penguin Books.

1973*c*. *Natural symbols.* New York: Random House, Vintage Books.

Dumont, Louis

1965. The modern conception of the individual: Notes on its genesis. *Contributions to Indian Sociology* 8:13–61.

1970 [1966]. *Homo hierarchicus.* Chicago: University of Chicago Press.

Durkheim, Emile

1886. Revue générale: Les études de science sociale. *Révue Philosophique de la France et de l'Etranger* 22:61–80.

1887. La science positive de la morale en Allemagne. *Révue Philosophique de la France et de l'Etranger* 24:33–58, 113–42, 275–84.

1912. *Les formes élémentaires de la vie religieuse.* Paris: Alcan.

1947 [1912]. *The elementary forms of the religious life.* Glencoe, Ill.: Free Press.

1949 [1893]. *The division of labor in society.* Glencoe, Ill.: Free Press.

1950*a* [1895]. *The rules of the sociological method.* Glencoe, Ill.: Free Press.

1950*b* [1895]. *Les règles de la méthode socio-logique.* Paris: Presses Universitaires de France.

1951. *Sociologie et philosophie.* Paris: Presses Universitaires de France.

1960 [1914]. The dualism of human nature and its social conditions. In *Emile Durkheim,* ed. Kurt H. Wolff, pp. 325–40. Columbus: Ohio State University Press.

1965. *Montesquieu and Rousseau.* Ann Arbor: University of Michigan Press, Ann Arbor Paperbacks.

Durkheim, Emile, and Mauss, Marcel

1963 [1901–2]. *Primitive classification.* London: Cohen and West.

Engels, Frederick

1940 [1927]. *Dialectics of nature.* New York: International Publishers. (Written mainly between 1872 and 1882.)

1972 [1891]. *The origin of the family, private property and the state,* ed. Eleanor Burke Leacock. New York: International Publishers.

Epistemon

1968. *Ces idées qui ont ébranlé la France.* Paris: Fayard.

Evans-Pritchard, E. E.

1937. *Witchcraft, oracles and magic among the Azande.* Oxford: Clarendon Press.

1940. *The Nuer.* Oxford: Clarendon Press.

1954. *Social anthropology.* Glencoe, Ill.: Free Press.

Firth, Raymond

1963. *Elements of social organization.* Boston: Beacon Press.

1965. *Primitive Polynesian economy.* 2d ed. London: Routledge and Kegan Paul.

1972. The sceptical anthropologist: Social anthropology and Marxist views on society. *Proceedings of the British Academy* 18:3–39.

Fortes, Meyer

1945. *The dynamics of clanship among the Tallensi.* London: Oxford University Press.

1949. *The web of kinship among the Tallensi.* London: Oxford University Press.

1957. Malinowski and the study of kinship. In *Man and culture,* ed. R. Firth, pp. 157–88. New York: Humanities Press.

1969. *Kinship and the social order.* Chicago: Aldine.

Fox, Robin — 1967. *Kinship and marriage.* Harmondsworth, Middlesex: Penguin Books.

Friedman, Jonathan — 1974. Marxism, structuralism, and vulgar materialism. *Man,* n.s., 444–69.

Furet, François — 1967. A report on the French Left: from Marxism to structuralism. *Dissent* (March–April), pp. 220–33.

Gaboriau, Marc — 1970 [1963]. Structural anthropology and history. In *Structuralism: A reader,* ed. Michael Lane, pp. 156–69, London: Jonathan Cape.

Garaudy, Roger — 1965. Structuralisme et "Mort de l'homme." *Pensée,* no. 135 (Oct.), pp. 107–24.

Geertz, Clifford — 1973. *The interpretation of cultures.* New York: Basic Books.

Gifford, Edward — 1924. *Tongan myths and tales.* Bernice P. Bishop Museum Bulletin no. 8.

1929. *Tongan society.* Bernice P. Bishop Museum Bulletin no. 61.

Gilson, Richard P. — 1963. Samoan descent groups. *Journal of the Polynesian Society* 72:372–77.

Godelier, Maurice — 1972 [1966]. *Rationality and irrationality in economics.* London: NLB.

1973. *Horizon, trajets marxistes en anthropologie.* Paris: Maspero.

Graves, Maitland — 1951. *The art of color and design.* New York: McGraw-Hill.

Gregory, R. L. — 1966. *Eye and brain.* New York: McGraw-Hill.

Greimas, A. J. — 1966. Structure et histoire. *Les Temps Modernes,* no. 246 (Nov.), pp. 815–27.

Groves, Murray — 1963. The nature of Fijian society. *Journal of the Polynesian Society* 72:272–291.

Habermas, Jurgen — 1971. *Knowledge and human interests.* Boston: Beacon Press.

Harris, Marvin — 1968. *The rise of anthropological theory.* New York: Crowell.

Hart, Keith — In press. The development of patrilineal institutions in an open economy: Tallensi 1900–1970. *Proceedings of the Internal Congress of Economic Anthropology,* Florence.

Henson, Hilary — 1974. *British social anthropologists and language.* Oxford: Clarendon Press.

Hering, Ewald — 1964 [1920]. *Outlines of a theory of the light sense.* Cambridge: Harvard University Press.

Heusch, Luc de — 1971. *Pourquoi l'épouser?* Paris: Gallimard.

Hocart, A. M. — 1915. Chieftainship and the sister's son in the Pacific. *American Anthropologist* 17:631–46.

1929. *Lau Islands, Fiji.* Bernice P. Bishop Museum Bulletin no. 62.

1952. *The northern states of Fiji.* London: Royal Anthropological Institute, Occasional Publication no. 11.

1970 [1936]. *Kings and Councillors: An essay in the comparative anatomy of human society,* ed. Rodney Needham. Chicago: University of Chicago Press.

Horn, Marilyn J. — 1968. *The second skin: An interdisciplinary study of clothing.* Boston: Houghton Mifflin.

Huntsman, Judith W. — 1971. Concepts of kinship and categories of kinsmen in the Tokelau Islands. *Journal of the Polynesian Society* 80:317–54.

Hurvich, Leo M. — 1960. The opponent-process scheme. In *Mechanisms of color discrimination,* ed. Y. Galifret, pp. 199–212, New York: Pergamon Press.

Hurvich, Leo M., and Jameson, Dorothea — 1957. An opponent-process theory of color vision. *Psychological Review* 4:384–404.

Jameson, Frederic — 1972. *The prison house of language.* Princeton, Princeton University Press.

Jarré, Raymond — 1946. Marriage et naissance chez les Fidjiens de Kadavu. *Journal de la Société des Océanistes* 2(2):79–92.

Jarvie, I. C. — 1969 [1967]. *The revolution in anthropology.* Chicago: Regnery.

Kaeppler, Adrienne L. — 1971. Rank in Tonga. *Ethnology* 10:174–93.

Kamakau, Samuel M. — 1964. *Ka Po'e Kahiko: The people of old.* Bernice P. Bishop Museum Special Publication 51.

Kelly, Raymond C. — 1968. Demographic pressure and descent group structure in the New Guinea highlands. *Oceania* 39:36–63.

Kinter, Minnie — 1940. Color trends in daytime dresses, 1935–39. M.S. diss., Home Economics and Household Administration, University of Chicago. (Available at University of Chicago Libraries.)

Kolakowski, Leszek   1969. *Toward a Marxist humanism.* New York: Grove Press.

Krader, Lawrence   1972. Introduction to *The ethnological notebooks of Karl Marx,* ed. L. Krader. Assen: Van Gorcum.

1973*a*. Karl Marx as ethnologist. *Transactions of the New York Academy of Sciences,* ser. 2, 35(4):304–13.

1973*b*. The works of Marx and Engels in ethnology compared. *International Review of Social History* 18:223–75.

Kroeber, A. L.   1948. *Anthropology.* New York: Harcourt, Brace.

Kuper, Adam   1973. *Anthropologists and anthropology: The British school 1922–1972.* New York: Pica Press.

Langer, Susanne   1957. *Philosophy in a new key.* 3d ed. Cambridge: Harvard University Press.

Leach, E. R.   1951. The structural implications of matrilineal cross-cousin marriage. *Journal of the Royal Anthropological Institute* 81:23–55.

1954. *Political systems of highland Burma.* Cambridge: Harvard University Press.

1957. The epistemological background to Malinowski's empiricism." In *Man and culture,* ed. R. Firth, pp. 119–38. New York: Humanities Press.

1960. The Sinhalese of the dry zone of northern Ceylon. In *Social structure in southeast Asia,* ed. G. P. Murdock, pp. 116–26. Viking Fund Publications in Anthropology, no. 29. Chicago: Quadrangle Books.

1964. Anthropological aspects of language: animal categories and verbal abuse. In *New directions in the study of language,* ed. Eric H. Lenneberg, pp. 23–63. Cambridge: MIT Press.

1966. *Rethinking anthropology.* London School of Economics Monographs on Social Anthropology no. 22 (corrected paperback edition).

1970. *Claude Lévi-Strauss.* New York: Viking.

1972. The structure of symbolism. In *The interpretation of ritual,* ed. J. S. La Fontaine, pp. 239–75, 283–84. London: Tavistock.

Lee, Richard B., and DeVore, Irven, eds.   1968. *Man the hunter.* Chicago: Aldine.

Lenin, V. I.	1972 [1920]. *Materialism and empirio-criticism.* Peking: Foreign Languages Press.
Lester, R. H.	1939–40. Betrothal and marriage customs of Mbau, Fiji. *Oceania* 10:273–85.
Lévi-Strauss, Claude	1963*a. Totemism.* Boston: Beacon Press.
	1963*b. Structural anthropology.* New York: Basic Books.
	1965. *Tristes tropiques.* New York: Atheneum.
	1966. *The savage mind.* Chicago: University of Chicago Press.
	1969 [1967]. *The elementary structures of kinship.* Rev. ed. London: Eyre and Spottiswoode.
	1971. *L'homme nu.* Paris: Plon.
	1972. Structuralism and ecology. *Barnard Alumnae* (Spring 1972), pp. 63–14.
	1973. Religion, langue et histoire: A propos d'un texte inédit de Ferdinand de Saussure." In *Méthodologie de l'histoire et des sciences humains* (Mélanges en l'honneur de Fernand Braudel), pp. 325–33. Paris: Privat.
Levy, Sidney	1968. Symbols by which we buy. In *Consumer behavior,* ed. James F. Engel. Homewood, Ill.: Irwin.
Linksz, Arthur	1952. *Physiology of the eye: Vol. 2. Vision.* New York: Grune and Stratton.
	1964. *An essay on color vision and clinical color-vision tests.* New York: Grune and Stratton.
Linton, Ralph	1936. *The study of man.* New York: Appleton-Century.
Livergood, Norman D.	1967. *Activity in Marx's philosophy.* The Hague: Martinus Hijhoff.
Lukács, Georg	1971. *History and class consciousness.* Cambridge: MIT Press.
Lukes, Steven	1972. *Emile Durkheim: His life and work.* New York: Harper and Row.
Lynes, Russel	1957. *A surfeit of honey.* New York: Harper.
Lyons, John	1968. *Introduction to theoretical linguistics.* Cambridge: Cambridge University Press.
Mabuchi, Toichi	1960. Two types of kinship rituals among Malayo-Polynesian peoples. *Proceedings of the IXth International Congress for the History of Religions,* pp. 51–61. Tokyo: Maruzen.

1964. Spiritual predominance of the sister. In *Ryukyan culture and society,* ed. Alan H. Smith, pp. 79–91. Honolulu: University of Hawaii Press.

McLellan, David

1970. *Marx before Marxism.* New York: Harper and Row, Harper Torchbooks.

1971a. *Marx's Grundrisse.* London: Macmillan.

1971b. *The thought of Karl Marx.* New York: Harper and Row.

Macpherson, Crawford Brough

1962. *The political theory of possessive individualism.* Oxford: Clarendon Press.

1973. *Democratic theory: Essays in retrieval.* Oxford: Clarendon Press.

Malinowski, Bronislow

1912. The economic aspect of the Intichiuma ceremonies. *Festkrift tillegnad Edvard Westermarck.* Helsingfors: J. Simalji.

1921. The primitive economics of the Trobriand Islanders. *Economic Journal* 31:1–16.

1930. Kinship. *Man* 30(17):19–29.

1931. Culture. *Encyclopedia of the Social Sciences,* 6:621–46.

1949 [1923]. The problem of meaning in primitive languages. Supplement to *The meaning of meaning,* ed. C. K. Ogden and A. I. Richards, pp. 296–336. International Library of Psychology, Philosophy and Scientific Method. London: Routledge and Kegan Paul.

1950 [1922]. *Argonauts of the western Pacific.* London: Routledge and Kegan Paul.

1954. *Magic, science and religion.* Garden City, N.Y.: Doubleday, Anchor Books.

1960 [1944]. *A scientific theory of culture and other essays.* New York: Oxford University Press.

1964 [1936]. The dilemma of contemporary linguistics. In *Language in culture and society,* ed. Dell Hymes, pp. 63–65. New York: Harper and Row.

1965 [1935]. *Coral gardens and their magic.* 2 vols. Bloomington: Indiana University Press.

1966 [1926]. *Crime and custom in savage society.* London: Routledge and Kegan Paul.

1967. *A diary in the strict sense of the term.* New York: Harcourt, Brace and World.

Malo, David
1951. *Hawaiian antiquities.* Bernice P. Bishop Museum Special Publication no. 2.

Marie, Alain
1972. Parenté, échange matrimonial et récipro-cité. *L'homme* 12(3):5–46; 12(4):5–36.

Marx, Karl
1904 [1859]. *A contribution to the critique of political economy.* Chicago: Kerr.

n.d. [1869]. *The eighteenth brumaire of Louis Bonaparte.* Moscow: Foreign Languages Publishing House (2d ed., Hamburg, 1869).

1933 [1849]. *Wage-labor and capital.* New York: International Publishers.

1961 [1844]. *Economic and philosophical manuscripts of 1844.* Moscow: Foreign Languages Publishing House.

1964. *Pre-capitalist economic formations,* ed. E. J. Hobsbawm. London: Lawrence and Wishart.

1967 [1867, 1893, 1894]. *Capital.* 3 vols. New York: International Publishers.

1968 [1847]. *Misère de la philosophie.* Paris: Editions Sociales.

1972. *The ethnological notebooks of Karl Marx,* ed. L. Krader. Assen: Van Gorcum.

1973 [1857–58]. *Grundrisse.* Harmondsworth, Middlesex: Penguin Books (translation by Martin Nicholaus of notebooks composed in 1857–58).

Marx, Karl, and Engels, Friedrich
1936. *Correspondence: 1846–1895.* New York: International Publishers.

1965. *The German ideology.* London: Lawrence and Wishart.

Mathews, Mitford M.
1951. *Dictionary of americanisms.* 2 vols. Chicago: University of Chicago Press.

Mauss, Marcel
1966 [1923–24]. Essai sur le don. In *Sociologie et anthropologie.* Paris: Presses Universitaires de France.

Maxwell, James Clerk
1970 [1872]. On color vision. In *Sources of color science,* ed. David L. MacAdam, pp. 75–83. Cambridge: MIT Press.

Mead, Margaret
1930. *The social organization of Manu'a.* Bernice

P. Bishop Museum Bulletin no. 76.

Mészáros, Istvan — 1972. *Marx's theory of alienation.* New York: Harper and Row, Harper Torchbooks.

Mills, C. Wright — 1962. *The Marxists.* New York: Dell.

Milner, G. B. — 1952. A study of two Fijian texts. *Bulletin of the School of Oriental and African Studies (University of London)* 14(2): 346–77.

Monod, Jacques — 1972 [1970]. *Chance and necessity.* New York: Random House, Vintage Books.

Montesquieu, Baron de — 1966 [1748]. *The spirit of the laws.* New York: Hafner.

Morgan, Lewis Henry — 1868. *The American beaver and his works.* Philadelphia: Lippincott.

1963 [1877]. *Ancient society,* ed. E. B. Leacock. Cleveland: World Publishing Company.

Murdock, George Peter — 1949. *Social Structure.* New York: Macmillan.

1960. Cognatic forms of social organization. In *Social structure of Southeast Asia,* ed. G. P. Murdock, pp. 1–14. Viking Fund Publications in Anthropology, no. 29. Chicago: Quadrangle Books.

1972. Anthropology's mythology. *Proceedings of the Royal Anthropological Institute of Great Britain and Ireland for 1971,* pp. 17–24.

Murphy, Robert F. — 1970. Basin ethnography and ethnological theory. In *Languages and cultures of western North America,* ed. E. H. Swanson, Jr., pp. 152–71. Pocatello: Idaho State University Press.

1971. *The Dialectics of Social Life.* New York: Basic Books.

Murray, David C., and Deabler, Herdis L. — 1957. Colors and mood-tones. *Journal of Applied Psychology* 41:279–83.

Nadel, S. F. — 1957. Malinowski on magic and religion. In *Man and culture,* ed. R. Firth, pp. 189–208. New York: Humanities Press.

Needham, Rodney — 1963. Introduction to Emile Durkheim and Marcel Mauss, *Primitive Classification,* pp. vii–xlviii. London: Cohen and West.

1972. *Belief, language and experience.* Chicago: University of Chicago Press.

Ollman, Bertell	1971. *Alienation.* Cambridge: Cambridge University Press.
Panoff, Michel	1970. *La terre et l'organisation sociale en polynésie.* Paris: Payot.
Parain, Charles	1965. Structuralisme et histoire. *Pensée,* no. 135 (Oct.), pp. 38–52.
Parsons, Talcott	1968 [1937]. *The structure of social action.* 2 vols. New York: Free Press.
Partridge, Eric	1967. *A dictionary of slang and unconventional English.* 6th ed. New York: Macmillan.
Paz, Octavio	1970. *Claude Lévi-Strauss: An Introduction.* Ithaca, N.Y.: Cornell University Press.
Peirce, Charles S.	1932. *Collected papers of Charles Sanders Peirce,* ed. Charles Hartshorne and Paul Weiss. Vol. 2. *Elements of logic.* Cambridge: Harvard University Press.
Peters, Richard	1956. *Hobbes.* Harmondsworth, Middlesex: Penguin Books.
Petrovic, Gajo	1967. *Marx in the mid-twentieth century.* Garden City, N.Y.: Doubleday, Anchor Books.
Piaget, Jean	1971 [1968]. *Structuralism.* London: Routledge and Kegan Paul.
Poffenberger, A. T., and Barrows, B.	1924. The feeling value of lines. *Journal of Applied Psychology* 8:187–205.
Pokorny, Joel, and Smith, Vivianne C.	1972. Color vision of normal observers. In *The assessment of visual function,* ed. A. M. Potts, pp. 105–35. Saint Louis: Mosby.
Polanyi, Karl	1944. *The great transformation.* New York: Rinehart.
Pouillon, Jean	1966. Présentation: Un essai de définition. *Les Temps Modernes,* no. 246, pp. 769–90.
	1975. *Fétiches sans fétichisme.* Paris: Maspero.
Quain, Buell	1948. *Fijian village.* Chicago: University of Chicago Press.
Radcliffe-Brown, A. R.	1948 [1922]. *The Andaman Islanders.* Glencoe: The Free Press.
	1950. Introduction to *African systems of kinship and marriage,* ed. A. R. Radcliffe-Brown and D. Forde, pp. 1–85. London: Oxford University Press for the International African Institute.

1952. *Structure and function in primitive society.* London: Cohen and West.

1957. *A natural science of society.* Glencoe: Free Press.

Radin, Paul

1966 [1933]. *The method and theory of ethnology.* New York: Basic Books.

Rappaport, Roy A.

1967. *Pigs for the ancestors.* New Haven: Yale University Press.

1971. Nature, culture and ecological anthropology. In *Man, culture and society,* ed. H. L. Shapiro, pp. 237–67. London: Oxford University Press.

Resek, Carl

1960. *Lewis Henry Morgan: American scholar.* Chicago: University of Chicago Press.

Richards, Audrey

1957. The concept of culture in Malinowski's work. In *Man and culture,* ed. R. Firth, pp. 15–32. New York: Humanities Press.

Richardson, Jane, and Kroeber, A. L.

1940. Three centuries of women's dress fashions. *University of California Anthropological Records* 5:111–54.

Ricoeur, Paul

1967. La structure, le mot, l'événement. *Esprit,* n.s., no. 360, pp. 801–21.

1970. *History and truth.* Evanston: Northwestern University Press.

Rosencranz, Mary Lou

1972. *Clothing concepts.* New York: Macmillan.

Rousseau, Jean Jacques

1964. *Oeuvres complètes. Vol. 3. Du contrat social; écrits politiques.* Paris: Bibliothèque de la Pléiade.

Rudolfsky, Bernard

1947. *Are clothes modern?* Chicago: Theobald.

Ryan, Mary Shaw

1966. *Clothing: A study in human behavior.* New York: Holt, Rinehart and Winston.

Sahlins, Marshall

1961. The segmentary lineage: An organization of predatory expansion. *American Anthropologist* 63: 322–45.

1962. *Moala: Culture and nature on a Fijian island.* Ann Arbor: University of Michigan Press.

1969. Economic anthropology and anthropological economics. *Social Science Information* 8(5):13–33.

1972. *Stone age economics.* Chicago: Aldine-Atherton.

1976. Colors and cultures. *Semiotica.* In press.

Salisbury, Richard — 1962. *From stone to steel.* Cambridge: Cambridge University Press.

Sapir, Edward — 1933. Language. *Encyclopedia of the social sciences,* 9:155–69.

Sargent, Walter — 1923. *The enjoyment and use of colors.* New York: Scribner's.

Sartre, Jean-Paul — 1968. *Search for a method.* New York: Random House, Vintage Books.

Saussure, Ferdinand de — 1966 [1915]. *Course in general linguistics.* New York: McGraw-Hill.

Schaff, Adam — 1967 [1964]. *Langage et connaissance.* Paris: Editions Anthropos.

1970. *Marxism and the human individual.* New York: McGraw-Hill.

Schmidt, Alfred — 1971. *The concept of nature in Marx.* London: NLB.

Schneider, David M. — 1968. *American kinship: A cultural account.* Englewood Cliffs, N.J.: Prentice-Hall.

1972. What is kinship all about? In *Kinship studies in the Morgan Centennial Year,* ed. P. Reining, pp. 32–63. Washington, D.C.: Anthropological Society of Washington.

Schwartz, Jack — 1958. *Men's clothing and the Negro.* M.A. diss. Committee on Communication, University of Chicago. (Available at University of Chicago Libraries.)

Sebag, Lucien — 1964. *Marxisme et structuralisme.* Paris: Payot

Silverstein, Michael — 1976. Shifters, linguistic categories, and cultural description. In *Meaning in anthropology,* ed. K. Basso and H. Selby. Albuquerque: University of New Mexico Press for School of American Research. Forthcoming.

Simmel, George — 1904. Fashion. *International Quarterly* 10:130–55.

Smith, Marian — 1959. Boas' "Natural History" approach to field method. In *The anthropology of Franz Boas,* ed. W. Goldschmidt, pp. 46–60. American Anthropological Association, Memoir no. 89.

Southall, James P. C. — 1937. *Introduction to physiological optics.* London: Oxford University Press.

Spengler, Oswald — 1956. *The decline of the West.* Vol. 1. New York Knopf.

Steiner, Franz — 1954. Notes on comparative economics. *British Journal of Sociology* 5:118–19.

Steward, Julian H.

1936. The economic and social basis of primitive bands. In *Essays in Honor of Alfred Lewis Kroeber,* ed. R. H. Lowie, pp. 331–50. Berkeley: University of California Press.

1938. *Basin-Plateau aboriginal sociopolitical groups.* Smithsonian Institution, Bureau of American Ethnology, Bulletin no. 120, Washington, D.C.: U.S. Government Printing Office.

1955. *Theory of culture change.* Urbana: University of Illinois Press.

Stocking, George W., Jr.

1968. *Race, Culture and Evolution.* New York: Free Press.

1974. *The shaping of American anthropology 1883–1911: A Franz Boas reader.* New York: Basic Books.

Stone, Gregory P.

1959. Clothing and social relations: A Study of appearance in the context of community life. Ph.D. diss., Sociology, University of Chicago. (Available at University of Chicago Libraries.)

Tambiah, S. J.

1969. Animals are good to think and good to prohibit. *Ethnology* 8:423–59.

Terray, Emmanuel

1972. *Marxism and "primitive" societies.* New York: Monthly Review Press.

Thompson, Laura

1940. *Southern Lau, Fiji: An ethnography.* Bernice P. Bishop Museum Bulletin no. 162.

Tippet, Alan Richard

1968. *Fijian material culture.* Bernice P. Bishop Museum Bulletin no. 232.

Tregear, Edward

1891. *The Maori-Polynesian comparative dictionary.* Wellington: Lyon and Blair.

Turkle, Sherry

1975. *Symbol and festival in the French student uprising (May–June 1968).* In *Symbol and politics in communal ideology,* ed. Sally Falk Moore and Barbara G. Meyerhoff, pp. 68–100. Ithaca, N.Y.: Cornell University Press.

Turner, Bryan S.

1974. The concept of social "stationariness": Utilitarianism and Marxism. *Science and Society* 38:3–18.

Turner, Terence S.

MS. The social structure of the Northern Kayapo.

Turner, Victor

1967. *The forest of symbols.* Ithaca, N.Y.: Cornell University Press.

Valeri, Renee

1971. Study of traditional food supply in the southwest of France. *Ethnologia Scandinavica,* pp. 86–95.

Valeri, Valerio

1970. Struttura, transformazione, "esaustivita": Un'esposizone di alcuni concetti di Claude Lévi-Strauss. *Annali della Scuola Normale Superiore di Pisa,* ser. 2, 39:347–75.

Vayda, Andrew P.

1965. Anthropologists and ecological problems. In *Man, Culture and Animals,* ed. A. P. Vadya. American Association for the Advancement of Science, Publication no. 78, pp. 1–5.

1969. An ecological approach in cultural anthropology. *Bucknell Review* 17(1):112–19.

Vayda, Andrew P., and Rappaport, Roy A.

1967. Ecology, cultural and non-cultural. In *Introduction to cultural anthropology,* ed. J. Clifton, pp. 476–97. Boston: Houghton Mifflin.

Veblen, Thorstein

1934 [1899]. *The theory of the leisure class.* New York: Modern Library.

Venable, Vernon

1966 [1945]. *Human nature: The Marxian view.* Cleveland: World Publishing Co.

Vološinov, V. N.

1973 [1930]. *Marxism and the philosophy of language.* New York: Seminar Press.

Vygotsky, L. S.

1962. *Thought and language.* Cambridge: MIT Press; New York: John Wiley.

Wagner, Roy

1972. *Habu.* Chicago: University of Chicago Press.

Wellmer, Albrecht

1971. *Critical theory of society.* New York: Herder and Herder.

Wentworth, Harold, and Flexner, Stuart Berry

1967. *Dictionary of American slang.* New York: Crowell.

Wexner, Lois B.

1954. The degree to which colors (hues) are associated with mood-tones. *Journal of Applied Psychology* 38:432–35.

White, Leslie

1942. On the use of tools by primates. *Journal of Comparative Psychology* 34:370–74.

1949. *The science of culture.* New York: Farrar, Straus and Cudahy.

1958. Man, culture, and human beings. Address of the vice president and chairman of Section E (Anthropology) of the American Association for the Advancement of Science, Washington, D.C., 27 Dec. 1958 (mimeographed).

1959*a*. The concept of culture. *American Anthropologist* 61:227–51.

1959*b*. *The evolution of culture.* New York: McGraw-Hill.

1960. Four stages in the evolution of minding. In *The Evolution of Man,* ed. Sol Tax, pp. 239–54. Chicago: University of Chicago Press.

Williams, Thomas, and Calvert, James 1959. *Fiji and the Fijians.* New York: Appleton.

Wolf, Eric R. 1964. *Anthropology.* Englewood Cliffs, N.J.: Prentice-Hall.

Worsley, Peter M. 1956. The kinship system of the Tallensi: A revaluation. *Journal of the Royal Anthropological Institute* 86:37–75.

Index